UP YOUR SCORE

2018 / 2019

SAT

The Underground Guide
to Outsmarting the SAT

by Larry Berger, Samantha Bindner,
Michael Colton, Manek Mistry, and Paul Rossi

Illustrations by Chris Kalb

WORKMAN PUBLISHING, NEW YORK

Copyright © 2017 by Larry Berger, Michael Colton, Manek Mistry, Paul Rossi

Interior illustrations: Chris Kalb
Cover art: John Ritter

Library of Congress Cataloging-in-Publication Data is available.

ISBN 978-0-7611-9365-4

SAT questions reprinted by permission of the Educational Testing Service, the copyright owner of the test questions.

Permission to reprint the SAT material does not constitute review or endorsement by the Educational Testing Service or the College Board of this publication as a whole or of any other testing information it may contain.

SAT is the registered trademark of the College Board, which has not endorsed this publication.

WORKMAN is a registered trademark of Workman Publishing Co., Inc.

Grateful acknowledgment is made for permission to reprint the following:

"You Can Call Me Al" by Paul Simon © 1986 Paul Simon.

Workman books are available at special discount when purchased in bulk for special premiums and sales promotions as well as for fund-raising or educational use. Special editions or book excerpts can also be created to specification. For details, contact the Special Sales Director at the address below or send an email to specialmarkets@workman.com.

Workman Publishing Co., Inc.
225 Varick Street
New York, NY 10014-4381
workman.com

Printed in the United States of America

First printing August 2017
10 9 8 7 6 5 4 3 2 1

TO OUR PARENTS

Florence and Toby Berger
Ellen and Clark Colton
Virginia and Nariman Mistry
Charline and Faust Rossi
Cindy and Jim Bindner

Acknowledgments

Many people have helped with *Up Your Score*. Our heartfelt thanks to:

Chris Arp for his vast store of SAT wisdom and for keeping us laughing. We could not have done this book without him.

David Bock, Ithaca High School, for being a terrific math teacher, for the valuable ideas he gave us for the guessing section, and for his editing assistance.

Mom, Dad, and Meme for giving Samantha some good brain genes.

Milton Kagan, one of the few SAT coaches who really knows his stuff, for sharing some of his excellent ideas with us.

Andrea Kochie, Ithaca High School, for being an amazing college admissions advisor, and for helping us acquire so much of the information that we needed.

Rita Rosenkranz, the agent John Grisham wishes he had, for scoring a perfect 1600 on the Super Agent Test.

Bob Schaeffer and FairTest, for advice and information.

The folks at Workman Publishing, for their astuteness, audacity, alacrity, and ardor—Margot Herrera and Evan Griffith for their brilliant editing, Kim Daly for her attention to detail, Orlando Adiao for great design work, and Noreen Herits for getting the word out.

CONTENTS

Introduction   **A Brief History of This Book**
One Afternoon in the Ithaca High School Cafeteria
    Way Back in the Late '80s viii
Years Later ix
Meet Samantha x

Chapter 1   **About the SAT**
Before We Begin, Any Questions? 2
The Story of the Evil Testing Serpent 14
SAT Scoring 16
SAT Services 19
SAT Mistakes 21

Chapter 2   **How to Study: A Primer for the Lazy,
the Anxious, and the Disorganized**
Getting in Gear 24
The *Up Your Score* Lower Your Stress Plan™ 25
Concentration 28
How Not to Get Stuck 32
Wean Yourself from Your Phone 34
Creating a Study Program . . . and Sticking with It 34
Practice, Practice, Practice 36
Building Endurance 37

Chapter 3   **The Evidence-Based Reading Test**
The Serpent's New Obsessions—
    Evidence and Analysis 40

The Nuts and Bolts of the Reading Test 42

The Seven Key Rules 44

So Many Passage Types, So Little Time 49

Reading Test Question Types 56

Different Readers, Different Strategies 69

A Very Serious Reading Passage 71

A Truly Serious Reading Passage—We Mean It This Time ... 75

Infographics 81

Vocabulary—Still Essential 92

Decodable Words 93

Memorization Strategies 94

The Word List 98

Chapter 4 | The Writing and Language Test: Embracing Your Inner Grammaniac

Know Your Enemy.. 158

Standard English Conventions 160

Expression of Ideas 184

Informational Graphics.................................... 195

Let's Put This All Together and Practice!.................. 196

Pithy Parting Wisdom 201

Chapter 5 | The Math Test

Welcome to Math... 204

Before We Begin 204

The Shape of the Test...................................... 205

How Is This Different from the Old SAT?.................. 205

Mental Math Tricks.. 206

Some Arithmetic Reminders 212

Problem Solving and Data Analysis 221

Interpreting Graphs....................................... 227

Statistics.. 233

Heart of Algebra.. 242

Passport to Advanced Math............................... 253

Additional Topics... 268

Grid-In Problems... 295

A Few Last Words 297

Chapter 6   **The Not-So-Optional Essay**

Does Optional Really Mean Optional? 300

Not *What* Is Said, but *How* It's Said 300

One Template to Rule Them All... 303

How Is the SAT Essay Scored?.. 314

How to Write Good.. 315

Why You Shouldn't Hate the Essay 318

Chapter 7   **Guessing, or Defeating the Impostors from Hell**

Impostors from Hell... 320

Guessing, the SAT, and the Specter of
    World Destruction.. 323

The Five Rules of Guessing 324

Some More Good Advice... 328

Chapter 8   **But Wait! You Also Get . . .**

Little Circles 330

Cursing Cursive 333

Yoga and the SAT... 333

The SAT and the Internet 335

Cheating 336

Is the SAT Biased? 338

A Test Taker's Guide to Proctors 340

What's the Best Way to Prepare the Day Before the SAT?.... 342

Sneaky Snacking.. 346

Fashion and Beauty Tips 347

Keeping Track of Time 348

Stick It in Your Ear 349

SATitis 349

Canceling Counseling 350

The SSS 351

SATing for Dollars 352

Some Other Thoughts on Getting into College...................... 352

Parting Words of Advice... 355

Who Are These People, Anyway? 356

Whiz Kids Wanted 358

A Brief History of This Book

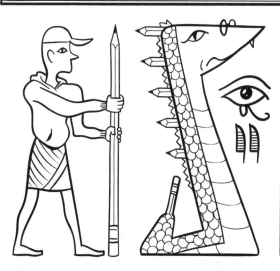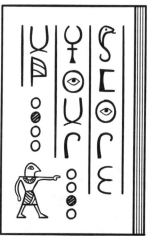

ONE AFTERNOON IN THE ITHACA HIGH SCHOOL CAFETERIA WAY BACK IN THE LATE '80s

"This book really stinks," Paul yawned as he pulled the crust off his sandwich, scattering Miracle Whip all over page 12 of Barron's SAT guide.

"Yeah, what's the point of the SAT, anyway?"

"To cause us pain and suffering," Manek mumbled.

"You know what's wrong with these SAT review books?"

"No, what?" asked Larry.

"They're all written by embalmed educators who were born before the invention of the number 2 pencil, before the SAT itself, and before *The Brady Bunch* went on the air."

"If I wrote an SAT review book, it wouldn't be so boring."

"I know what you mean. If I wrote an SAT review book, it would be erudite, yet not bombastic. It would elucidate the turbid depths of this baneful examination and carry students to new heights of academic self-actualization . . ."

"Yeah, and have lots of skin."

"You know, Larry's right. If we could write an awesome manual telling confused, bored, and frustrated students like us across this great land how to rock the SAT, we would—"

"We would be making a contribution to society that—"

". . . could bring us enough funds to pay for college."

". . . and a chance to get on *The Tonight Show*."

"*Tonight*? Do you really think so?"

A few months later, after Larry, Manek, and Paul each scored over 1500 on the SAT, they began work on a review book that shared their secrets of SAT success. It was called *Up Your Score*, and it helped many students get into prestigious colleges that cost more than they could afford.

YEARS LATER

Over the next six years, Larry, Manek, and Paul grew old and joined bingo and shuffleboard leagues, and the SAT also changed. Because too many students had read *Up Your Score* and outsmarted the test, the SAT was revised. In order to meet this new challenge, Larry, Manek, and Paul decided to seek out some young blood, searching long and hard for a new coauthor to update the book. Eventually, they decided upon Michael Colton, a brilliant young rebel from Massachusetts who achieved a perfect 1600 by reading *Up Your Score* and who also baked award-winning chocolate chip cookies.

Michael's revision of the book enabled a new generation of youngsters to follow in his footsteps at Harvard, but age eventually caught up with him as well. His references to *Full House* and Vanilla Ice (both of which were very funny, trust us) now fell on deaf ears. So every two years, *Up Your Score* found new students who had used the book to earn perfect scores. What emerged over time is a condensed volume of pure, unadulterated test-taking wisdom from kids who have aced the SAT. These student editors all went on to prestigious universities and careers, including a few who became professional test-prep gurus in their own right.

Then, in 2005, the SAT made a bunch of big changes. Instead of a perfect 1600, students now had to shoot for a 2400, thanks to the addition of a Writing section, which included an essay and grammar questions. Accordingly, the book was overhauled, and student editors who had scored all 2400 of those points were quickly found.

"Phew," said the *Up Your Score* editors. "That was a ton of work, but luckily the College Board will never, ever completely change the SAT again."

Then in 2016 the College Board completely changed the SAT again.

We are going to tell you all about those changes in the very next chapter. But first, some good news: We've found a ridiculously talented guest editor who will help guide us through the transition.

MEET SAMANTHA

Hey, readers! My name is Samantha, and I've been in your shoes. Many times. Too many times . . . and that's why I'm here as the new guest editor. Most of the comments, tips, and totally-not-lame jokes in the margins of this new, shiny edition of *Up Your Score* are my doing.

Though my perfect SAT score helped me get a full-tuition scholarship to my dream school, I had to work to get it—all the way from seventh grade to junior year (disclaimer from personal experience: You shouldn't have to take the SAT as many times as your grandmother's celebrated her birthday to get the score you want). Then . . . drum roll please . . . I met this book.

Up Your Score is designed to help you get the most done in the most efficient way possible. Great, right? Now, that doesn't mean it will be painless—the SAT doesn't work that way. But I *can* tell you that this book will make your Saturday morning practice sessions a lot more productive *and* a lot more fun. And you might just end up with an SAT score your mom will want to hang up on the refrigerator. Now start reading!

About the SAT

BEFORE WE BEGIN, ANY QUESTIONS?

WHY DO I HAVE TO READ THIS BOOK IF I WANT TO GO TO COLLEGE?

Good question. The answer is, you don't. You can choose not to read this book and halfway through the SAT have a nervous breakdown from which you never quite recover despite decades of psychiatric care, which will lead to all of your several marriages ending in bitter divorces that cost you every penny you make as a mediocre professional bowler, until your life is cut short by an agonizing fungal disease for which they find a cure a week after no one comes to your funeral. Next question?

WHAT IS THE SAT?

The SAT was developed in 1927 because colleges wanted an objective way of comparing students. It used to be that they had no way of knowing that Eggbert's D average at Impossible High School was actually much more impressive than Betty's B average at Easy Academy. The goal was for the SAT to give an accurate measure of a student's ability to do college work. A certain bunch of SAT prep book authors think that it fails miserably in its attempt to do this. The SAT has undergone several revisions to make it more relevant and useful, with mixed success. But through all these revisions, one thing has not changed: The SAT is and will continue to be an important part of the college application process. While there are a lot of factors that admissions officers look at in an application, the bottom line is that your SAT score can make the difference between acceptance to and rejection from a college.

WHAT EXACTLY IS ON THE SAT?

The SAT changed in 2016. The new test—the one you will be taking—is three hours long, plus an extra 50 minutes if you decide to take the optional Essay. It is broken into two sections, Evidence-Based Reading and Writing, and Math. The Reading and Writing section is further broken into two tests. The Reading Test is 65 minutes long and asks 52 questions; the Writing and Language

Trust me, it won't kill you to trade in your Saturday morning Netflix binge sesh for a chance to jump-start your future. Grey's can wait.

—Samantha

Test gives you 35 minutes to answer 44 questions. The Math Test asks you to answer 58 questions in 80 minutes, including a short section where no calculator is allowed. There is also an optional essay that comes at the end, and you will be given 50 minutes to analyze an argument and write about it.

The SAT also offers Subject Tests (or "SAT IIs") that cover individual subjects such as literature, foreign languages, history, math, and various fields of science. Some of the more selective colleges require applicants to take one to three of the SAT Subject Tests. They're completely different and separate from the SAT, which tests general "scholastic aptitude" and is the focus of this book. While good scores on Subject Tests can enhance your application, they are generally not as important as your SAT score.

While this book focuses on the main SAT, it is important to figure out which SAT Subject Tests (if any) you want to take based on your career interests and the requirements of specific colleges.

WHAT'S NEW ABOUT THE NEW SAT?

In 2014, the College Board announced that it was overhauling the SAT. It seems students—or at least those who read *Up Your Score*—were insufficiently afraid of the old test. So they found ways to make a new one that was even more hideous than the last one—albeit more related to the skills you actually need in college. The College Board describes all the changes they're making to the test on their website (collegeboard.org), but their description comes in the form of hyper-wonky PR speak. We'll tell you about the changes straight up.

Let's start with the Big Picture changes.

The SAT is and always has been a *reasoning* test. This means that the College Board is looking to test your ability to puzzle through, reason with, and analyze a problem. They are *not* testing your knowledge of facts. The big change in 2016 was that the SAT redefined what they mean by *reasoning*. The skills they want to test are:

The ability to back up your answer with evidence. You might have noticed that the new Reading and Writing Test is now called the Evidence-Based Reading and Writing Test. That's because the

SAT is now not only going to ask you a question about a passage, it's going to ask you to *prove* your answer. Sometimes this will mean a follow-up question where you point out which line of the passage supports your previous answer.

Knowledge of vocabulary that is actually used in the world. *Monadnock, crithomancy, limn.* These are all words that you might have seen on the old SAT, but you won't on the new one. The new SAT will definitely throw some tough words at you (like *obfuscate, paradigmatic,* or *puerile*), but they will be the kind of words you might use in a college paper. * There will also be a greater emphasis on the meaning of words in context. For example, the SAT might ask a question like the following about the seemingly simple word *interests.*

> "In the 2000s, the United States government had **interests** in the Middle East."
>
> As used in the above sentence, the word "interests" most nearly means which of the following?
> A) passions
> B) concerns
> C) hobbies
> D) curiosities

The correct answer is B. All four of the answers are synonyms of the word *interests,* but "concerns" is the only one that makes sense in this context. If you hadn't read the sentence, answering this question would be impossible. This emphasis on context is much more pronounced on the new SAT than it was on the old one.

Crithomancy, FYI, is the art of reading the future in uncooked dough. *

Math that colleges want you to know. When you go to college, you are going to be doing a lot more statistics and algebra than geometry problems. That's just a fact. The new SAT reflects this,

Key word: "might."
        —Samantha

I wonder if you can crithomancize your SAT score? Sure would have given me some relief back in the day.
        —Samantha

with a much greater emphasis on data analysis and algebra, and the inclusion of some new concepts, like (basic) trigonometry and complex numbers.

The ability to solve math with your brain. Another new, scary feature of the SAT is the No Calculator section. How will you know that you cannot use a calculator? Simple: There will be a big icon of a crossed-out calculator on the top of every page, and your proctor will be bellowing at you to put away your TI-84. This section often scares off potential SAT-takers, but it shouldn't. Most of these problems do not involve much hairy arithmetic. There is a greater focus on algebraic manipulation than on long division. But yes, you will need to sharpen your mental math game to get through this section in time. That's why we've included quite a few "mental math" tricks in our math chapter.

The Math test is also a reading test. If you're one of those students who skipped learning the ABCs and focused solely on SOHCAHTOA and completing the square, you're in for a bit of a shock. Many of the math questions on the new SAT are very, very wordy. It can be intimidating to turn the page and see that a math problem is TWO PARAGRAPHS long. Again, the bark here is worse than the bite. In some ways, the detailed, minutely explained problems are clearer than the shorter SAT problems of yesteryear. But pay attention during our Reading chapter. The same reading skills discussed there also apply to the new, wordy Math section.

There is also increased emphasis on science, history, and social studies—and a lot more infographics. While the old SAT included a variety of types of reading passages, they did not draw from natural science texts or include charts and graphs. Nor did they tend to be actual historical documents. Don't be surprised to see passages in the new reading test that include infographics, or excerpts from documents like *The Federalist Papers*. (The good news is that you aren't expected to be familiar with these documents.)

THE THINKER
the ANALYZER

Finally, the new optional Essay asks you to analyze, rather than emote or philosophize. The old SAT Essay asked students to answer very broad questions, like "Is violence ever justified?" and students were expected to write about their own ideas. The new, now "optional" (more on that in Chapter 6) Essay will provide you with a passage and ask you to analyze it. What claim is the author making? How does the author establish this claim? What evidence is used?

The big idea here is that the new SAT wants students to use the same kinds of skills they will use in college. When you sit down in Anthropology 101, the professor will not say, "Do you think violence is ever justified? Write a five-paragraph response in twenty-five minutes. Go!" What the professor will do is give you (a ton of) reading and ask you to analyze it. With every change to the test, the College Board has college readiness firmly in mind. Will the new test achieve this goal? Only time will tell.

There are also a few smaller changes that you need to know about.

- **You have much more time for the Essay.** The old Essay gave you an insanely short 25 minutes; the new one gives you a still-annoying-but-far-more-reasonable 50 minutes.
- **There is no guessing penalty.** * The old SAT deducted 0.25 point for each wrong answer. The new SAT does not. This means you MUST guess, because there is no downside and there's at least a 25 percent chance that you'll guess right. For more on best-practices guessing, go to Chapter 7.
- **The new score is out of 1600, not 2400.** If you are hoping to score a 2400, even the new perfect score will disappoint you.
- **The new score report will include a bunch of subscores.** We'll go over these on page 19.

* If you're just about out of time on a section and still have unanswered questions, fill in all of their bubbles with the same letter. I'm a "B" girl, myself.
—Samantha

WOW, THAT'S A LOT OF INFORMATION TO PROCESS. CAN YOU JUST TELL ME IF IT'S HARDER OR EASIER?

From the tests released so far (a few of which can be seen at collegeboard.org), the Math Test looks a little harder, primarily because it includes some new concepts from higher math and because the problems can be wordy. The Reading and Writing Tests look to be the same difficulty as before. You will need to get used to the old-timey English of the historical documents and not lose your mind when you see a chart. But after reading this book, neither of those changes will freak you out. The new Essay requires a bit more brainwork, but you have more time to do it, so this comes out equal as well.

AND WHAT ABOUT THE ACT? HOW IS THAT TEST DIFFERENT FROM THE NEW SAT?

Actually, the new SAT is a lot more like the ACT than it used to be. The ACT is designed to test whether a student gained the

	NEW SAT	ACT
Material Tested	Standard high school curriculum; Evidence-Based Reading and Writing Tests include tables and graphs; Math includes a No Calculator section and a section where students supply their answers	Standard high school curriculum; Science Reasoning section includes tables and graphs; Writing section has a greater emphasis on punctuation
Length	180 minutes plus 50-minute optional essay; 154 questions	175 minutes plus 40-minute optional essay; 215 questions
Format	Multiple-choice questions, grid-in questions, optional essay prompt	Multiple-choice questions, optional essay prompt
Highest Possible Score	1600	36
How the Test Is Scored	Evidence-Based Reading and Writing is worth up to 800 points, as is the Math section. These two scores are added together for a composite score.	Each of the four required sections (English, Math, Reading, Science) is scored out of 36, then averaged for the overall score.

skills taught in your average high school curriculum. It includes a Science section, in which natural science passages are presented along with graphs and charts. The new science passages in the SAT Reading Test resemble these ACT science passages. Like on the new SAT, the ACT Essay is optional.

Perhaps the biggest remaining difference between the tests is that the ACT requires you to answer more questions faster. Both tests are accepted at all universities and colleges. On the previous page is a handy chart that outlines the nitty-gritty details.

WHAT IS A "GOOD SCORE" ON THE SAT?

Each section of the test is scored on a scale of 200 to 800. So the perfect combined score is 1600 (Evidence-Based Reading and Writing plus Math), and the score you really, really don't want to get is a 400. ✱ The Essay, which is scored separately, is scored from 2 to 8 on each of three traits, and these numbers are *not* combined into an overall score. So you are hoping for an 8, 8, 8.

NO, SERIOUSLY, WHAT SCORE SHOULD I SHOOT FOR?

Well, that depends. First, you have to consider what your goals are. Some of you are reading this book because the NCAA rules require that you get a certain minimum score in order to be eligible to play on an intercollegiate team as a freshman. Some of you want to end up at Harvard, so you'll want to score in the high 1500s. Schools usually offer the SAT score range of the middle 50 percent of their freshman class to give an idea of what type of score they're looking for. You can typically find this information on a college's website.

And remember, these numbers are typical of the scores of the students entering these schools. They are not the minimum requirements, nor do they guarantee admission.

Admissions officers consider many other factors. High school grades and courses, work experience, extracurricular activities, application essays, leadership qualities, the admissions interview, ethnic background, athletic prowess, legacy

✱ *But look on the bright side—there's no possible way you can get a 0. People have tried.*

—Samantha

A long time ago, we asked Jim Wroth, then a sophomore at Yale, what his combined math and verbal scores were on the SAT. He said 1760. When we responded that it's impossible to score above 1600, he explained that he has Yale relatives who date back to the year 1760, so it didn't really matter what his scores were.

(having relatives who went to the school you are applying to), and many other things all have an impact on whether or not you get in. Although these other factors are important, your SAT score may be the most crucial. If you are president of every club in your school, the admissions officers may be so impressed with your extracurricular activities that they'll accept you even if you scored noticeably below the school's average SAT score. But if you don't have legacy, your grades are ho-hum, and you have a boring list of extracurriculars, then you will need SAT scores well above the average. (For more on college admissions, see page 352.) Many admissions officers would try to deny this claim, but the admissions records show that if you have an SAT score above the average for the school to which you are applying, and there's nothing flagrantly wrong with the rest of your application, then you will often get in at all but the most selective colleges. While the other factors on your application are subjective, your SAT score is a big, fat, hairy, "objective" *number*. Even an admissions officer who claims that the SAT score is not particularly important is going to be subconsciously influenced by this number. It categorizes your application in the admissions officer's mind as "smart enough" or "not smart enough." It has an impact on the way an admissions officer interprets virtually everything else on your application.

Your SAT score is what gets you the first glance. Whether the admissions officer keeps reading or not, well, that's a different story.
—Samantha

WHAT ABOUT THE PSAT?

If you've already taken the PSAT and you didn't study for it, don't read this. Reading about the awards, recognition, and money that a good PSAT score could have brought you will be depressing. *

* *Scholarships! Plaques! Ceremonies! Oh my!*
—Samantha

The PSAT follows a format similar to the SAT, but it supposedly contains fewer of the most difficult questions, and it's 15 minutes shorter. As in the SAT, you'll see one Evidence-Based Reading and Writing section, and one Math section. It will be scored on a similar scale to the SAT, and the score report will include the same subscores as the SAT. But there is one crucial

A good score on the PSAT makes you eligible for all sorts of scholarship programs, the most famous of which is the National Merit Scholarship Program.

* Your bank account will thank you for this when you find yourself trying to strike a balance between caffeine level and size value on the dollar-menu coffees at the campus McDonald's.
—Samantha

difference: The PSAT has a *P* as its first letter. Here's why:

The *P* in PSAT stands for three things. The first (and official) thing is easy—Preliminary. The PSAT is a preliminary look at the real SAT. It's a sneak preview of what the real thing is going to be like and a good chance to practice (which also begins with a *P*). In fact, your PSAT score report will come with your test book and a computer printout telling you, for each question, the correct answer, your answer, and the level of difficulty of the question. You can use this information to help prepare for the SAT.

But the PSAT is more than just a chance to practice. In our mind, the second thing the *P* stands for is *Programs*, as in scholarship*s* and special *p*rograms. A good score on the PSAT makes you eligible for all sorts of scholarship programs, the most famous of which is the National Merit Scholarship Program. The National Merit Scholarship is based on your *Selection Index score*, which is double the sum of your reading, writing, and math scores. Recognition by the National Merit Program is a big plus on your college applications, and it can even win you some money. The top 50,000 scorers are recognized by the National Merit Program. The top 16,000 scorers become semifinalists, and 15,000 of *them* become finalists. About 7,500 of the finalists get big bucks toward college. Sometimes, even if you don't become a finalist, or you're not one of the finalists to receive a scholarship from the National Merit Corporation, you still may be eligible to get money from one of your parents' companies. Also, if you score well on the PSAT but don't make the final cut, some colleges still might offer you scholarships to attend their school so they can get bragging rights to educating the greatest number of National Merit semifinalists or finalists, and you get your college education for less than you planned on spending— sometimes for free. * This program is described in depth in the "PSAT/NMSQT Student Guide," which also lists the corporate and college sponsors of the program. You can pick up a copy in any guidance counselor's office or find it at nationalmerit.org.

The third thing the *P* stands for is A*pp*lications. The College Board says the PSAT is not used as a college admissions test. But some schools have a space for PSAT scores on their applications. Of course, it's optional whether or not you tell them your PSAT scores, but it's impressive if you have good ones.

BACK TO THE SAT. WHAT ABOUT SUNDAY TEST DATES?

The College Board offers the SAT seven times a year between August and June; most students take the test on a Saturday morning. However, those students who cannot take the SAT on a Saturday for religious reasons have the option of taking it on Sunday, usually the day after the scheduled Saturday test. On your registration form you need to fill in the special 01000 test center code, and you must also send in a signed letter from your clergyperson on official letterhead explaining that religious convictions prevent you from taking the SAT on a Saturday. When you sign up for one Sunday test, you must take the rest of your tests on Sundays as well.

Because the test given on Sunday is exactly the same as the Saturday test, you cannot register for both. The test is scored on the same scale, and percentages are calculated the same way for Sunday test takers as for Saturday test takers. In the end, therefore, there is no advantage or disadvantage to registering for a Sunday test. Only do it if you have to, or if you are convinced that being one day smarter is going to make the difference.

WHAT IF I WANT TO APPLY FOR EARLY DECISION OR EARLY ACTION?

Many students now take the SAT in October and/or November of their senior year in order to meet the deadlines for Early Decision or Early Action. Under these programs, seniors generally know by the end of December whether they will have a low-stress second semester. By applying for Early Decision, you commit to attending the school if your application is successful. (This means that you can apply for Early Decision at only one

Taking the SAT in your junior year can cut down on stress and make maximum use of any studying you did for the PSAT. You also then have time for a do-over (not that you'll need it, of course).

*This is one of the worst causes of blacklisting, right under wearing socks with sandals and accidentally calling your teacher "Mom."
—Samantha

school.) There is no such restriction with Early Action policies, which in general means you can apply for Early Action to more than one school. Some schools, however, have a "Single-Choice Early Action" policy—you aren't obligated to accept their offer of admission, but you can't apply to any other schools under Early Action. If you're seeking early admission anywhere, make sure you know what the school's policy is.

Note: Some schools that are eager to attract good students may send you their "Priority" or "Distinguished Student" applications. These can also count as early admission options. If you've already applied for Early Decision or Single-Choice Early Action elsewhere, check to see that these don't violate the agreement. Don't be one of those "broke the early admission rule and got themselves blacklisted" kids. * So not cool.

WHAT SPECIAL SKILLS WILL I NEED TO TAKE THE SAT?

Several abilities are necessary. First, you must be able to stay awake, which can be difficult even though you will be sitting for upward of four hours in the most uncomfortable chair imaginable. (This is the reason for the sections on yoga in Chapter 8 and concentration in Chapter 2.) Second, you have to be able to sign a statement in cursive alleging that you, not some cyborg clone, are taking the test (see page 333 for practice). Third, you must be able to read. (And if you're reading this, you've probably already cleared that hurdle, unless you're just looking at the pretty design of the pages.) Fourth, you must know a lot of math and reading and writing stuff so that you can answer the questions correctly. (That's what most of this book is about.) Fifth, you need to understand the proper strategies for taking the SAT and the many ways you can outsmart the test. (We explain all the tricks.) Sixth, you need to be able to fill in all the little circles on the computerized answer sheet, without going out of the lines. (We've provided several columns of little circles for practice and have done extensive experimentation to identify the most efficient way to fill them in. See page 330.)

★Good bladder control is also a great trait to have. Utilize the bathroom breaks wisely.
—Samantha

★This is a real phenomenon. Print two admission tickets and put one in your (or your parent's) car and one in your bag the night before. Then you will have virtually no excuse for not having it the next day.
—Samantha

Other useful skills are eating for endurance and stealth snacking. ★ These skills are covered on pages 38 and 346.

SO ALL I HAVE TO DO IS READ THIS BOOK?

That, plus practice tests. In the extremely unlikely event that you do that and still do miserably on the SAT, do not whine. Just make the best of going to college in the Australian outback. In addition, there are a number of small details that could go wrong during the test regardless of what you learn (or do not learn) from this book. A few examples:

1. You fall asleep the night before the test and do not wake up until it is over.
2. You lose your admission ticket, so they never even let you into the testing center. ★
3. You fall asleep during the reading passage about the history of celery.
4. You fall asleep while the proctor is reading the directions.
5. All four of your number 2 pencils break, and you end up having to use chalk.
6. You don't know the answer to question 6 on the test, so you skip it. However, you forget to leave number 6 blank on your answer sheet. Then, you put the answer to question 7 in the space for question 6, the answer to question 8 in the space for question 7, etc. You don't realize that you have done this until you wake up in the middle of the passage about the history of celery and try to find your place. (Seriously, if you mess up your answer sheet like that, the proctor will probably give you some time to rearrange your answers after the test is over. Raise your hand and ask.)

Some distractions can be remedied. For example, if your desk squeaks, it's too hot, there's a fan blowing your papers around, or you're left-handed and the desks are made for right-handed people—tell the proctor! Although some proctors bite, most don't carry any dangerous diseases, and the occasional proctor will even try to help you. (See "A Test Taker's Guide to Proctors" on page 340.)

WHO MAKES UP THE SAT?

The conventional answer to this question is that it is made up by the College Board, a shadowy nonprofit based in New York City. However, we have discovered that this answer is a cover-up. The real truth about who makes up the SAT is revealed here for the first time in history. . . .

THE STORY OF THE EVIL TESTING SERPENT

In the beginning, there was no SAT. Students frolicked in their high school paradise without knowledge of evil, able to pick freely from the Tree of College.

But then the Evil Testing Serpent silently slithered into the high school through the hot-lunch loading dock. The Serpent, an unfathomably long, mighty, mucus-encrusted beastie, was determined to bring evil and pain into paradise. So it devised a plan that would put an end to the happiness of high school students.

This is how the Testing Serpent's plan was to work. For more than three hours, students would have to answer an incessant string of questions. The questions would be both boring and tricky. Students who gave too many wrong answers would have miserable futures and then die. It called this hideous ordeal the Slimy and Atrocious Torture (SAT).

The Serpent inflicted the SAT on the oppressed masses of students for many years, and its power increased as it drained their meager life forces. Gradually, all resistance was crushed, and the tormented youths became accustomed to taking the SAT. Parents and teachers began to view the SAT as a national institution. Long, bleak years of misery appeared to lie ahead for civilization.

Could no one defeat the Testing Serpent? Would this

merciless beast continue to strangle its victims into submission? Would *Saturday Night Live* ever be funny again? Was there no hope for humanity? Well, it turned out there was. Four ordinary students, born under the tyranny of the Serpent, suffered through the unholy SAT with the rest of their comrades. But afterward, they made a secret blood vow to avenge the misery they had suffered at the fangs of the Serpent. They delved into the mysteries of the SAT in the hope of uncovering its weaknesses and defeating it. They soon discovered many ways of psyching out the Testing Serpent and outsmarting the SAT. They transcribed their revelations in a stirring document wherein they demonstrated that although the Serpent was mean, their readers would be above the mean. The high school paradise was soon restored, and students once again were able to pick freely from the Tree of College.

Since these SAT warriors published their manifesto, the Evil Testing Serpent has undergone two devious transformations in order to rule the high school world once more.

One night, as it lay stewing in its miserable cave in midtown Manhattan, an idea formed in its so-called mind. Why not make the test *harder*? Maybe add some statistics and obscure scatterplot graphs! Add some reading passages from 1783! Add a 50-minute Essay, but make it optional so that kids either feel the misery of taking it, or the misery of guilt for not taking it! The Evil Testing Serpent quivered with delight! But not to worry. With the help of a new guest editor, the gallant fighters vowed to fight the Serpent, no matter what form it took. Once again.

So they stealthily searched for its cave, found its secrets, and revised the document. *It is that document you now hold in your sweaty, trembling hands.*

Here, the cruel tricks of the Serpent will be revealed and you will be shown how to use your understanding of its methods to your own advantage. Throughout this book, the Serpent will make loathsome appearances and will secrete foul venom all over the pages to protest our revelations of its weaknesses and its trickeries. Fear not. Soon you will be able to recognize the Serpent's infamous tricks and you will live forever free of the fear of the Slimy and Atrocious Torture.

SAT SCORING

Fewer people know how the College Board really derives an SAT score than know whether or not the government has UFOs buried in a bunker in Nevada. This information hovers in a cloud of confidentiality and "we'll call you back" messages. The College Board claims that this information is known only by a few members of their statistics department and that no single person knows the entire system. On one occasion, they even told us that we can't call the department that could explain this system because they don't have a phone. *

*Come on. It's the 21st century. We don't buy that anymore.
—Samantha

Despite this veil of secrecy, by piecing different information together, we were able to find out quite a bit about how the College Board takes the number of questions you got right and translates them into a percentile and SAT score.

WHAT IS A RAW SCORE?

The raw score is a number based solely on how many questions you got right.

WHAT IS A PERCENTILE?

Your percentile is based on the percent of test takers who had a lower raw SAT score than you. If, for example, you're in the 64th percentile, your raw score was higher than the scores of 64 percent of the other people taking the test.

$$\left(\frac{\sqrt{\pi}}{\theta}\right) \times n - \left(\left[2\pi r^2 - x\right] \div\right.$$

$$\Sigma \div \theta \left(2x - \sqrt{3n}\right) -$$

$$\left(n \div x\right) + \left[\frac{(4xy - n) \cdot 2}{\pi + 4}\right]$$

$$-\sqrt{\pi r^2} + 2xr^3 - y \cdot$$

$$+\Sigma x + \theta + \left(\frac{2\pi}{n-x}\right) \div$$

$$\sqrt{\Delta} - 2\left(\frac{x-n}{\pi}\right) - ny$$

$$\hookrightarrow + \left(\frac{y \div 2}{3n}\right) - \pi\sqrt{\infty} \div$$

$$\left(\left[2\pi r^2 - x\right] \div \sqrt{\sigma}\right) \cdot \left(\frac{2\pi}{n-x}\right)$$

$$\Sigma\left[\frac{(4xy - n) \cdot 2}{\pi + 4}\right] \cdot \sqrt{3n} -$$

$$\left[\left(2x - \sqrt{3n}\right) + \Sigma \div \theta\right] \cdot n\pi^2$$

$$-\left(\frac{\sqrt{\pi}}{\theta}\right) \times n - \left(\left[2\pi r^2 - 2\right] \times \theta\right)$$

$$-2(\theta x) - \pi\sqrt{\Delta} + \left(\frac{y \div 2}{3n}\right)$$

$$\div \frac{2}{\pi} - \left(\frac{xy}{z}\right) - 4xyr^2\pi \div$$

$$\left(\frac{3x + xy -}{n \div}\right)\left(\frac{xy}{-y}\right) - \pi\right]$$

$$-\left(\sqrt{x} \quad -2xy\right) = \text{SCORE } 1320$$

WHAT ABOUT THE OTHER SCORE—YOU KNOW, THE IMPORTANT ONE?

The other score you receive is the numerical score, which is on a scale of 200 to 800 for each section. This is the score that is shrouded in so much mystery.

Many people believe that SAT scores are set up on a bell curve, which means that most people would get a score just above or below a 500 and that an equal number of people would get scores an equal distance from the average. This would mean that if 620 people got an 800 on the Math section, 620 people would also get a 200. And it would mean that the average score on the test should be 500. But none of these things is true. The College Board admits that the average score on each section is not 500. For the class of 2015, the average math score was 511, the average reading score was 495, and the average writing score was 484.

The College Board uses a lot of averaging and shady crypto-math to determine their curved scores. The National Center for Fair and Open Testing—a watchdog group that believes that all of this information should be available to the public—has suggested that the College Board takes a standard bell curve and shifts it up slightly, allowing more 800 than 200 scores. They also go through a complicated process of evaluating which questions on the test were the most difficult and comparing your performance to that of other people who took the same test and to other people who took the test in the last few years.

ARE PERCENTILES AND SAT SCORES CONNECTED?

Your score and percentile are definitely connected, although the exact relationship will probably be discovered around the same time as the cave in which Tupac and Elvis have been hiding all these years.

HOW MANY QUESTIONS CAN I GET WRONG AND STILL GET A PERFECT SCORE?

That varies from year to year. Traditionally there has been more leeway on the reading and writing scores than the math scores. On the old SAT, during an average year, you could get one or two reading or writing questions wrong and still score 800, but an 800 in math usually required a true, no-errors perfect performance. But on the new SAT, at least so far, it looks like you need to get all the questions right on all sections to score that sweet 1600.

WHY ARE SCORES ON A SCALE OF 800 INSTEAD OF 100?

When the SATs were first invented, the College Board decided that if scores were on a scale of 0 to 100, people might start to complain that their SAT scores were not on a par with their regular school grades: "I got a 96 in math but only a 90 on the SAT Math section." To avoid problems like this (and in our opinion to make the test seem more grand and precise than it really is), they set it up on a scale of 200 to 800. Because no one ever gets a 705 or a 692, many people wonder why scores are not on a scale of 20 to 80, the same way PSAT scores are calculated. Again, this is probably a marketing ploy. It sounds better to get an 800 than an 80, and the SAT needed to set itself apart from other tests in order to get thousands of colleges to force kids to pay millions of dollars to take it.

WILL I SEE ANY OTHER SCORES ON MY SCORE REPORT?

Yes, you will see three other test scores. A Reading Test score, a Writing and Language Test score, and a Math Test score will all be given in a range from 10 to 40. You will also see "Cross-Test Scores," which will range from 10 to 40 and grade you in "Analysis in History/Social Studies" and "Analysis in Science." And that's not all! You will *also* receive subscores, including "Command of Evidence," "Words in Context," "Expression of Ideas," "Standard English Conventions," "Heart of Algebra," "Problem-Solving and Data Analysis," and "Passport to Advanced Math" (seven total). The new SAT is not skimping: You get a lot of scores for your buck!

But do any of these other scores *matter*? Well, if you want to learn which types of problems you got wrong to prepare for your next attempt, then sure. But in terms of college applications: Heck no. The college admissions officer, and hence you, will primarily care about that composite score in the 400 to 1600 range.

SAT SERVICES

SCORES ONLINE OR BY PHONE

Your scores will be available online about three to four weeks after you take the test. You can also hear them over the phone by calling 866-756-7346, but you won't get them any earlier this way, and it also costs an extra $15. You might be wondering, How could it possibly cost $15 per student? According to our local phone company, the College Board is probably paying about 50 cents for each toll-free call—so most of the $14.50 left over would seem to be pure profit for the supposedly nonprofit College Board. If every student in America used this service, the Testing Serpent could make more than $20 million a year off it. That's enough to gold-plate the elevators in the College Board's office building.

Why should you give the College Board even one more measly dollar? Hasn't the Serpent already wrung enough moolah out of you, not to mention blood, sweat, and tears? The better option, by far, is to get your scores over the Internet. For no additional fee, you can go to collegeboard.org, click on "SAT," put in your username and password, and click on "Scores" to see your entire score history. There is one hitch: You must sign up for a College Board account before you take the test. Make sure you do this! ✱

SCORE SENDER

When you register, you are given the option of requesting that your score report to be sent to up to four colleges at about the same time the report is sent to you. You will need to send score reports when you apply to colleges, so if you have an idea of where you're going to apply when you take the test, you might

✱ Once you sign up, make sure you save your password in a safe place—or multiple safe places. I lost mine approximately seven times.
　　—Samantha

as well use the Score Sender option. It saves a step later on. And it's free. However, if you don't know where you're applying and/or you have time to get your scores first (and take the test again, if necessary), you can wait and request score reports for your colleges later. The score report is cumulative and shows all of your scores for up to six SATs and six SAT Subject Tests.

The College Board lets you request score reports over the phone, by mail, or on the Internet, and once again the Internet is much more convenient. Using the College Board's site (sat .collegeboard.org/scores/send-sat-scores), you can send as many reports as you want for the extortionate cost of $12 per report.

Remember, it takes about three weeks for your scores to be mailed after you request them. So if you have a college admissions deadline, plan ahead. But if you forget, there is a rush reporting service. It costs $31 (a price established by a national committee of organized crime bosses), in addition to $12 for each report. Scores are mailed out within two to four business days of your request.

Tip: Be careful when you're tempted to use the rush reporting service. Some colleges specifically state that they will not accept rushed scores.

SCORE CHOICE

Though normally all of your SAT scores will be sent to a college when you send a score report, you can use a service called Score Choice to pick which SAT and SAT Subject Test scores will be sent. While Score Choice doesn't cost any extra, it still has some pros and cons. In the pro column, if you took the Biology Subject Test twice, you can choose to send only your higher score. However, Score Choice allows you to omit entire tests only—meaning you can't choose to send your 800 in Reading and Writing and not your 580 in Math from the same test. Additionally, some colleges don't allow Score Choice. But never fear! Many colleges will "super score" (or look only at the best score you have received in each section) anyway.

REGISTERING ONLINE OR BY PHONE

If you have already registered for any SAT, you can register for another by phone. Just call 866-756-7346. But, if we haven't beaten it into you by now, here it is again: Registering online is a much better way to go. All you have to do is go to sat.college board.org/register and follow the instructions.

Why should you register online? For one thing, it's a lot faster. (And cheaper! There's a $15 fee to register by phone.) Just a few clicks and you're done. You will also know the moment you sign up where your testing center is. In the event that you lose your admission ticket, all you have to do is print out a new one. And, just when it couldn't get any better, you can also see your scores online the day they come out, instead of waiting three weeks for the paper report to come. You can also see a copy of your own essay online.

SAT MISTAKES

If you really think something went wrong with the grading of your test, the College Board offers a score verification service for $55.

The College Board is human after all! Well, not exactly "human," but it does make mistakes.

On the SAT given in October 1996, the Math section contained a flawed question. A student much like you realized that, depending on how one interpreted the unclear (and mean and nasty) problem, there could be different answers. The College Board acknowledged its treachery and rescored the exam, raising the scores of about 45,000 tormented students (13 percent of those taking the exam on that day) an average of ten points.

For the SAT in October 2005, about 4,600 tests were scored wrongly, due to scanning problems with the machines. While this affected only a tiny proportion of students taking the test that day, you can imagine how you'd feel if you were one of the unlucky ones.

These mistakes just prove that no one (not even the Evil Testing Serpent) is perfect. If you really think a question is unfair—not just that you don't know the answer, even though we all think those are unfair—there is a (slim) possibility that it is a mistake. The procedure for challenging a question is in the registration bulletin, and your proctor should be able to help you as well.

That should answer most of your practical questions about the SAT, but we did leave one big question still hanging: HOW DO I GET A HIGHER SCORE ON THE SAT?!?!

The answer, of course, is simple: Study.

But, like most simple answers, that is not nearly enough. First and foremost, you need to study more effectively and efficiently than you have before. There are good ways of studying, and there are bad. To learn about the best ways to study for the SAT, check out the next chapter.

How to Study

A Primer for the Lazy, the Anxious, and the Disorganized

How does one become a track star? It's very simple: Go to the track, run, go to the track again, run again. Repeat. So why are we not all track stars? Because in another sense, all of that practice is incredibly hard. You have to motivate yourself to go every day, even on the days that you are sick, even on the days when there is a *RuPaul's Drag Race* marathon on TV.

Studying for the SAT is similar. Really, there are only two things you need to do. One is read—read this book certainly, and it's a good idea to read high-quality material in general. Two, take practice tests and practice sections. But in truth, actually doing the reading and studying is the easy part. The hard part is finding the motivation to get started.

GETTING IN GEAR

HOW DO I GET PSYCHED TO STUDY FOR THE SAT?

So how can you realistically motivate yourself to study for the SAT? Here are a few ideas.

1. Try to convince yourself that it is fun and challenging to develop your critical reading skills and learn mathematical facts. (Ha-ha-ha-ha-ha. Nope, no way.)
2. Try to convince yourself that the things you learn in today's study session will enable you to think critically and to sound articulate for the rest of your life. (Oh, please.)
3. Realize that your crush is attracted to equations and big words. (Keep dreaming.)
4. Note that the average teenager burns approximately 115 calories during an hour of intense studying. (Maybe so, but walking up and down stairs for an hour is much more interesting and burns 350 calories.)

The above techniques do not work because they use positive thinking. The SAT does not inspire positive thinking. You must learn to think negatively. For example:

1. Recognize that if you do not do well on the SAT you will not get into a good college. You will have to go to school in the Australian outback and your studies will be constantly interrupted by kangaroo migrations.

AUSSIES 101

2. Go to the kitchen. Press your tongue against the metal freezer tray and hold it there for ten minutes. Then rapidly yank it away. By comparison, studying for the SAT may actually be pleasurable.

3. Most of the dweebs who deserve to get into the colleges of their choice are probably too busy playing with their TI-89 calculators to have time to read this book. It's fun to watch dweebs get mad when they don't get into a college that you get into.

4. The SAT is expensive:

$57.00	test fee for the SAT (with essay)
14.95	this book
24.99	*The Official SAT Study Guide*
5.00	transportation to and from the test
.50	four number 2 pencils
5.00	food brought into the test

$107.44	Total

You don't want to waste that kind of money. *

It might seem counterintuitive, and it is certainly not guidance-counselor approved, but you need to learn how to dwell on these negative thoughts. Let them gnaw at your insides. Begin to feel a hatred of this test and all it stands for. Hate is a powerful emotion: It will give you the drive and determination you need for intense study. But be careful! If you get the balance wrong, you could get *too* negative and slip into anxiety mode. This might happen. In fact, this *will* happen. But not to fear, because you are about to learn about . . .

Sit back, close your eyes, and imagine that you are on a beach next to the bluest of oceans. The sun warms your skin and your toes wriggle in the soothing sand. The smell of coconut suntan lotion washes over you in a delicate sea breeze. As you take deep breaths of this beautiful air, you feel more and more at peace.

*With that, you could have bought 160 hot and ready Krispy Kreme donuts, 21 Venti Caramel Frappuccinos, or 470 number 2 pencils.

—Samantha

THE *UP YOUR SCORE* LOWER YOUR STRESS PLAN™

That sure would be relaxing. But the SAT isn't anything like that. The SAT is when you get up from the beach and stroll into the blue ocean and a black cloud of stingrays surrounds you and stabs you until ravenous sharks smell your blood mixing with the salt water and begin a feeding frenzy on your flesh.

The SAT will never be a day at the beach, but it doesn't have to be a gruesome drowning, either. To help manage your stress, we have developed a multipart *Up Your Score Lower Your Stress Plan™*.

KNOW YOUR ENEMY

Because people are frightened of the unknown, the best thing you can do to lower your stress is to prepare yourself. If you've memorized the test directions, know how to approach all the question types, and have taken a number of practice tests, then there won't be any unknowns to stress you out. (You can even pick a Saturday morning to get up early, go through the routine you have planned for test day, and take a full practice test. There, there, it's not that bad.)

INHALE, EXHALE

This might sound pretty stupid, but a lot of people forget to breathe normally because they are so nervous. If you find yourself holding your breath subconsciously, take some long, deep breaths. A pretty useful method is called "square breathing": First, exhale all of the bad air out of your lungs. Hold that for four seconds. Then, slowly inhale all of the air you can for four seconds. Hold it for four seconds. Then, repeat the sequence. (Four-four-four-four—that's why it's called Square Breathing, get it?) This is a great test-day technique, but can also be used any time anxiety strikes.

No, of course this isn't a surefire way to ruin Saturdays for the rest of your life.
—Samantha

MEDITATE

Concentration meditation is a simple technique that could really help you home in on what's important—like the history of celery. To meditate, simply sit in a relaxed, but upright position and focus your attention on a single object (say, the tree outside your window, your bedside lamp, or even this wonderful book). Keep your attention on the object. Increase your awareness of the object. Think of it as zoning in, not zoning out. Do this for ten minutes twice a day and you'll be surprised at what it can do for you.

SEE THE TEST

Another way to reduce your anxiety is to do what is called "positive visualization." Each night before you go to bed, make a movie in your mind about exactly what it will be like to arrive at the test center, show your admission ticket and ID, sit down, get your answer sheet, listen to the incomprehensible proctor read the directions, hear the smelly kid in front of you crack his knuckles. Then visualize yourself being completely relaxed throughout the whole ordeal. No, you are beyond relaxed—you are totally focused with intense energy on the test. You're in the zone. You're breathing deeply, your palms aren't sweaty, and your pulse is slow. If you visualize this scenario numerous times before the real test, you'll be amazed at how similar to your visualizations the real test will be. Of course, you'll be more nervous than you were in your imagination, but you won't feel any need to panic, and that extra bit of nervous energy might help keep you alert. *

*Nervous energy isn't bad. That adrenaline is what helped us escape lions on the savanna thousands of years ago. Use it now to rock the SAT.
—Samantha

REMEMBER, YOU'RE NOT EXPECTED TO KNOW IT ALL

Another relaxing thing is realizing that you are not supposed to know all the answers. Sure, an occasional whiz gets a perfect score, but the SAT is not like a classroom test on which your teacher will be disappointed in you for each question you get wrong. In fact, you can get tons of questions wrong and still do just fine. For example, you can miss 30 questions and still score around 1300. You can miss about half the questions and still get a score that is around the national average. So, don't worry about whether or not you can solve a particular problem. Work on it for a reasonable amount of time, then say, "It just doesn't matter. I'm not supposed to know all the answers." Mark it in the test book so you can go back to it if you have time, use one of our guessing techniques to make an educated guess for the time being (see Chapter 7), and then go on with the test.

BIG PICTURE

Finally, we checked with the heads of the world's major religions, and they all agree that while a poor performance on the SAT might make it less likely that you will get into the college of your choice, it will not have any effect on your chances of getting into the heaven of your choice.

CONCENTRATION

A man walks down the street
Says, "Why am I short of attention?
Got a short little span of attention
But, oh, my nights are so long."
—Paul Simon

Now that you're totally relaxed and feeling groovy, we're going to teach you how to increase your *concentration span*. Your concentration span is the length of time that you can direct your attention to a given task without spacing out. Every task also has what is called a distraction potential. The higher the distraction potential of a given task, the more difficult it is for you to concentrate for long periods. We all know that the distraction potential of the SAT can be very high indeed. Not only is the test itself difficult and boring, but the test hall atmosphere, complete with creaking chairs, strange odors, ticking watches, squeaking pencils, sneezes, and shuffling papers, can be distracting.

Imagine the following scenario. It's 19 minutes into the first Math section, and you're on the second-to-last question:

The equation $\dfrac{12x^2 - 5x - 7}{ax + 3} = -3x - 1 - \dfrac{4}{ax + 3}$

is true for all values of $x \neq -\dfrac{3}{a}$, where a is

a constant. What is the value of a?

A) -4

B) -2

C) 4

D) 16

This type of problem is not that hard if you recognize what's required. But when you're under pressure—particularly time pressure—you can really lose focus. If someone were to take a "brain transcript" of you trying to do this problem, here's what it might look like:

"What is THIS monstrosity? Wait . . . ooooh-kay. It looks like one of those rational functions that I have to divide. Yeah, poly . . . Polly . . . no-mials. Yeah. What the hell does Polly know? Probably more than me. . . . All right, all right, what am I looking at? I don't know a, so how can I divide by the denominator? Crap. Well, what's this garbage on the right side? I can never remember what the result of division is called. Dividends? Divisors? Shoot! I'm losing time. What do I have left? Two minutes? If I don't get this right, I'll probably lose like 20 points. Maybe I should guess. But I have no frickin' idea. Hmm . . . What about if I divide? In that case, the $12x^2$ part is going to become $-3x$ after it's divided by the "ax." I wish that idiot in front of me would stop tapping his foot. *Tap. Tap. Tap. Tap.* There he goes again. What's up with his hair? *Tap. Tap.* He looks like he just came from the gym. Gross! Hey, guy, you know, gyms have these great things called "showers." Okay, okay, okay. Back to this problem. If $12x^2$ is $-3x$, then $12/a$ is going to be -3. What does a have to be, in order to get -3 as the first term? Well, $12/a = -3$. So I can multiply both sides by a to cancel, and then divide both sides by -3. That gives me -4. So I don't need to care about ANY of the rest

I like to call the ability to concentrate for long periods of time "superfocus." Yes, it is a superpower.
—Samantha

Practice makes perfect. Concentration is no exception. The earlier you hone your concentration abilities, the better.

of this, the remainder and all that, because *a* is just –4. Bam, the answer's A. Fill in A."

Well, you got the answer right, but only after much wasted thought. The worst mistake was checking the time. Do this only between problems, never in the middle of a problem.

And never let the slightest distraction bother you—foot tapping, slimy hair, or whatever. Of course, this is much easier said than done. Simply deciding to concentrate can leave you with a brain transcript that looks like this:

"Concentrate. Concentrate, damn it. Okay. I'm just gonna focus my brain like you wouldn't believe. This is the most important four hours of my life and I am going to concentrate intensely for the whole time. Ooooh, I'm really concentrating now. His slimy hair isn't bothering me a bit. This is total concentration—no distractions. And the *tap-tap-tap* noise that guy's foot is making right now—which I wish would stop—isn't bothering me, either. You could stick me with pins and I wouldn't feel it. Okay, what problem am I on . . . ?"

You're concentrating so hard on concentrating that you're not concentrating on what you need to be concentrating on: the test. The trick is to learn to concentrate without thinking about concentrating. Your mind should be effortlessly focused. To learn to do this, you must practice. Training your brain is just like training any other part of your body—you have to exercise it.

Concentration exercises are usually pretty lame. They're the kind of thing you read, then say to yourself, *That's lame*, and move on without even trying them once. Typical concentration exercises are things like trying not to space out while running through the multiplication tables in your head. Any mental task that can be done for 20 consecutive minutes but is tedious enough that your brain is tempted to space out makes for a good concentration exercise.

We have discovered that drinking games make much better concentration exercises. If you practice these games for 20 minutes a day for a month, you will find that your concentration span will improve dramatically. You will also be admired when you go to parties in college because you will be so good at these games.

Important Note: Usually, these games are played in groups, and whenever someone screws up, that person has to take a drink. You, however, should play them alone and without doing the drinking. You will kill the whole value of the concentration game if you stop every few minutes to drink. You will also kill off so many brain cells after a month of these games that you will have no brain left with which to concentrate.

We've provided you with guidelines for two drinking games. We suggest that you play Game 1 for ten minutes, then Game 2 for ten minutes. It is good practice to try to do these games with the television on to see if you can concentrate so intensely that you are not even aware of the TV.

Game 1: *Kerplunk!* This one starts off simply but gets difficult. Say to yourself, in a steady rhythm, the following sequence of sentences:

1. One frog—two eyes—four legs—in a pond—*Kerplunk!*

(Then multiply everything by two.)

2. Two frogs—four eyes—eight legs—in a pond—*Kerplunk! Kerplunk!*

(Then do it with three frogs.)

3. Three frogs—six eyes—twelve legs—in a pond—*Kerplunk! Kerplunk! Kerplunk!*

As you can see, the basic pattern is

X frogs—2 X eyes—4 X legs—in a pond—repeat the word *kerplunk* X times

Keep doing the sequence. Whenever you say something wrong (i.e., saying 12 legs when you should have said 16 legs or forgetting to say "in a pond" or not knowing how many times you have said the word *kerplunk* or forgetting which number is next) or whenever you lose the mental rhythm and have to pause to think of what to say next, you have to divide the nearest even number of frogs that you are on by two and then start again. For example, if you were on 10 frogs and you said that they had 40 eyes, you would have to go back to "5 frogs—10 eyes—20 legs—in a pond . . ."

Game 2: *Buzz*

This is a counting game. Pick a number between 2 and 10, not counting 2 and 10. Then start counting in a steady rhythm. Whenever you come to a number that

   is a multiple of the number

or

   has the number as one of its digits

you don't say the number; instead you say the word *buzz*. The best way to explain this is to give an example.

   Suppose the number is 4, then you count

1, 2, 3, *buzz*, 5, 6, 7, *buzz*, 9, 10, 11, *buzz*, 13, *buzz*, 15, *buzz*, 17, 18, 19 . . .

   If you miss a *buzz* or lose the rhythm, you have to go back to the number that is half of the last even number you counted up.

Game 3: SAT Practice Tests

This game hasn't gained widespread popularity in bars, but it is the most useful concentration game. If you take a lot of practice tests and really concentrate on each section from start to finish, you will concentrate better on the real test.

HOW NOT TO GET STUCK

A common concentration-related problem you might encounter is an inability to move right on to the next question if you have not been able to solve the previous one. This difficulty arises because your mind is unwilling to accept that it is unable to do the problem and wants to keep working on it. A brain transcript might look like this:

OLD PROBLEM

"Okay, screw this. Too difficult. Can't figure it out."

NEW PROBLEM

NOT LOOKED AT YET

"This one looks easy. I can do this one. Choice D looks good but . . ."

"But wait! I can do this one. If I just knew what this part was. I've already spent two minutes on it. I might as well finish it. No. That's stupid. Move on to the next question."

"Where was I? Oh yeah. Choice D looks good."

"Hey, maybe choice D is also right on this problem. No, that can't be right. Move on to the next problem."

"Okay, it was D. I'll fill that in on the answer sheet."

This sort of zigzagging really wastes time. When your brain tries to occupy itself with two problems at the same time, it doesn't work well on either of the problems. ＊ You have to trick your subconscious mind so that it will move on to the next problem without trying to go back. Three things will help you do this:

1. **Skip and come back after two problems**. Zigzagging is a bad way to toggle between problems. Instead, you should leave the problem and work on two problems before returning. When you come back to the problem, it will be with a fresh(er) mind, and you'll be able to take a new swing at it. **Pro Tip**: Circle the problem number in your test booklet to remind yourself to come back!

2. **Guess**. When you guess, your subconscious is satisfied that it has found an answer and is more willing to move on. Again, mark the questions you've guessed on so if you have time you can go back and check your answers.

＊Even if our success with studying while Snapchatting our progress on a footlong sub has us convinced that we are professional multitaskers, we are not. Brains can't split in two.
—Samantha

3. **Practice**. The more timed practice tests you take, the more relaxed your brain will become with moving on.

WEAN YOURSELF FROM YOUR PHONE

It goes without saying that your phone will have to be off and out of sight in the testing room. But if you're like us and you keep a smartphone with you at all times, turning it off isn't always enough to take your mind off of it. You'll still be thinking about the sports scores you can't check, anxiously wondering why that photo of yesterday's omelet got only two likes, or responding to the ghost vibrations in your pocket. These are not things you want going through your head when you need to focus. So we recommend getting some distance from your phone the day before you take the SAT. We call this the *Up Your Score* Phone Challenge. Keep that sucker silent and inert for 24 hours before the test until the minute you walk out of the testing center. That's when you can take your "I Survived the *Up Your Score* Phone Challenge" selfie. *

*Do not live tweet the SAT. I repeat, do NOT live tweet the SAT.
—Samantha

CREATING A STUDY PROGRAM ... AND STICKING WITH IT

Needless to say, there are thousands of things you'd rather do than prepare for the SAT, beginning with weeding and ending with sticking hypodermic needles in your eyes. But after you've given yourself some motivational talks and calmed your anxiety, exactly how do you make yourself sit down and study?

1. SET A SCORE GOAL

Establish a specific score as your goal. Pick a score that you think you can achieve but that will require some preparation. (A good score goal is one a bit above the average SAT score for students at the schools you're considering.) Once you've set this goal, don't stop factoring quadratics and locating the use of irony until you consistently achieve the score (or even a smidge higher) on practice tests.

2. BLOCK OUT TIME IN YOUR SCHEDULE

Make appointments with yourself to study and take practice

Put it on the same level as a date with your lifelong crush, or a 5-hour uninterrupted nap. —Samantha

tests. Don't compromise this time; treat it as a serious commitment that you can't break. * Find a quiet, secluded place, and don't let yourself be disturbed—that means no food breaks, no texting, no checking Facebook, no pat-the-cat sessions. When you're finished, go outside and yell for a while to release your tension. Then reward your hard work and self-discipline by bathing in melted milk chocolate.

3. STUDY WITH FRIENDS

Anything is more fun if you do it with friends (except maybe body piercing). Read this book out loud. The jokes will be funnier and the tips will make more sense.

Another advantage to studying with friends is that you can help one another with some of the harder math concepts and argue over which sentence provides evidence for a particular answer in a reading passage. Just make sure that you don't get carried away fooling around and forget to study. Also, don't have too good a time or the Evil Testing Serpent will hunt you down, hide under your bed, and stab a number 2 pencil into your little toe while you sleep. The College Board doesn't like students to have any fun with the SAT.

4. TREAT IT LIKE THE REAL THING

When you are taking the practice tests, don't go too soft on yourself. This means taking the practice test within the time limit and not letting it go on for three days. If time's up, time's up. Sorry, you just have to be your own proctor.

Don't be tempted to cheat on the practice test (what's the point, anyway?), like sneakily whipping out a pocket dictionary at the sight of hard vocabulary. You can review the difficult questions after the test. If you've been conditioned to easier standards, you'll just have a harder time when the real SAT comes around.

Remember, if you don't prepare the first time, you'll just have to take the test again, and eventually you'll have to study.

Take practice tests in the morning if you can. You're never going to be taking the SAT at 8:00 p.m., unfortunately.

PRACTICE, PRACTICE, PRACTICE

Don't hold this against him. He means well.
—Samantha

As we mentioned earlier, you will need to practice on *real* SATs in addition to reading this book. Don't waste your time on fake SATs designed by test-prep companies. A lot of the time, questions on those tests are totally unlike the ones that are on the real SAT. Also, in many books, several of the given answers are *wrong*! So get the genuine article. Here's how:

Take the practice tests available online at khanacademy.org /sat or at collegeboard.org and in *The Official SAT Study Guide*, published by the College Board. The book and sites offer full-length practice SATs, with in-depth explanations for each question. They also have extra practice questions, many with clear explanations. The hints and strategies they provide are also worth reading. Of course, because the material is all sponsored by the College Board, it doesn't tell you how foolish the SAT can be, it doesn't show you any of the tricks on how to beat it, and it's not nearly as funny as we are.

In addition to practice tests, Khan Academy, which is partnering with the College Board, offers diagnostic tools that identify your strengths and weaknesses. It will also create a personalized playlist of videos to help you study. Your big sister and cousin Abner didn't have anything like this when they were studying for the SAT. But you do, and they're free so you might as well take advantage of them.

The founder of Khan Academy, Sal Khan, with help from his associates, walks you through each type of question on the test, just like we do in this book. He is genuinely determined to level the testing playing field with his free, high-quality study materials. But to do so he had to sell his soul to the College Board; he is now a minion of the Evil Testing Serpent. Khan pretends the test is your friend, but it is not. *

Also, before watching Khan's videos, we recommend that you shotgun a few Red Bulls because, although he is a good teacher, his voice is about as exciting as cottage cheese. But if you follow our advice, it will be as exciting as cottage cheese with Red Bull.

Finally, take advantage of the College Board SAT services.

Even though you'll probably walk out of the test with a couple of questions you're pretty sure you missed in mind, chances are you missed others, too. Whether it was because of a simple error or because you didn't understand the problem, it's always good to know what you got wrong and why so you can avoid the mistake next time.

—Samantha

BUILDING ENDURANCE

Since many colleges consider only your highest score, you can take the SAT more than once. For example, if you are planning to take the test in June, you can also register for the March test date and sign up for one of the services that the College Board offers to help you learn from your first test (and to make themselves more money). The Question-and-Answer Service provides you with a copy of the test you took, your answers, the correct answers, scoring instructions, and information about the type and difficulty of each question. * The service costs $18.00, and you can order it either when you register for the test or up to five months after your test date. It takes three to seven weeks after your test is scored for you to receive the materials, but if you are willing to pay the $18.00 and wait a bit, you'll know exactly which areas of the SAT you need to practice. Unfortunately, the College Board does not offer this valuable service for all of the test dates. If you want to use it, be sure it's available on your test date.

For the test dates on which the Question-and-Answer Service is not available, the College Board offers the Student Answer Service. For $13.50, you receive a computer-generated report that tells you for each question what type it was (vocabulary in context, geometry, etc.), whether you answered it correctly or incorrectly or skipped it, and the level of difficulty on a scale of 1 to 5. You can order this service the same way you order the Question-and-Answer Service, and you'll receive the materials three to six weeks after your test is scored. Although it doesn't provide you with as much information, you can still use it to gauge the areas in which you need work.

The SAT is a nearly four-hour test (if you include the optional Essay), which is tough for anyone. But it will be especially tough for those of us who were raised on a steady diet of Instagram and Facebook. Even if you are the kind of person who is easily able to focus on a given task, it is an altogether different challenge to focus for such a long period of time.

The best way to improve your stamina is to do it by phases.

Don't frantically study the day before. Maybe review any areas that have been giving you trouble, but there's no need for panicked cramming or last-minute practice tests. Rest your brain.

—Samantha

In the month before your test, try following this schedule:

Week One: Do one practice section per day, three days a week.

Week Two: Transition to two sections per day on one of those days.

Week Three: Now, add one three-section day on a Saturday or Sunday.

Week Four: You can scale it back to sections on only two weekdays, but on the weekend, do a WHOLE TEST. The more whole tests you can get done before the real thing, the more accustomed you will be to the endurance challenge.

On test day, a great way to improve your stamina is to simply calm down. Don't distractedly look up (or sideways or over your shoulder) too often. Force yourself to look only at the test—and your trusty watch (see page 348). If some kid next to you accidentally stabs himself in the hand, then runs around shrieking and spraying blood across the walls, don't look up. Let someone else tell you about it afterward.

Bring snacks. (See our extra-scrumptious and totally healthy recipe on page 346.) One of the sneakiest ways to lose endurance is due to hunger and thirst. Keep yourself well fed and well hydrated (but not too well hydrated), and you will be surprised by how much easier it is to concentrate.

Finally, you should know that losing focus or energy is another sneaky sign of stress. If you feel suddenly, inexplicably fatigued, try the breathing and meditation exercises mentioned earlier. There is a good chance this will help.

And if all else fails, bring a CamelBak backpack filled with 5-Hour ENERGY Shots to the test. Good luck going to sleep that night, though.

The Evidence-Based Reading Test

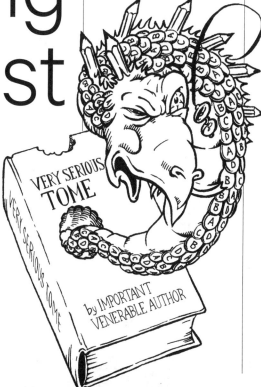

What used to be called "The Verbal Section" has gotten a grander—and more terrifying—new name: The Evidence-Based Reading and Writing Test. It is considered bad luck to say this full name in public. You may whisper it, or use its acronym: the EBRAWT. This might be a scary section, but there is no denying that it is fun to say the word *EBRAWT*.

Like death by lethal injection, the EBRAWT has two—or you can opt for three—phases. The first (designed to put the inmate to sleep) is the Reading Test. The second (designed to stop the inmate's breathing) is the Writing and Language Test. The third part is an optional Essay Test (designed to stop the heart from beating should phase two fail).

In this and the upcoming chapters, we will explore these three sections of the SAT. Each of them is an expression of the Evil Testing Serpent's new obsessions.

THE SERPENT'S NEW OBSESSIONS— EVIDENCE AND ANALYSIS

Lest you think that the gruesome features of the EBRAWT are the result of the Serpent's hatred for high school students, you should know that the EBRAWT is actually the product of LOVE. Yes, in the process of inventing the new SAT, the Serpent fell head-over-claws in love. The Serpent's new crush object, about whom it talks all the time and to whom it sends gushy Sexts (Serpent texts), is named *Evidence*. It isn't clear if Evidence likes, or even notices, the Serpent, but the Serpent just can't stop asking questions about Evidence:

- How does this piece of evidence contribute to the overall argument?
- This evidence could be used to support which of the following claims?
- If this evidence were to change, how might the overall argument change?
- The author uses which piece of evidence to support the claim made in paragraph three?

Even when the Serpent tries to play it cool by not saying

the word *evidence,* the Serpent is still secretly, obsessively talking about Evidence with words like *claim* and *point*:

- Which of these facts would most directly support the claim made in paragraph three?
- A student claims that the pace of economic growth in developing countries does not benefit from government regulation. Which of the following statements in the passage contradicts the student's claim?
- Which point about the noodles that are highly valued in lasagna is implicit in Passage 1 and explicit in Passage 2?

Indeed, if we wanted to summarize in one sentence what's new about the new verbal SAT, we might say: The Serpent decided to be "just friends" with its previous passion, Vocabulary, and is now hitting on Evidence nonstop. (You'll notice, however, that Vocabulary has not been posting revenge pictures on Instagram. That's because the Serpent still gets with Vocabulary when Evidence isn't around. So it may be more accurate to say that Vocabulary and the Serpent are now "friends with benefits.")

In light of all this drama, we realized that in order to master the EBRAWT, we had no choice but to make friends with Evidence. The things we do for you. We went up to Evidence one day and whispered, "You know, that Serpent is just *using you* to support a claim. As soon as the Serpent is done using you, it'll start flirting with the next face that comes along. In fact, people saw the Serpent sitting suspiciously close to Analysis in the library. . . ."

In exchange for this gossip, we have learned a lot about the Serpent and even the secret things it does when it is alone with Evidence. We'll teach you everything we know. But the fact is that Evidence gets around—you can find Evidence in any number of scientific and historical texts and you should probably read more and more such texts to learn how writers in each field use Evidence.

If you want to get with Evidence, you have to start reading. There's no way around it. Unlike the good old days when you could learn a few hundred words and watch your score go up, there's no tricky substitute for being a reader. Consider trying to get yourself to read 1,000 words of serious, college-level science and history every day. No? Okay, 900. Maybe 850?

Analysis— A Fancy Word for Thinking

Confirmed—
analyze is just a
fancy word for
"explain what's
going on."
xoxo, gossip girl

As rumored, the Serpent's other emerging fascination is with *Analysis.* The Serpent might ask you to:

- Analyze the argument.
- Analyze what would happen if the author used this word instead of that word.
- Analyze this pattern across two texts. Analyze the tone, analyze the change, analyze the conclusion, analyze the analysis.

When you get to the Writing Test, you will almost certainly be asked to analyze a topic based on evidence in the passage.

Yes, it is all a bit scandalous—the Serpent is frequently seen doing things with both Evidence *and* Analysis. And you, too, will have to join in the fun.

What is analysis? It's largely the task of comparing evidence, evaluating evidence, combining evidence from different sources, and thinking about what claims you can make from the evidence. You know: thinking. It also includes analyzing language or "rhetoric"—what is the effect of using this word instead of that word?

So, let's begin tracking evidence and analysis through the first part of the EBRAWT—the Reading Test.

THE NUTS AND BOLTS OF THE READING TEST

The Reading Test is 65 gruesome minutes long. An hour and five minutes of your life that you will never get back. All of the questions on the new Reading section take the format of a passage followed by questions about the passage.

There are FOUR passages of 500–750 words, and ONE pair of related passages (which will add another 500–750 words total). There will be 10 or 11 questions after each. For the paired passage, you'll be asked questions about each of the passages and about the relationship between the passages.

Luckily, there will be some variety. One passage will be an excerpt from a work of U.S. or world literature. Two passages (or a stand-alone passage and a pair of passages) will be about a topic in history/social studies. Usually one of these will actually be about a social science topic, for example, economics or law. Two passages (or one stand-alone passage and one pair of passages) will focus on science.

All passages are from previously published sources, and the Evil Testing Serpent assures us, with a sadistic gleam in its eye, that they represent the top writing and thinking in their respective fields. You're also going to see something a little strange: Informational graphics will accompany one or two of the passages, and questions will be asked about the graphics. Don't worry—we'll talk about this later. **Literature passages** can be old or new, American or international—they will always be written in English. If you encounter a passage written in Serbian, please show it to a non-Serbian proctor.* **Science passages** can be about scientific concepts that have been around for a long time, or more recent discoveries. **History/social studies passages** come from articles and book excerpts on social science topics such as education, anthropology, and sociology, as well as from founding documents in U.S. history and, in Serpent-speak, "texts in the Great Global Conversation." Although you could argue that the Great Global Conversation is happening on Twitter these days, we would recommend you shelve those arguments while you're taking the SAT. These passages are from speeches and other important documents about political philosophy or ethics. They will probably be about justice, freedom, rights, the tension between equality and liberty, or the best way to keep your wig powdered and fresh during a long Continental Congress.

Unfortunately, all of the passages will be much longer than a tweet.

We'll go over each type of question that you'll encounter on the Reading Test, so you know what to expect. But first, there are seven essential rules that you should familiarize yourself with.

*If all your proctors are Serbian, we cannot help you.
—Samantha

THE SEVEN KEY RULES

It's like cruise control—once you find your speed, you won't have to even think about it anymore. That is, until you come to the red light that is the proctor announcing the end of the section—then it might be time to stop.

—Samantha

RULE 1: KNOW YOUR SPEED.

One of the most important strategies for improving your score on the Reading Test is to use the time well. You can lose a lot of points if you don't get through all the passages, but you'll also be penalized if you work too quickly and make dumb mistakes. If you get the timing just right, then you'll read with the right balance of care and speed, and you'll answer questions with the right amount of precision and time to check your work. Most important, knowing your speed helps you relax and feel like you are "in the zone." The two key aspects of getting your speed right are to know your reading speed and your answering speed.

THE RIGHT READING SPEED

But you may be asking, "Is my speed the *right* speed? Because it feels a bit . . . *slower* than the right speed."

Look, you're going to have to read about 3,000 words in the reading passages on this section of the SAT. This means the ability to read quickly can be a big advantage.

So we recommend that you read only those words that start with the letter *w*. "Hold it," you say, "but then I won't understand anything." To which we respond, "Oh yeah, you're right, sorry," and then suggest, "Try reading everything very carefully and make sure you comprehend it all." To which you respond, "But then I won't have time to finish the test."

This is the heart-wrenching conflict you must deal with on the Reading Test: To speed or not to speed? All we can say is: Do as many practice tests as you possibly can so that you know how fast you can read while still understanding as much as possible of the passage. It would be great if you could get your "time per passage" to under six minutes.

Fancy speed-reading tricks probably won't help much. Psychologists have found that speed-reading tricks really only teach you how to skim a text by skipping details. But for reading questions on the SAT, you have to know the details.

There's no substitute for practice—practice reading the kinds

of texts that will be on the SAT, and take enough practice tests that the right reading speed becomes natural to you.

THE RIGHT ANSWERING SPEED

Remember, you've got 65 minutes to answer the 52 reading questions. This is more time than previous versions of the SAT allowed per question, but don't be fooled: The Serpent isn't being generous. The questions are a bit more demanding now—all because of the pesky focus on evidence.

The math-berts among you have already done some calculating and thought: *Great, I have about 75 seconds per question.* Wrong, math-bert! You have to subtract about 20 minutes for the amount of time you need to read the reading passages. Then subtract another minute for the time you spend watching the kid in front of you pick his nose and maybe another half second for the time you spend picking your own nose. Now you have only about 50 seconds per problem. That's just about the amount of time most people need if they work efficiently. If you find yourself finishing ten minutes early, then you're probably working too fast and being careless (or you didn't spend enough time picking your nose). If you aren't on track to finish all the questions before the time runs out, you might have to be a little less careful.

If, after lots of practice and long hours spent in libraries, you are having serious trouble getting to the end of the test, you might need to take the extreme "amputation strategy." This is where you don't even try one whole passage of the test. You don't read it. You just enter guesses for each question. Which passage should you amputate? * Whichever one is generally hardest for you. If you know you hate the science passage, skip the science passage and just guess at the questions. If you know you hate the paired passages or the passage with the infographic, skip that one. All other things being equal, skip the LAST passage on the test because it may be a bit harder. But remember: Enter guesses even if you didn't read it. (For more on guessing, patiently wait for Rule 3—and see Chapter 7, page 323.)

*As in medicine, amputate only if absolutely necessary. Your score will lose a limb . . . or at least a foot.
—Samantha

*Truth exists in layers. Chocolate cake also exists in layers, but that's a different story.
—Samantha

RULE 2: TRUST THE PASSAGE MORE THAN YOUR OWN KNOWLEDGE.

Reading questions refer to what is "stated or implied in the passage." You do not need any outside information beyond general background knowledge. So if the passage is about the history of celery and you happen to be an expert on stringy green vegetables, you still have to read the passage. However, the passages almost never contradict accepted outside knowledge. You won't ever see a passage that claims that the earth is flat or that celery is good. So never choose an answer that you know is making a false statement.

On the other hand, never assume that you know the right answer just because you know that one of the statements is true. There might be other true statements among the choices that are more applicable to the passage. *

RULE 3: ALWAYS GUESS.

If you skip a question because you don't know the answer, you should always give it your best guess (there is no penalty for guessing wrong and you might just get lucky). Then put a mark next to it in the test booklet. We suggest an "X" for the questions you don't think you'll be able to figure out and a "?" for the ones you think you'd get if you have time left over at the end. If you want to be really organized, put a "☆" next to the ones you did answer but aren't sure about. Then, when you get to the end of the test, do the "?" ones first, the "☆" ones next, and the "X" ones last. (For more good guessing strategies, see Chapter 7.)

RULE 4: KNOW THAT, FOR THE MOST PART, QUESTIONS WILL BE IN THE ORDER OF THE PASSAGE.

That is, the answers to the first questions tend to be at the beginning of the passage, the answers to the middle questions tend to be in the middle of the passage, and the answers to the last questions tend to be at the end of the passage. So if the answer to question 1 is about line 12 and the answer to question 3 is about line 20, then the answer to question 2 can often be found between line 12 and line 20.

This usually works even if a question is not asking about a particular line. For example, imagine three consecutive questions:

1 The reference to the "dusty" butter (line 65) most directly emphasizes . . .

2 The author of the passage believes that . . .

3 In line 73, "dingbat" most nearly means . . .

Clearly, the answer to question 1 is in line 65, and the answer to question 3 is in line 73. While you might think that the answer to question 2 could come from anywhere in the passage, the College Board knows that you don't have enough time to skim through several paragraphs in search of the answer. So there should be something between line 65 and line 73 that clearly supports one of the multiple-choice answers to question 2. This method often works, but just in case, you should do your best to keep the entire passage in mind.

RULE 5: KNOW THE DIRECTIONS.

The directions are generally the same for any given edition of the new SAT. Memorize them from the practice tests on the College Board website.

Don't waste precious time carefully reading directions during the test unless they seem different from the ones you've seen before.

RULE 6: ADOPT A POSITIVE ATTITUDE.

The reading passages are the one place where you should abandon the negative thinking we recommended on page 24. As impossible as this may sound, it is important to assume a positive attitude toward the Reading Test. Why is this? Well, remember the chapter on oral hygiene in the health textbook

This is a prime reason why you should familiarize yourself with the test before test day: the smug feeling you'll get when all the other kids are still reading the directions but you're already on question #3.
—Samantha

There's a psychological theory that if you force yourself to smile you will become happy. Smile while reading the passages. Ignore the weird looks from the guy next to you.

—Samantha

you had in sixth grade? No, because it was boring and you didn't want to read it. But do you remember the chapter on sex? Yes, because sex is more interesting than tooth decay. This is an eternal rule of reading. You don't remember passages that you find boring. Instead, you need to learn to trick yourself, to convince yourself that you are passionately interested in whatever the passages are about. Get psyched to read them. Treat them as you would a love letter. Ponder them as you would a passage from a piece of great literature. Cherish them as you would a section of *Up Your Score*.

There is sound psychological backing for this claim. Scientists have shown that comprehension and retention levels are much higher when people are interested in what they are reading than when people aren't. Your brain just doesn't bother remembering stuff that it considers totally dull.

RULE 7: READ, READ, READ.

The sad fact remains, the best preparation for the Reading Test is to have read widely and deeply. We'll give you all our best tips, but you still need to invest time in reading a variety of texts of increasing complexity. If your reading matter is limited to cereal boxes and the school's bathroom stalls, it's time to explore new possibilities—like a newspaper, perhaps. **Caution**: Do not attempt to switch cold turkey! Many a student has gone into intellectual shock after attempting to jump straight from Snapchat captions to *The Plasma Physicist's Quarterly*. We suggest that you work up to quality reading material using this one-week plan:

Day 1: *Outlaw Biker* (This is a real mag!)

Day 2: *The National Enquirer*

Day 3: *Seventeen*

Day 4: *People*

Day 5: *Entertainment Weekly*

Day 6: *Time*

Day 7: *Vanity Fair*

Now you should be ready to tackle the kind of reading you are likely to find on the SAT. Read things like the *New York Times*, the *Economist*, the *Atlantic*, *National Geographic*, *Sports Illustrated*, *Outside*, *The New Yorker*, *Harper's*, *Lapham's Quarterly*, and *Scientific American*.

Reading these high-caliber publications is useful for many reasons. First of all, you get to impress your friends with all the lofty vocabulary and syntax you'll pick up. ("Dude, evanescence is my MO—one minute I'm here, the next minute I'm gone.") Secondly, you'll start to think that SAT-type passages are familiar, almost normal. And on the Essay, the more you mimic the sort of writing featured in these kinds of publications, the happier the Essay scorers will be. And lastly, if you can survive an eight-page article on interest rates in the Middle East, you can survive anything the Evil Testing Serpent throws at you. Of course, if you're feeling ambitious, you might also try reading a full book, but please consult a doctor before any extreme, unfamiliar exertions.

It's never too late to become a good reader. Just think about things that interest you—really, *anything*—and start reading all the high-quality material on the subject that you can find. Look for it online. You should also look at what your school and local libraries have to offer. And suggest magazine subscriptions and books if someone asks what you want for Flag Day. *

*Magazine subscriptions can be found in app form. We realize this is not the sixteenth century.
—Samantha*

Once you get your reading endurance up, you may have to transition from topics you like to read about to those that are going to make you good at the SAT. Remember, the Serpent likes passages about history and science, and excerpts from works of literature. We wish there was a way to avoid having to read these things and still do well on the SAT, but it doesn't seem that there is. So just suck it up and get in touch with your inner nerd.

SO MANY PASSAGE TYPES, SO LITTLE TIME

The reading passages on the old SAT used to be about anything at all, as long as it was boring and harmless. There could be a passage about a person who knitted mittens from the lint in his navel. There could be a passage about pastries.

Now the reading passages are much more "academic." They are examples of the kinds of things you will read in college—science, history, social science, literature. And what is the Serpent looking for when selecting a passage? You guessed it: evidence. The passages are heavy with bits of evidence that support an argument. There wasn't much evidence in the breezy passages about lint mittens. But scientific and historical arguments are often presentations of evidence and a claim about how the evidence should best be interpreted.

So don't spend a lot of time asking yourself, "How does this passage make me feel?" or "What's my opinion about this passage?" The SAT isn't at all concerned with your feelings or opinions. It wants to know whether you can find the evidence and understand how the author uses evidence to support her argument.

SCIENCE PASSAGES

For the scientific passages, the College Board selects articles written for a wide audience. The passages assume no prior knowledge of the particular topic, but they do use alarming words like *vulcanization* and *flagellates* and employ the kind of thinking that comes from having studied high school science and read good prose about science. The *New York Times*, *Discover*, *Wired*, *Science*, and *New Scientist* all feature articles of this type.

You don't have to be a science whiz to handle the science passages. You just need to pay attention.

A few questions, we're sorry to say, might test your ability to think scientifically. You may need to understand and evaluate the scientist's hypothesis and methods of experimentation, and make sense of data to identify what conclusions can and cannot be validly drawn from an experiment. The passage might cite other related experiments by different scientists, and you might be asked whether the findings of the different researchers support or contradict one another.

How to handle: Do not be intimidated by scientific jargon. The scientific passage will inevitably have some far-out scientific terms that you have never heard of. Don't worry. You don't need to know these terms. They will either be explained or go untested. Take, for example, the following excerpt from an actual SAT question:

> . . . Kinematic studies of such objects show them to be receding from us at a rate proportional to their distance . . .

Some students might panic when reading this sentence because of the word *kinematic*. Relax. You don't have to know what kinematic studies are to answer the questions correctly. ✱

The second reason this sentence could be intimidating is that it refers to proportions. Proportions are math, and math is terrifying. Once again, there is no need to worry. If you read the sentence that follows the difficult sentence, you'll see that it explains the math, so you don't have to do any thinking:

> That is, those galaxies most distant from us have larger recessional velocities.

The expression "that is . . ." clues us in to the fact that this sentence is going to explain the previous sentence. This is a good rule of thumb: If you don't understand a sentence, look at the sentences that precede and follow it and read it like you would read anything else. Chances are, these tactics will disarm the fancy scientific language.

Science passages will often get an infographic that you have to understand as part of the passage—we'll talk about how to handle those a bit later in this chapter.

HISTORY/SOCIAL STUDIES PASSAGES

The history/social studies passages will feature one of three different kinds of texts.

1. **Founding documents** (e.g., the Declaration of Independence, *The Federalist Papers*, the Constitution, the Bill of Rights, majority/minority opinions from key

✱ *In a scientific passage, if you encounter an impossible word, replace it with something more familiar. "Certain studies of such objects show them to be receding from us . . ." sounds much better, doesn't it? The only reason you'll have to worry about the impossible word is if it appears in a test question, which is unlikely.*
—*Samantha*

Some prior knowledge about these documents may be useful, but you should be able to find the answers in the text. So unless you're looking for an intriguing hobby for your résumé, no need to read all of The Federalist Papers.

—Samantha

Supreme Court decisions, etc.) Luckily, you paid complete attention in civics class, took rigorous notes, and have a photographic memory.

How to handle: The founding documents are about all kinds of things, but they are mostly about how we should live together, how we should govern ourselves, what our values and principles are or should be. Their language is extremely formal: "We hold these truths to be self-evident . . ." The nice thing about founding documents is that because they are written in olden-times-speak, the questions will be very straightforward. The Serpent will not be asking about some deep, hidden meaning. The questions will ask about what the author is saying and how he says it.

2. **The Great Global Conversation** These will also be primary sources. Some of these are speeches and essays by famous Americans like Abraham Lincoln and Martin Luther King Jr. Others are by noteworthy people from other countries, like Mahatma Gandhi, Margaret Thatcher, or Sia. But all of them will be about important and lofty ideals like freedom and justice and Top 40 pop.

How to handle: These will also be challenging texts, so you can expect most of the questions to be literal—just figure out what the passage says, not the deeper things it doesn't say. Many of these passages are taking a stand against something that is wrong. They gather the evidence of how wrong that thing is, and they argue for a solution. It is highly unlikely that these passages will argue for murder, hatred, injustice, or anything bad, so if you have to guess, embrace your newfound positive thinking and choose the positive, idealistic answers.

3. **Social sciences** The third type of history/social studies passages will draw from topics in the social sciences, including anthropology, economics, political science, and psychology. These are similar to science passages

in that they might drop some spine-tingling words like *zeitgeist* and *commodification*. The bad news is that the Serpent *does* expect you to learn these words because you will be using them in college. The good news is that we have defined many of them beginning on page 98.

How to handle: Many of these passages will use social science evidence, such as statistics, charts and graphs, or academic studies, to make a point about the world. Just like with the science passages, pay attention to the evidence and how the author uses it. Again, do not form your own opinion about whether the article is right or wrong or whether you like it. Just read it on its own terms and pay attention to the evidence it assembles and how it analyzes that evidence.

LITERATURE PASSAGES

The literature passage will be a piece of literary prose. It could be anything from a classic by Mark Twain to something by a contemporary author you've never heard of. It will most likely be realistic, rather than science fiction or fantasy or mystery. So those ten months you spent reading all of *A Song of Ice and Fire* might not be as helpful as you thought. The good news is you don't have to know anything about the author or the time period.

The passage won't be radical or sexy or violent because that would trouble some students and help the rest of us stay awake. *

Anything remotely entertaining is against the Serpent's very goal in life and therefore illegal.
—Samantha

Again, the questions will not ask what you think or feel about the work of literature. They will ask what the passage says and how the author says it and they will want you to notice details and subtlety.

How to handle: The literature passage may seem like a welcome break from all that evidence. Literature rarely makes a direct argument from facts or statistics. There won't be any infographics. But the literature passage probably will have an evidence question. Often, these questions are spread out over two questions. First there's a question that you answer based on your understanding of the passage:

1 Based on the passage, the primary problem with the initial bowl of porridge is that

A) it is too hot.

B) it is too cold.

C) it is too just right.

D) it has gluten.

Then there is a sneaky follow-up question that asks what evidence (what lines from the passage) best supports the answer you gave to the previous question. That means you have to remember what you just answered and identify where in the passage you found the answer.

2 Which choice provides the best evidence for the answer to the previous question?

A) lines 3–4 ("Goldilocks . . . sonorous.")

B) lines 8–9 ("Papa Bear . . . belch.")

C) lines 11–12 ("Mama Bear . . . taxidermy.")

D) lines 14–15 ("Gluten . . . despair.")

If you don't see an answer choice on the second question offering good evidence for the answer you provided to the first question, then reconsider your answer to the first question. (For more on follow-up questions, see page 63.)

Other than the evidence question, most of the questions about the literature passage will focus on what the text says or implies—and on *how* the author says it or implies it. There will certainly be a couple of vocab-in-context questions that ask what a word means or what effect a word has in a passage. There is often a symbol or metaphor in these passages, and a few questions will ask if you understand the metaphor. This can be particularly tough, as metaphors are often "open to interpretation." Just remember, the Serpent stays *very* close to the text. So don't get all deep. It is almost never asking about some mystical hidden meaning. It is asking about things that you can find in the passage if you read it carefully.

For literary passages, it can be smart to skim the questions *first* so you know what parts of the passage you should focus on. Read every word of the passage, but keep those questions in mind.

PAIRED PASSAGES

The paired passage consists of two separate passages, both focusing on science, history, or social science. According to the College Board, the passages will "oppose, support, or in some way complement" each other. They are usually short and the questions will be less about one passage or the other and more about how the two passages relate, how they draw different conclusions from the same evidence, or how they draw the same conclusions from different evidence.

The key to the paired passages is figuring out how they relate to each other.

How to handle: The heart of answering the paired passage questions is figuring out the relationship between the passages. You should be able to tell easily whether the two passages agree or disagree.

If you're having trouble figuring out the relationship, follow this general rule: If the context and subject matter of the two passages seem quite different, then their main points will almost certainly be similar. For instance, the Evil Testing Serpent once paired a speech from ancient Greece and a speech from the Civil War (two different historical eras and locales). These disparate passages had the same view on war. An essay on silent film and one on mime (two different art forms) showed the similarities between the two forms.

By contrast, another selection had two passages on architecture, both from the twentieth century, and they disagreed. So if the two passages were written in different times or places or if they concern different subjects, they probably agree conceptually. If they talk about the same subject and were written in the same time or place, they probably disagree.

READING TEST QUESTION TYPES

Luckily for you, the Serpent can ask only a few different types of questions on the Reading Test. After all, it has promised to offer subscores on very specific reading skills, and it needs to be able to show that one year's score is comparable to a score the next year. What this means for you is that once you get comfortable with the question types, you can rest assured that nothing will surprise you.

There are a few different types of questions, but they fall into four broad categories and one mini-category. The broad categories are main idea questions, meaning questions, structure questions, and rhetoric and vocabulary questions. The mini-category is comparison questions, which you will see only on the paired passages.

Main Idea Questions

There is almost always a question that asks about the central idea of the passage.

- The author is primarily concerned with . . .
- Which of the following titles best summarizes the passage?
- The primary purpose of the passage is to . . .
- Over the course of the passage, the main focus shifts from . . .

If you're not sure what the passage's main idea is, look at the first paragraph, especially the first and last sentences, where you are most likely to find the "topic sentence" or thesis statement, then look at the concluding paragraph, as well as the first sentence in each of the other paragraphs. The clues should be there. If you are still confused, try this: Look away from the page. Look out the window, or, if you are taking the test in an underground bunker, look at the concrete wall. Ask yourself: "Self, what was that about?" You'll be surprised how good your brain is at summarizing the main idea when it is freed from searching through each word.

But not all of the main idea questions are about the passage as a whole. So watch out for questions like "The main purpose of the third paragraph is . . ." These questions about a particular paragraph are often asking: What is the main piece of evidence brought forward in that paragraph or what is the analysis offered by it?

Pro Tip: "Main idea" questions are not about "deeper meaning." Some people overthink these questions. They've just read about the Celery Rebellions in medieval Europe and they conclude that the passage is really about "the long struggle between ignorance and justice" (a deep theme never mentioned). The main idea is often more literal. It is a straightforward statement that is supported by the article: "The Celery Rebellions were a failed attempt to win human rights for people who like celery."

Other main idea questions might ask you to **summarize** a passage or paragraph. The idea here is exactly the same as any other main idea question: Pick the answer that includes the thesis and primary argument of the passage but does *not* include any extraneous information.

Pro Tip: If one of the summaries includes *more* language from the original passage than the other options do, it probably *is not* the right answer. When the question writers craft a summary, they make sure it is mostly in different words than the original. But when the Serpent writes the impostors (tempting wrong answer choices—see Chapter 7) it knows that including a lot of words from the original passage might convince an unsuspecting student who recognizes the words, but doesn't understand that they are being used in ways that do not summarize the passage.

Some main idea questions try to disguise themselves using scary analysis-speak. The two most common disguises are **main purpose** questions and **author's point of view** questions.

A "main purpose" question might look like this:

The main purpose of this paragraph is to
A) address a misconception.
B) justify an opinion.
C) identify a solution.
D) share a memory.

On others, the choices will be a little more specific:

The main purpose of the passage is to
A) emphasize the value of snail eggs as an unorthodox pizza topping.
B) describe the intensity of the New York/Chicago pizza rivalry.
C) question the feasibility of making an even deeper dish pizza.
D) warn readers about the dangers of superheated Hawaiian Volcanic Pizza.

After you read these questions, you might think that you need to *dig deeper* into the passage, to find the true, hidden nugget of meaning beneath all the verbiage. But put that shovel away! These are just asking for the main idea. Look over those topic sentences, glance at those first and last paragraphs. Look away from the page and ask your brain what the passage is about. Then, pick the answer that accounts for the thesis of the passage.

Main purpose questions test your knowledge of academic vocabulary as much as your ability to determine the purpose behind what you've read. If all the choices were written in everyday English, most students could probably skim the passage and answer these questions without giving them much thought. But the questions that employ top-shelf vocabulary can throw people off, even when they really *do* understand the purpose of

The best way to answer reading comprehension questions is to spot the key words of the answer choices. In this case, look at the verbs: Emphasizing is very different from describing is very different from questioning is entirely different from warning. If you feel your brain starting to get bogged down, look only at the key words of the answer choices and see if that helps you narrow it down.

—Samantha

the text. Spend some time with our academic vocabulary section that starts on page 98 to help ensure that you won't get tripped up by these words.

An **author's point of view question** can also look more challenging than it really is.

> In the passage, the stance that Nicki Minaj takes is best described as
> A) a woman who is proud of her body.
> B) a philosopher contemplating the nature of celebrity.
> C) an artist exploring new modes of self-expression.
> D) an idealist dreaming of a better future.

After reading this question, you might think that you need to ponder Minaj's preexisting conceptions, her attitude, or her tone. Nope! This is just a disguised main idea question. By now you know the drill: Check those topic sentences, those first and last para-greezies, look away from the page.

Pro Tip: In general, it is a good idea to SKIP main idea questions and do them after you've answered the more specific questions on any passage. This is because the specific questions force you to read the passage over and over; plus they often give you valuable clues as to the overall meaning. By the time you go back to the big picture questions, you will be in a much better position to answer them.

Meaning Questions

Meaning questions are very straightforward. They ask you what the text says, so the answer is always right there in the passage. Unfortunately, the SAT has found a few ways to make these questions more difficult.

To start off, there are two types of meaning: explicit and implicit. **Explicit meaning questions** ask you what the text *literally* states. These are a bit easier, so let's start with them.

Here are some explicit meaning questions:
- According to the fourth paragraph, some economists feel that . . .
- According to the passage, an atom of which of the following substances will split, releasing energy and more neutrons?
- The narrator asserts that Margaret asked Mrs. Horn's opinion because Margaret . . .

The primary strategy for answering explicit meaning questions is to first locate the relevant part of the passage, reread it, then formulate your *own* answer before heading to the answer choices. This is crucial. Don't forget, the answer choices are trying to trick you (for more on "impostor" answer choices, see page 320). Coming up with your own answer is like putting on a suit of armor before heading into battle.

Note that you may have more luck with the explicit meaning questions if you skim the questions in advance and mark the relevant evidence while you read the passage. (See the strategies that start on page 69 for other useful approaches to these questions.)

Explicit meaning questions will often ask about trickier parts of the passage. They might ask about a part of a paragraph that discusses a counterexample. Like this:

> While alien spacecraft do not generally have human-butt-shaped seats or nail clippers sized for human toes, the *Starship Magnarax* was surprisingly comfortable. It even served palatable food and piped in music that sounded very similar to smooth jazz.

Those butt-shaped seats and nail clippers were a counterexample. It is a thing that most alien spacecrafts lack. The rest of the paragraph is about all the great things that the *Starship Magnarax* has. The Serpent likes to ask questions that require you to understand that the counterexample is not like the rest of the evidence. It contradicts the argument the author is making. So if the question were to say:

> What is a reason that the author brings up
> the example of "nail clippers"?

Then you would want to reject the answer that said:
A) To provide an example of the convenient features aboard most alien spacecraft.

and instead look for an answer like:
B) To illustrate the types of features that most alien spaceships lack.

Implicit meaning questions are slightly more difficult. These ask about something that is never stated outright, but is reasonable to conclude based on what *is* stated in the passage. These questions will look like this:

- It can be inferred that the guilds were organized as they were because . . .
- It can be inferred that each of the following applies to cognitive behavioral therapy EXCEPT . . .
- With which of the following statements about marketing would the author most likely agree?

The secret to these questions is that the Evil Testing Serpent will never ask you to infer very much. The correct answer is the one that is closest to the literal meaning of the text. Let's try this out. Read this passage:

> While traditional roach poisons such as hydramethylnon are undoubtedly effective, they cause levels of pain and suffering far beyond what is necessary. Not only is fipronil more eco-friendly, but it takes only minutes to kill the insect, as opposed to hydramethylnon's medieval six hours of suffocation and organ erosion.

If there are two answer choices that seem to be almost perfect opposites, like these two, go back and check the passage to make sure that the one you chose is what the text is <u>actually</u> saying.
—Samantha

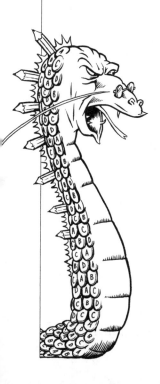

If the question were to say:

> It can be inferred that the author would agree with which of the following opinions about roaches?

then you would reject the answer that says
A) Roaches have long been unfairly vilified.

and would also reject
B) Those who use hydramethylnon are heartless.

and would instead pick
C) The purpose of poisons is to eliminate pests, rather than torture them.

You should be able to pinpoint exactly where you found evidence for your answer. Prove this to yourself by circling or underlining the evidence in the text.

—Samantha

The point here is that you *could* go down the inference rabbit hole and arrive at choices A or B. "Well," you could say, "he *does* call hydrametha-whatever medieval, and in medieval Europe outsiders were often vilified as an excuse to torture and kill them, so *perhaps* we can say that he is arguing that roaches were similarly vilified." Do you see how many twists and turns we had to take to arrive at that answer? The correct answer will require no more than one, and most often zero, brain-twists to arrive at the correct inference. Stick to the text!

Both explicit and implicit meaning questions might be followed by questions that look like this:

> Which choice provides the best evidence for the answer to the previous question?
> A) "There are many ways to skin a cat, and many ways to kill a bug." (line 1)
> B) "Scientists agree on one thing . . . studies have shown." (line 7)
> C) "Not only is fipronil . . . organ erosion." (line 13)
> D) "Famous last words." (line 25)

Time Saving Tip: As soon as you see a follow-up evidence question, jot down the line numbers next to the passage. Like so:

1
7
13
25

This will save you time, frustration, and the paper cuts that come with flipping back and forth.

We call these **follow-up evidence questions**, because they ask you to point at the line that proves your previous answer. If you answered the previous question correctly, then this should be no problem, but if you did not, then you might just double-down on wrong answers! Be careful! In the previous question, it is C, the line about fipronil, that proves the answer to the previous implicit meaning question.

Pro Tip: You can *use* the evidence-based follow-up question to check if your previous answer was correct. For example, if you picked an answer that cannot be proven with *any* of the sentence options, then you know that you were wrong, and you should go back and reconsider the other answer choices.

Finally, you might see one more type of meaning question: **the analogy**. These are pretty bizarre. The questions take forms like:

- Which situation is most similar to the one described in lines 71–78 ("The eel . . . ascent")?
- Which of the following is most like the fear Constanza expresses in the beginning of paragraph 2?

These questions require that you abstract from the specifics of a particular passage and turn it into a template. Then apply that template to the answer choices to see which one fits. Take this passage:

> The composition of Martian soil might not factor into the everyday concerns of your average citizen. But the number of tax dollars allocated to Martian eco-science means that every one of us is actively participating in this area of research. If we're paying for this, then we should be giving Mars more thought.

First, let's abstract from the specifics and turn it into a template. Here, a distant, seemingly unimportant thing is shown to be more important than it initially appeared. The question might look like this:

It can help to look at the answer choices while you figure out the abstract template. Your brain will start to form connections.
—Samantha

Which of the following situations is most similar to the one described?

A) A volcano in Hawaii causes the local bird population to decline.

B) A new element is discovered after a long process of experimentation.

C) An obscure financial regulation causes all citizens to lose a portion of their savings.

D) A long-accepted theory on evolution is questioned when new evidence arises.

Told you these questions were weird. Luckily, they are also pretty rare. Here, the only answer that fits our abstracted template is C, where a seemingly unimportant thing turns out to be very important.

Structure Questions

Just as buildings are made of beams and joists, passages are made from logical sequences and cause-and-effect relationships. Take this classic kids' story:

> One bright summer morning, Bubbles the Bear invested two-thirds of his life savings in total stock market index funds. Forty-five years later, Bubbles retired with enough savings to afford a modest condo in the Strawberry Forest.

The structure of that story is that Bubbles first invested his savings, then he retired with those savings. This relationship between elements of a story is all we mean when we talk about structure. Most structure questions will either be about cause and effect or, similarly, sequences of events.

Cause-and-effect questions explore the relationship between something that happens in the passage and whatever caused it. They can be about the small actions of an individual person or larger trends in an entire society.

Why was Bubbles the Bear so prepared for retirement?

A) He had created a stable network of family and friends.

B) He lived in an area where summer mornings were bright, and thus easier on his cataracts.

C) He had made sound financial decisions earlier in life.

D) He had managed to save much of his income.

Notice how the Testing Serpent will try to disguise C, the correct answer, in vague terms? That is Serpentine Deviousness 101. Also, did you catch the answer choice that used the words *bright summer morning* from the text? That was a classic trap. So was answer choice D, which referred to something mentioned in the passage. Sure, Bubbles had saved some of his income, but it was not the saving that directly caused the retirement preparation, it was the investment.

Sequence questions will test your understanding of the chronological order of events in a passage, or in the historical background contained in the passage.

But watch out! Often, the Serpent will pick sentences where, due to tricky syntax, events do not occur in the order you'd expect. So a sentence like this:

Before there were circuit breakers, there were fuses.

inverts the time sequence—the fuses came first, the circuit breakers came second.

Or you might have a cause-and-effect sentence like:

Before Dwight Eisenhower was elected president, he won the admiration of millions as the Supreme Commander for the Allied Powers.

This would be accompanied by a question asking:

Why was Eisenhower known to most
Americans before his presidential campaign?

If you zone out and see "elected president" followed by "Supreme Commander," you could think that Eisenhower served as the Supreme Commander after his presidency. Not only would your history teacher feel a sudden chill pass through her chest, but you would get the answer wrong! So look out for critical direction and causality markers like "before," "unless," "despite," "after," etc.

Rhetoric and Vocabulary Questions

Rhetoric is a very fancy word. When the Duchess of York wakes up each morning, she says the word *rhetoric* in a slow drawl, before eating a breakfast of crumpets, Darjeeling tea, and rose petals. But in truth, rhetoric just refers to the way words are employed.

While the old SAT asked you for the meanings of words, the new test will ask you about how words are being used in the context of the passage.

- The main effect of the phrase "before his eyes" is . . .
- With which of the following phrases does the author shift from telling a story to establishing an argument?
- If the word "irony" were replaced with "earnestness" in the opening sentence of the passage, how would it change the meaning?

The crucial strategy here is to read the phrase or word IN THE CONTEXT of the passage. Words can mean many different things in different contexts (for example, you can inhale air and you can also air your grievances—same word, different contextual meaning). Carefully read the sentence in which you find the phrase. If the word's meaning is still elusive, go ahead and reread the whole paragraph.

No matter how well you know the word, it's wise to go back and look at the sentence or paragraph rather than answer based

It's safe to assume that the Serpent will try to trip you up whenever possible. Sometimes the answer will be the word's most well-known meaning, but make sure you can really justify that answer.
　　—Samantha

solely on your knowledge of the word because maybe the author used it in some unusual way (for example, sarcastically).

Note that while the SAT used to test students on very obscure words you were unlikely to ever encounter in real life (ever heard of *bloviate* or *gobemouche*?), many of the questions on the revised SAT will ask about short, seemingly simple words, like *taste*. The Serpent is NOT trying to do you a favor. These little words are sneaky because they have multiple meanings depending on the context, so don't assume that *taste* means "flavor" just because that's the first definition that comes to mind—it could also refer to experience ("He finally got a taste of real life") or preference ("Pink plaid is really not my taste") or social customs ("Farting at the dinner table is in bad taste").

Many vocabulary-in-context questions pick out a certain word from a passage and ask you to choose the correct synonym. For example, the passage may have a line like "Harold was positive that the offending BO in the boys' locker room was coming from Stinky Steve," followed by the question:

> In line 14, "positive" most nearly means
> A) cheerful
> B) encouraging
> C) confident
> D) optimistic

While "positive" can mean any of these things in different contexts, "confident" is the only synonym that makes sense here. Usually, the SAT questions are about loftier themes than body odor, but the logic is the same.

You should also expect some questions that ask about hypothetical variations in word choice and what the impact might be on meaning:

> If instead of the word "passion" the author had used the word "toothpaste" in line 7, what would have changed about the meaning of paragraph 3?

Also note that the tricky vocabulary word is not always in the question. Sometimes it is in the answer choices. For example:

> Which of the following words best describes
> the mood that Toby was in when he invented
> the ketchup milk shake?
> A) exhilarated
> B) inspired
> C) lugubrious
> D) ambivalent

As you can see in this question, you can't always rely completely on context. This means that you have to learn some vocabulary. While we cannot tell you all of the words tested on the new SAT, we have created a list of some frequently used words, which you can find beginning on page 98.

Bonus: Comparison Questions (Paired Passages Only)

Were you worried that we were done with the question types? Never fear, for there is one last type of question you might see on the SAT: comparison questions.

Comparison questions are usually not terribly difficult, but they *are* terribly annoying. This is because they require that you summarize the argument of one passage, in order to compare it to a point made in the second passage. Take a look at these:

> *Passage 1*
> Today, film critics write to assert their own
> preconceived opinions, to reinforce their own
> unwavering stance. These days, the critic is a brand, and
> brand management is considerably more important—
> and more lucrative—than earnest evaluation,
> open-minded consideration, or plain thought.

> *Passage 2*
> When *Passionate Hearts* opened, the filmerati were
> unimpressed. The *Los Angeles Times* called it "a paean

to stupidity," and A. O. Scott of *The New York Times* wrote a notorious, one-word review: "Dreck."

The author of passage 1 would most likely agree with which of the following statements about the "filmerati" in passage 2?
A) They are often mischaracterized as vindictive.
B) Their opinions, though logically sound, are stylistically questionable.
C) They dumb themselves down for their readership.
D) Their critical goals are insincere.

To answer this question, we need to summarize passage 1 (critics care more about their reputations than the act of reviewing) and apply this to passage 2. Here, the answer choice that best accounts for passage 1 is D.

DIFFERENT READERS, DIFFERENT STRATEGIES

There are many different types of readers. Some skim through *The Wall Street Journal*, searching for the most important percentages and tables. Others luxuriate over a page of James Joyce's *Ulysses* repeating each pun and portmanteau. Reading, in other words, is a rich activity, and there are many ways to do it. Similarly, there are a few different strategies that may be useful for taking the test. Try them all and determine which ones work for you. We recommend, however, that you not *luxuriate*, as you only have a few minutes.

STRATEGY 1: SKIM THE QUESTIONS BEFORE READING THE PASSAGE.

This gives you an idea of what to look for while you read. Follow the five guidelines below if you use this method.
- Read *only* the questions; do not read the answers, too, because that takes too much time.
- If the question is about a specific line number in the passage, mark that line so that when you read the

Make sure you don't mix up the passages and attribute something you read in passage 2 to passage 1. Again, circling and underlining here will help you avoid that.
—Samantha

passage you will know to pay close attention to it. (This is especially helpful for the vocabulary questions.)

- When you see a question that asks for something general, such as "Which is the best title?" or "The main idea of the passage is . . ." quickly go on to the next question. Why? Because you should always assume that there will be at least one main idea question, so you don't even have to bother reading it.

- As you read the passage, circle anything that might be an answer to one of the questions. Don't immediately go and answer the question because that will break your concentration and interfere with your comprehension.

- Don't get so caught up in looking for the answers to the questions that you fail to understand the overall meaning of the passage.

STRATEGY 2: MENTALLY SUMMARIZE.

After you read each paragraph, ask yourself, "What was that paragraph about?" Spend a couple of seconds summarizing the contents of the paragraph in your head. If you want, take a moment to jot down notes and paraphrases in the margins or underline key phrases. This can save time later when you have to look for the answers. If you are a flake who, like Larry, can read an entire passage before realizing that you weren't paying attention and that you have no idea what it was about, then this strategy might help force you to concentrate, paragraph by paragraph.

Remember this rule of thumb: If you can't summarize it, you don't understand it. If you head into the questions with an inadequate understanding of the passage, you are like a ball of dough heading into a pasta machine: You *will* be shredded into delicious strands.

STRATEGY 3: CIRCLE THE MAIN IDEA.

Usually, the passage will include a few sentences that state the author's main idea. As you read the passage, underline these sentences.

Not only will this reinforce your understanding of the main argument, but it will help you locate important sentences when you face those main idea questions.

Again, this technique functions as a warning sign if you are not getting the passage. If you cannot locate the main idea sentences, then you are lost on this passage and need to do some rereading, or, if you are hopelessly lost, tackle another passage and come back later.

STRATEGY 4: READ THE PASSAGE, THEN TRANSLATE THE WHOLE THING INTO SWEDISH.

This will help only if you are Swedish.

Two bonus tips, at no extra charge:

- When in doubt, lean toward the politically correct. Never pick an answer that seems too extreme or countercultural. The College Board tries to be as politically correct and mainstream as possible.
- Even when you find a question totally baffling, remember that the answer—or, at least, clues to it—is always in the passage, just sitting there, waiting for you to find it. Even if you can't find the definitive answer, anything that improves your guessing will help your score.

A VERY SERIOUS READING PASSAGE

Now it's time to attempt a sample reading passage. Following the passage are examples of the different types of questions and the answer choices that will accompany them. The passage is an excerpt from a scientific magazine about an astonishing technological breakthrough.

FROM *ROVER ON THE ROCKS* by Dr. Emilio Sziklas, et al. © 1998. Originally published in *Consumer Trends*.

Modern science has brought us many wonderful inventions—the television, the waterbed, and "I Can't Believe It's Not Butter!" Many more marvelous technological breakthroughs loom on the horizon. The latest development in the field of applied science is no exception. Today, scientists have invented a process through which

Line
5

deceased family pets can be freeze-dried and saved for millennia.

Every pet owner knows that pets are integral parts of the household. When they have been around for so long and have had such an influence on family members, it's hard to let them go when they pass on. Now, through freeze-drying, Fido or Fluffy can remain a household member forever.

When your pet dies, its lovable body is kept intact. You can keep it on the mantel and take it down to pet it at your leisure—and a dehydrated pet does not require feeding, walking, or litter boxes. It emits much less of an odor than regular dead pets, and it looks much better, too.

The projected uses for freeze-dried pets are numerous. If Spot happens to have died in a crouched pose, he can be placed on your lawn as a security device. Snookums can be used as a decorative centerpiece. Market analysts predict a boom in gerbil paperweights, goldfish refrigerator magnets, and poodle hood ornaments.

Detractors claim, however, that the dehydration wears off after several years, as moisture from the air enters the animal corpse and causes decomposition. This, it is feared, would attract bacteria into the home. Another flaw in the freeze-drying process is that the pet becomes brittle and breaks easily. For a young child, finding Fluffy shattered on the living room floor could be extremely traumatic. Finally, it is feared that people who dislike their pets might have them freeze-dried prior to death.

Furthermore, leading dehydration ethicist Thornton McFrackleberry believes that "a freeze-dried pet would be subjected to an eternity of humiliation and mistreatment at the hands of uncaring owners." He argues that moisture should not be removed from pets without their prior consent. However, a reliable way to gauge a pet's willingness to be freeze-dried after death is yet to be discovered. Other experts, such as Dr. Lisa Furrycorpse at Harvard's Mammal Mummification Institute, have voiced support of this new preservation technique. Furrycorpse polled more than 1,000 pet owners and found that 89 percent of them would be greatly comforted by the presence of their pet's physical form even after its life had ended.

Although there are problems with the procedure, the concept of freeze-dried pets is a valuable one. If the method is perfected, it will allow a pet to remain an everyday part of the lives of its loved ones and, indeed, it will permit pets to be passed from generation to generation as family heirlooms.

1 This passage is primarily

A) a scientific description of the freeze-drying process.

B) an exploration of the religious and moral ramifications associated with a proposed technological development.

C) a general discussion intended to acquaint the reader with a new service.

D) an expression of opinion.

(Question Type: Main Idea)

2 The first paragraph is best described as

A) descriptive.

B) introductory.

C) argumentative.

D) conciliatory.

(Question Type: Structure)

3 The word "detractors" in line 22 most likely refers to

A) farm implements.

B) critics.

C) supporters.

D) pet owners.

(Question Type: Vocabulary in Context)

4 According to the passage, one of the specific problems associated with the process is

A) a freeze-dried pet attracts viruses.

B) the lack of qualified individuals to perform the task.

C) freeze-dried pets are not shatterproof.

D) the fear that freeze-dried pets will stick to the wallpaper.

(Question Type: Explicit Meaning)

You've been writing essays for a while now. Think about it: What do first paragraphs usually do?
—*Samantha*

5 The author seems to believe that
A) the difficulties of freeze-drying outweigh the benefits.
B) the likely outcomes of freeze-drying are unforeseeable at this point.
C) critics of the freeze-drying process are tainted by their business associations.
D) the goals of freeze-drying are worth striving for.
(**Question Type:** Implicit Meaning)

6 How does the fourth paragraph of the passage ("Detractors claim . . . prior to death.") contribute to the author's overall argument?
A) It reveals the author's personal stake in the success of freeze-drying pets.
B) It demonstrates the author's inability to decide between pro and con arguments.
C) It shows that the author has considered both the pros and cons of freeze-drying pets.
D) It reveals the author's unstated biases.
(**Question Type:** Structure)

7 McFrackleberry and Furrycorpse offer _____ views toward pet freeze-drying.
A) opposing
B) compatible
C) aligned
D) concurrent
(**Question Type:** Implicit Meaning)

8 The data from Lisa Furrycorpse's study suggests that
A) preserving a pet's body after death is appealing to most pet owners.

*Note: The SAT will not provide a handy line of answers after each set of questions. Sorry.
—Samantha

A TRULY SERIOUS READING PASSAGE— WE MEAN IT THIS TIME

B) freeze-drying would be a profitable business venture.

C) the majority of Americans approve of freeze-drying a pet.

D) the majority of people approve of freeze-drying a pet.

(**Question Type:** Explicit Meaning)

Answers: 1. C; 2. B; 3. B; 4. C; 5. D; 6. C; 7. A; 8. A. *

The following is an excerpt of the late Nelson Mandela's opening address at his 1964 trial in South Africa. It is often called "An Ideal for Which I Am Prepared to Die." Like your typical SAT passage, the speech makes use of evidence. Also, like an SAT global conversation passage, it is considered an important part of history. Sure, it is more serious than freeze-drying your pets, but most SAT passages won't be a barrel of laughs. And take a deep breath, because this one is a full 680 words long.

"An Ideal for Which I Am Prepared to Die"
by Nelson Mandela, his address from the dock as accused
number 1 at the Rivonia Trial, April 20, 1964

Our fight is against real, and not imaginary, hardships or, to use the language of the State Prosecutor, "so-called hardships." Basically, we fight against two features which are the hallmarks of African life
Line in South Africa and which are entrenched by legislation which we
5 seek to have repealed. These features are poverty and lack of human dignity, and we do not need communists or so-called "agitators" to teach us about these things.

South Africa is the richest country in Africa, and could be one of the richest countries in the world. But it is a land of extremes and
10 remarkable contrasts. The whites enjoy what may well be the highest standard of living in the world, whilst Africans live in poverty and misery. Forty per cent of the Africans live in hopelessly overcrowded and, in some cases, drought-stricken reserves, where soil erosion and the overworking of the soil makes it impossible for them to live

Quick refresher: Nelson Mandela was a South African revolutionary who fought against racism and segregation (apartheid) in his country. After being imprisoned for 27 years, he became the first black president of South Africa in 1994. He also was awarded the Nobel Peace Prize. (Thanks, Wikipedia!)
—Samantha

15 properly off the land. Thirty per cent are labourers, labour tenants, and squatters on white farms and work and live under conditions similar to those of the serfs of the Middle Ages. The other 30 per cent live in towns where they have developed economic and social habits which bring them closer in many respects to white standards.

20 Yet most Africans, even in this group, are impoverished by low incomes and high cost of living.

The highest paid and the most prosperous section of urban African life is in Johannesburg. Yet their actual position is desperate . . . 46 per cent of all African families in Johannesburg do not earn

25 enough to keep them going.

Poverty goes hand in hand with malnutrition and disease. The incidence of malnutrition and deficiency diseases is very high amongst Africans. Tuberculosis, pellagra, kwashiorkor, gastro-enteritis, and scurvy bring death and destruction of health. The

30 incidence of infant mortality is one of the highest in the world. According to the Medical Officer of Health for Pretoria, tuberculosis kills forty people a day (almost all Africans), and in 1961 there were 58,491 new cases reported. These diseases not only destroy the vital organs of the body, but they result in retarded mental conditions and

35 lack of initiative, and reduce powers of concentration. The secondary results of such conditions affect the whole community and the standard of work performed by African labourers.

The complaint of Africans, however, is not only that they are poor and the whites are rich, but that the laws which are made by the

40 whites are designed to preserve this situation. There are two ways to break out of poverty. The first is by formal education, and the second is by the worker acquiring a greater skill at his work and thus higher wages. As far as Africans are concerned, both these avenues of advancement are deliberately curtailed by legislation.

45 The present government has always sought to hamper Africans in their search for education. One of their early acts, after coming into power, was to stop subsidies for African school feeding. Many African children who attended schools depended on this supplement to their diet. This was a cruel act.

50 There is compulsory education for all white children at virtually no cost to their parents, be they rich or poor. Similar facilities are not provided for the African children, though there are some who receive such assistance. African children, however, generally have to pay more for their schooling than whites. . . .

55   The Government often answers its critics by saying that Africans in South Africa are economically better off than the inhabitants of the other countries in Africa. I do not know whether this statement is true and doubt whether any comparison can be made. But even if it is true, as far as the African people are concerned, it is irrelevant. Our

60 complaint is not that we are poor by comparison with people in other countries, but that we are poor by comparison with the white people in our own country, and that we are prevented by legislation from altering this imbalance.

1 What is the most likely reason Mandela addresses the common perception that "Africans in South Africa are economically better off than the inhabitants of the other countries in Africa"?

A) To reassure his audience that Africans in South Africa have sufficient resources and social mobility.

B) To counter the South African government's attempts to downplay the hardship and injustice faced by African citizens.

C) To voice the Africans' gratitude that their lives are better than residents of neighboring countries.

D) To dismiss the international community's sympathy for Africans in his country.

(Question Type: Implicit Meaning)

2 Which choice provides the best evidence for the answer to the previous question?

A) "Our fight is against real, and not imaginary, hardships or, to use the language of the State Prosecutor, 'so-called hardships.'"

B) "There is compulsory education for all white children at virtually no cost to their parents, be they rich or poor."

C) "Poverty goes hand in hand with malnutrition and disease."

D) "The present government has always sought to hamper Africans in their search for education."

(Question Type: Follow-Up Evidence)

3 In the passage, Mandela states that

A) South Africa is the poorest of the African nations.

B) legislation in South Africa prevents Africans from getting education and better jobs.

C) the South African government relies primarily on misinformation as a tool of oppression.

D) Communists are a threat to social equality in South Africa.

(Question Type: Explicit Meaning)

4 As used in line 4 "entrenched" most nearly means

A) contained.

B) drained.

C) reinforced.

D) installed.

(Question Type: Vocabulary In Context)

5 Which of the following can be inferred from the final paragraph?

A) South Africa is making progress toward racial equality.

B) Economic statistics inadequately compare poverty in African nations.

C) South Africans do not sympathize with the plight of other African nations.

D) The South African government cares less

about the well-being of its African citizens than about its white citizens.

(**Question Type:** Implicit Meaning)

6 The main rhetorical effect of the phrase "Our complaint is not that we are poor by comparison with people in other countries, but that we are poor by comparison with the white people in our own country," is to

A) localize the issue of racial inequality in South Africa.

B) demand a new strategy for political action.

C) renounce the policies of other African nations.

D) condemn Africans' concern with obtaining material wealth.

(**Question Type:** Rhetoric)

7 In the context of the passage, the last paragraph serves to

A) give concrete examples of an abstract idea.

B) question some of the points already made.

C) challenge a potential objection and restate his thesis.

D) shift the tone from one of criticism to one of celebration.

(**Question Type:** Structure)

Okay, let's dig into this a bit deeper and analyze why each correct answer is the right choice.

Question 1. The answer is B; Mandela brought up this false perception of Africans' quality of life in anticipation of what the South African government would say in response to this speech. The other choices falsely imply that Africans are not experiencing hardship.

Question 2. On the SAT, the second halves of these question pairs will include options that support some of the wrong answers from the first question, but you won't get points if both of your answers are incorrect, even if they "match." There is only one answer that really backs up the correct answer to Question 1 ("To counter the South African government's attempts to downplay . . ."). Choice A mentions the "State Prosecutor" and shows how he refuses to refer to the poor quality of life Africans experience as real hardship.

Question 3. A is false; Mandela says that South Africa is better off than many of its neighbors. C might be tempting because he does accuse the government of peddling misinformation, but he does not state that this is the *primary* means of oppression. D is false; Mandela mentions communists, and while we might be able to infer some negativity from his tone, we do not have reason to believe he sees them as a threat. That leaves B as the answer. It is the choice that most strongly supports Mandela's argument, and also the only statement found explicitly in the text.

Question 4. This one is tricky because several of the choices are associated with the word *entrenched*. The context is key here. Mandela does not say that legislation alone created (or "installed") the poverty and lack of human dignity experienced by black South Africans. What he means is that laws have supported (or "reinforced") traditions of racism. The answer is C. ✱

Question 5. What is Mandela implying when he says that whites in South Africa are significantly wealthier than Africans and that the government is doing nothing to fix this? Basically, he is implying that the government doesn't care about its African citizens. The correct answer is D because it best crystallizes the underlying meaning

✱With vocabulary questions, it always helps to plug the answer choices right into the sentence to try them out for fit. Feel free to imagine the sentence being read aloud by Nelson Mandela for authenticity.

—Samantha

of the paragraph. It might be tempting to choose C, since Mandela states that the condition of other countries is "irrelevant" for present purposes. However, he says this to emphasize the importance of the fact that "we are poor by comparison with the white people in our own country."

Question 6. This question is really just a test of whether you were able to follow the passage from beginning to end. Choice A is the only one that has a basis in the text. This portion of a sentence is Mandela's way of getting his audience to focus on South Africa and not let other nations influence the world's perception of his own.

Question 7. In the last paragraph, Mandela raises the usual objections made by the government in order to refute them. While the government might claim that South Africa is wealthier than other African nations, he restates his central argument that Africans are poorer than white South Africans and are denied the same opportunities. The answer is C.

INFOGRAPHICS

As we've mentioned, the SAT now includes questions about informational graphics that accompany the passages on the Reading and Writing Tests. It might be jarring, at first, to see a bar graph in your reading passage. But really, these graphs are just more pieces of evidence. What's more, once you get used to these infographics, they become some of the easiest questions in the section.

The test will generally use the kinds of bar, line, or circle graphs that you might see in a textbook, at lectures in a college course, or in a magazine like *Bar, Line, and Circle Graphs Quarterly*. They are never fancy or obscure. Sometimes a graphic might look unusual at first, but the unusual-looking ones are often easier to interpret as long as you don't get flustered.

But can the nonspectacled understand the utter pain of not being able to read the menu at Panera?? I didn't think so.
— Samantha

However they might try to fancy it up, these graphs always get back to one of two things:

1. distributions
2. variable relationships

These sound like the kinds of words you might say while pushing your glasses up on the bridge of your nose, but really they are basic concepts. Even the nonspectacled can understand them. *

Distributions

A *distribution* illustrates how much of something exists in varying places or conditions, or how much there is of one thing compared to other things.

Does that sound too abstract? Well, let's look at an example that charts one misguided young woman's attempt to woo her crush via texting.

The following is a text retrieved from a cell phone found in the hallway of a high school in Kalamazoo, Michigan.

Hey Johnny
I think ur really cute
I made this bar graph that compares your hotness to the average hotness of guys in our school, county, and state

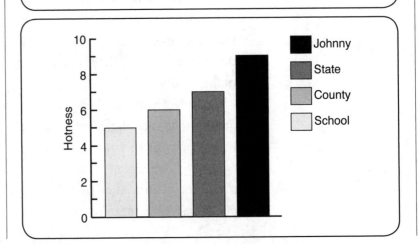

Here is another that shows how hot I am compared to the other 3 girls at our school who like u (trust me I know who all of them r and i am arranging for them to be transferred to another high school, ha ha, no srsly though I know the superintendent)

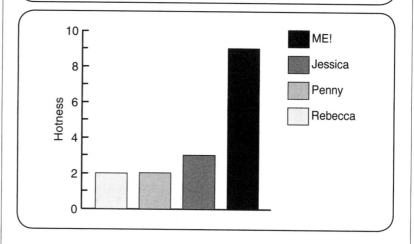

Ur super special! Im not kidding, look at this pie chart

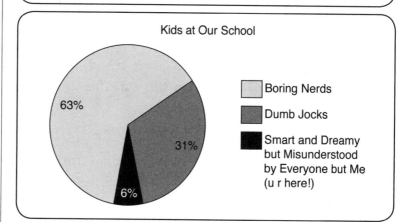

LMK if you wanna hang out :)

If the SAT were to write an SAT-style question about this text, it would probably look like this:

> Which of the following claims is supported by the data?
> A) Johnny is the hottest guy in the state.
> B) The number of hot guys in the state is higher than the number of hot guys in the county.
> C) The average hotness of guys in the county is less hot than Johnny.
> D) The hottest guy in school is less hot than the hottest guy in the county.
> (Answer: C)

In order to answer this question, you have to pay close attention to *precisely* what the first graph is recording. If we look at the preceding text, we see that our anonymous texter is comparing Johnny's individual hotness to the *average* hotness of guys in the school, county, and state. Does this mean that Johnny is the hottest? No! There could be someone hotter in the state, but also enough disgusting manimals (to use the technical term) to drag down the average. So A is wrong. Similarly, we know nothing about the *number* of hot guys at the state or county level, so B is out as well. Finally, we know nothing about the hottest individual guy in school, nor the hottest individual guy in the county, so D is out. That leaves us with C, our correct answer. Let's try another:

> The author's efforts to woo Johnny are best advanced by her claim that she is hotter than
> A) Jessica and Penny's combined hotness.
> B) Rebecca, Penny, and Jessica's combined hotness.
> C) Rebecca and Penny's combined hotness.
> D) none of the three girls who like Johnny.
> (Answer: B)

Don't pick the first answer that seems right. A, B, and C are all true, but B is the most compelling claim and the one that takes the whole graph into consideration.
—Samantha

As you can see, most infographic questions are straight-forward, but they require close, careful reading of the graph AND the question. If you were speeding through, you might accidentally pick A or C. Let's try another:

> According to the author's measurements, the boys at the author's high school are
> A) hotter than the average for the state, but not the county.
> B) hotter than the average for the county, but not the state.
> C) hotter than the county and state averages.
> D) less hot than the county and state averages.
> (Answer: D)

All of these questions ask about distribution. Graphic 1 is about how hotness is distributed in different regions. Graphic 2 is about how hotness is distributed among the texter and her rival bachelorettes, and graphic 3 is about how nerds, jocks, and people who resemble the hot textee are distributed in the school.

Variable Relationships

A variable relationship looks at how much one thing changes as another thing changes.

The most frequently graphed relationship between variables is change over time. The most common graphic is the line graph. You've seen a million of these in weather and stock market reports and probably on many of your science tests at school. Time is most often shown on the horizontal *x*-axis, and a *dependent variable* is most often shown on the vertical *y*-axis. Together, the two axes show how the amount of something changes over time. Or how it doesn't change. Take, for instance, this useful graph from the U.S. Census Bureau, which tells you exactly how many seats Wyoming has been allotted in the House of Representatives across the decades.

Good news—you don't have to memorize your state's congressional representation for the SAT. Though it would be easy for you Wyomingites (Wyomans? Wyomingians? Wyomes?).
—Samantha

WYOMING'S CONGRESSIONAL REPRESENTATION, 1880–2000

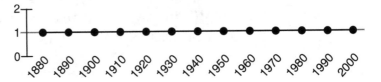

The graphs on the SAT will show more variation over time than this one (at least, we sure hope so). Here we present an example with more typical graphs.

WHY YOU SHOULDN'T PROCRASTINATE: A GRAPHICAL ANALYSIS

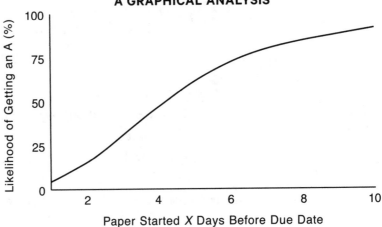

This graph is an example of the SAT sneaking into your subconscious. Don't procrastinate.
—Samantha

According to the above graph, students become less likely to get an A on a given paper if

A) they start writing the paper earlier.
B) they wait longer to start writing the paper.
C) they take mostly math classes.
D) they follow the Kardashians on Twitter.

We made this question intentionally tricky! When you think of procrastination, you probably think of a clock ticking downward. But the way this graph is presented, the *x*-axis counts *upward* from one day before the due date to ten. Even though you should start by reading this graph from left to right, time is moving from right to left. So, if you follow the line in that direction, you'll see that the likelihood of getting an A on the paper decreases the longer students wait to start it (as common sense and experience should tell you). So the correct answer is B.

Note: We actually didn't mean to make the graph so confusing. We just couldn't figure out how to reverse the values on the *x*-axis because . . . well . . . we procrastinated.

Let's try another question:

> A student sees the sharpest increase in the likelihood of getting an A between:
> A) 0–2 days.
> B) 2–4 days.
> C) 4–6 days.
> D) 6–8 days.

Here, the SAT is asking about the greatest increase between the various two-day periods charted on the *x*-axis. Between 0–2 days, it increases from about 5 percent to around 15 percent, or a 10 percent increase. Between 2–4 days, it increases from about 15 percent to about 45 percent, or a 30 percent increase, which is greater than the increase between either 4–6 or 6–8 days. Answer choice B, then, is our answer.

Some SAT graphics show change over time differently by presenting two different "distributions," taken at two different times, side by side. The following pie charts, for example, show the

POLL: FAVORITE PROCRASTINATION METHODS, 1618

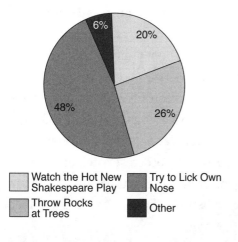

Watch the Hot New Shakespeare Play
Throw Rocks at Trees
Try to Lick Own Nose
Other

POLL: FAVORITE PROCRASTINATION METHODS, 2018

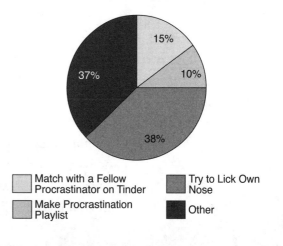

Match with a Fellow Procrastinator on Tinder
Make Procrastination Playlist
Try to Lick Own Nose
Other

results of two surveys that asked teenagers to select their favorite method of procrastinating, conducted four centuries apart.

Note: Students who named an activity that was not one of the three most popular procrastination methods were classified as "Other."

How does the information in the pie charts relate to the author's claim that students' procrastination preferences have become more varied since 1618?

A) It does not support the claim because trying to lick one's own nose was the most popular procrastination choice of teenagers in 1618 and 2018.

B) It supports the claim because the second and third most popular procrastination methods in 2018 were not available to teenagers in 1618. ✳

C) It supports the claim because the top three procrastination methods were favored by a combined 94 percent of teenagers in 1618, whereas the top three claimed only 63 percent of the total in 2018.

D) It does not support the claim because fewer students chose to procrastinate by watching Shakespeare plays in 2018.

✳Wait . . .
they didn't have
Tinder? How did
they find their
soul mates?!
—Samantha

Graphics on the SAT that show distributions separated by time will either be noticeably different or, maybe, remarkably similar. You should focus on these obvious differences or similarities. Here, the question asks about a difference between the two distributions—according to the author of the passage (not included here), teens' procrastination preferences are more varied today than they were 400 years ago. In other words, the author claims that the teen population selects a wider array of activities as their favorite way to procrastinate than it did in Shakespeare's day. Looking at the pie charts, you can see that the most noticeable difference between them is that the number of students who chose one of the "other" procrastination methods increased from 6 percent to 37 percent. Logically, this supports the author's claim. Technology has created so many new ways to procrastinate that teens aren't overwhelmingly choosing a few favorites anymore. Even if they still haven't given up on trying to lick their own noses. *

Attempting to lick your own nose will never go out of style.
—Samantha

Now you should look for the answer that makes note of this major difference. It's choice C, which points out that the top three activities in 2018 made up a smaller portion of the procrastination pie than the top three activities in 1618—that's because "Other" now occupies more than one-third of the pie.

There's a good chance that you will see graphs where the independent variable is not time, but the quantity or quality of something else that is described in the passage. When an unusual variable is used, the graphic they present might be unusual, too. For instance, these gauges show the stress and confidence levels of SAT takers who read *Up Your Score*, and of those who did not.

STUDENTS WHO READ
UP YOUR SCORE

STUDENTS WHO DID NOT READ
UP YOUR SCORE

From the above graphics, it can be inferred that reading *Up Your Score*

A) increases confidence and decreases stress.
B) increases confidence and stress.
C) decreases confidence and increases stress.
D) decreases confidence and stress.

You should know the answer to this already if you have read this far! But even if you just flipped to this page, it's clear that the answer is A just from looking at the numerical values in the graph. Although this is a rather elementary example, it has many qualities of the funkier graphics you'll find on the SAT. Instead of using a nice, clean bar graph, we've thrown in these weird gauges. As long as you read the labels above each pair of gauges, you're in the clear; otherwise you could accidentally mix up the outcome that they are trying to represent. And you need to realize that the qualities being measured are the same in each pair and that they are being represented in exactly the same way.

Let's take a look at a few more informational graphics questions, to really nail this down:

This is a good trend if you like buying bags of mostly air.
—Samantha

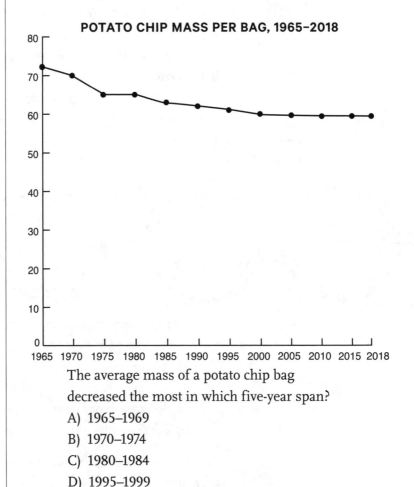

POTATO CHIP MASS PER BAG, 1965–2018

The average mass of a potato chip bag decreased the most in which five-year span?

A) 1965–1969
B) 1970–1974
C) 1980–1984
D) 1995–1999

(Answer: B)

ENTHUSIASM LEVEL DURING SAT

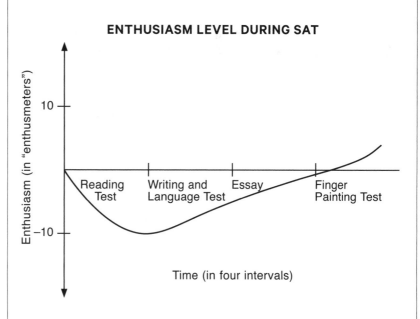

Enthusiasm (in "enthusmeters")

10

−10

Reading Test   Writing and Language Test   Essay   Finger Painting Test

Time (in four intervals)

From the graph, it can be reasonably inferred that students maintained the highest levels of enthusiasm during the

A) Reading Test.

B) Writing and Language Test.

C) Essay.

D) Finger-Painting Test.

(Answer: D, obviously)

You made it through infographics! Only one more section of this chapter to go. Let's move on to brushing up our vocabulary.

VOCABULARY— STILL ESSENTIAL

Hold up! Why do we have to brush up on our vocabulary? Didn't the SAT remove vocab questions from the test?

Unfortunately, there is still plenty of vocab tested on the SAT. First, we still have the "vocabulary in context" questions that are often easier if you already know the meaning(s) of the word. But more important, the reading passages will include a lot of "academic vocabulary" of the sort you would find in college textbooks and lectures, so even if there is no question about a specific word, you need to have a good vocabulary to comprehend these passages. And then, if you choose to do the Essay section, it's not a bad idea to use a few big words in your essay (as long as you use the words correctly). Technically, the test scorers won't give you points for fancy vocabulary, but in practice it signals to them that you are a sophisticated intellectual, and that makes them give you the benefit of the doubt.

So let's start with these essential words:

hypogyrrationalrhombocuboids

diffeomorphism

supermartingale

myelomeningocele

dacryocystorhinostomy

floccinaucinihilipilification

In first grade, I misspelled "supercalifragil- isticexpialidocious" by one letter, and I'm still not over it.
—Samantha

You probably don't know what any of these words mean. You probably don't care what they mean. Once you have finished this book, you still won't know what they mean. These words may be interesting and useful to someone. But they will not be on the SAT. The SAT tests you on the type of words that a college student would be likely to run into. A college student who ran into any of these words would suffer a concussion. If the SAT ever uses a huge, obscure word in a reading passage, it will define it for you in the context of the passage.

The new world of SAT words is defined by the concept of "academic vocabulary." There are various ways of formally defining this term, but for the most part it comes down to the idea that these are words one finds in the general language of college-level texts. So they aren't the specialized astronomy terms one is taught in an astronomy textbook, but they are all the general words that the astronomy textbook (and other college texts) assumes you know. For the most part, they are words that you look at and say, "Man, I should know what that word means, but I don't. I remember reading it in that article about such and such, but I can't quite . . ." Another characteristic of an SAT word is that it isn't particularly controversial. It won't have much to do with sex or violence or religion or anything that could offend someone. In all probability, you know more offensive words than the College Board does.

DECODABLE WORDS

One way to get a leg up on SAT vocabulary is to develop a knack for decoding "decodable" words. These are words that you figure out from some combination of the context and the roots and stems. For example, the word *decodable* is a decodable word. You could decode it like this:

de = take out; reverse

code = words or symbols with secret meanings

+ able = capable of being

---

decodable = capable of being taken out of its secret meaning

Here's a list of prefixes that are handy to know:

Prefix	Meaning	Example
a-	without	amoral
ante-	before	antecedent
anti- *	against	antibody
auto-	self	autobiography
bene-	good	beneficial

*Some more examples: anti-testing, anti-Saturday-wasting, anti-sitting-down-for-three-hours . . .
    —Samantha

Prefix	Meaning	Example
bi-	two	bicycle
circum-	around	circumnavigate
contra-	against	contradict
corp-	body	corpulent
di-	two	dichotomy
dict-	speak	diction
dis-	apart	disparity
homo-	same	homogeneous
hyper-	above	hyperactive
hypo-	below	hypothermia
inter-	between	interstate
mal-	bad	malevolent
micro-	small	microscope
mis-	wrong	mispronounce
multi-	many	multiple
neo-	new	neophyte
poly-	many	polytheism
pro-	for	protagonist
re-	again	redo
retro-	back	retroactive
un-	not	unconditional

This is practical stuff. Now you will understand all the dislocations, hyperextensions, and microfractures from ESPN's injury reports.
—Samantha

MEMORIZATION STRATEGIES

There are a lot of techniques that can help you memorize words. But one of the key tricks is to read the kind of books and articles that use the academic vocabulary words that you will be memorizing. If you just study a list of words and definitions, it can be hard to get the meanings to stay in your head. But if you encounter the words in real contexts, then they are more likely to become part of your personal vocabulary.

Someone needs to make a mnemonic device to help me remember how to pronounce mnemonic.
—Samantha

*We are teenagers. Admit it— this is what we remember.
—Samantha

The other important concept in memorizing things like vocabulary words is the mnemonic ("nuh-MAHN-eck") device. A mnemonic device is any technique, other than pure repetition, that helps you memorize something. So for each vocabulary word that you learn, close your eyes for a few seconds and think of a mnemonic device.

Research has demonstrated that for most people the most successful mnemonic devices are visual. If you can associate a word with a picture, you will be more likely to remember the word. For example, if you are trying to memorize the word *opulence* (luxury, great wealth), you could visualize a giant mansion surrounded by manicured lawns and lavish gardens. Above the gold-leaf front door, the word *opulence* would be spelled out in precious gems. Within, you might imagine well-groomed fat gentlemen, the word *opulence* stitched in diamonds across their chests, eating huge amounts of caviar molded into the shape of the word *opulence*. If you make your mental pictures extreme in some way, they will be more memorable. So make your pictures extremely bizarre, extremely gross, extremely obscene, extremely comical, or extremely whatever you are likely to remember. * (Detail is important in mental images like this one. The more details you are able to dream up, the more likely you are to remember the word.)

Move on to the other senses. Hear the chorus of castrati in the ballroom singing the word *opulence* over the gentle strains of Chopin played by an 80-piece symphony. Feel the silks you are wearing as your jeweled fingers trace the word *opulence* with champagne over your desktop. Smell the delicate and costly perfumes.

After you have seen, heard, felt, smelled, and tasted the word, you can open your eyes. You're still not done, though. Research has also shown that the more you do with a word, the more likely it will stay in your brain. So first read the word and its definition, then write the word and its definition, then sing the word and its definition, then make up a story about the word, then use the word in a conversation, then tattoo the word and its definition on your elbow, then Velcro the word and its definition to your goldfish.

Clinical tests have also proven that the pun is a very helpful memory technique. We have used puns to illustrate many of the words in the vocabulary list. (Note: Since we want to make sure that no one misses our subtlety, we have <u>pun</u>derlined each one.)

If none of these techniques works, there is one foolproof method. Neurologists say that if the word and its definition are repeated over and over during sexual activity, they will never be forgotten. There is no scientific explanation for this, but it is a widely accepted fact. Of course, we wouldn't know.

Another phenomenon you should be aware of is the serial position effect. Suppose you have a long list of words to memorize and you spend the same amount of time studying each word. According to the serial position effect, you will remember the words at the beginning of the list best, the words at the end of the list next best, and the middle words the worst. Therefore, spend the most time on the middle of the list.

Your chances of memorizing something improve if you study it right before you go to bed. ✱ While you sleep, your brain sorts out what occurred during the day. The last thought that goes into your brain right before you go to sleep gets special attention while your brain is doing its nightly sorting.

Finally, nobody studies better with music. Experiments have been done with people who swear that they study better with Rihanna playing in the background. But chances are slim that this will lead to more efficient work, work, work, work, work.

✱*Force your mom to recite vocabulary words to you as you fall asleep. Inform her that this is what she gets for making you take the SAT.*
—Samantha

Essential Tools

✳Actually a lifesaver. 11/10 would recommend.
—Samantha

When you come to a word you don't know, look it up and devote a few seconds to thinking up a mnemonic device, be it a sentence, a quick drawing, or a bit of song lyric—whatever works for you. Then transcribe it into a flashcard app like Quizlet ✳ or onto a real three-by-five-inch card, the word on one side and the definition + mnemonic device on the other.

Take your word list with you everywhere and study it during the ride to school, while you wait at the dentist's office, and during particularly boring classes. Every night before you go to sleep, test yourself on your words.

Do a similar thing with an audio recorder (many phones have one). When you come to a word that you want to remember, record the word, its definition, and either the example sentence that we give you or one that you make up. Then you can listen to the recording while you are in the shower or brushing your teeth. If you can rap or sing some of your words and definitions, it's more fun to listen to. If your friends ask you what you're listening to, respond casually, "It's Gretchen and the Vocab Lists—they're new out of Seattle." If your friends ask to listen, say, "The band asked me not to play it for anyone until it's been officially released."

Then, after you've aced the SAT, you can sell your recordings, flashcards, and notebook to your younger sibling.

THE WORD LIST

A

Don't be intimidated; there are only about 375 words here, and you probably know some of them already.

Bear in mind that some of the words on this list could appear in another form. You therefore should learn to recognize various forms of a word, like *refute* and *refutation*. The sentences and illustrations that follow the definitions are examples of the memorization techniques we described. Enjoy, and may you be blessed by the almighty vocabulary god until you get to *zyzzyva*.

aardvark

Aardvark is the first real word in the dictionary, so we figured that we should start with it even though it has never been and probably never will be on the SAT.

abase

lower; humiliate

"I will not abase myself by admitting that I don't even have a basic knowledge of vocabulary," said Paul.

abate

to lessen

Abigail's sister screamed, "Ab ate all the cookies!" Later, of course, her anger abated.

abstruse

profound; difficult to understand

When Abraham Lincoln wrote a confusing peace agreement to end the Civil War, people commented that Abe's truce was abstruse.

acclivity

an upward slope (as in a hill)

A cliff is an example of a steep acclivity.

accolade

award; honor

When Coolio received an accolade for his acting, he just smiled and asked for a Kool-Aid.

acne

zits

adroit

skillful

C-3PO is an adroit android.

adulterate

to make impure

Never trust an <u>adult</u> with your belly button lint collection. He will definitely <u>adulterate</u> it.

adverse

hostile; opposed; unfavorable (see AVERSE)

"It's tough writing a national anthem during a British attack," complained Francis Scott Key. "The only light you have is the rockets' red glare. You have to <u>add verses</u> under <u>adverse</u> conditions."

advocate

to urge; recommend

<u>Advertisements</u> <u>advocate</u> products.

aesthetic

artistic; pertaining to a sense of what is beautiful

<u>As the tick</u> was sucking blood from my arm, I squashed it. The dead insect smeared on my arm was not <u>aesthetically</u> pleasing.

affected

fake (think: a-FAKE-ted)

His <u>affected</u> personality negatively <u>affected</u> our <u>affection</u>.

affinity

attraction

There was a natural <u>affinity</u> between him and his new <u>Infiniti</u>.

affluent

rich

<u>A flu went</u> around the <u>affluent</u> passengers of the yacht; their diamond tiaras and Rolexes sparkled when they sneezed.

agenda

a schedule; a plan (sometimes of a secretive or devious nature)

Next up on Secret <u>Agent A</u>'s <u>agenda</u>: Defeat the SAT, no matter the cost.

aghast

horrified

We were <u>aghast</u> when he "passed <u>gas</u>." (See EUPHEMISM. *Passed gas* is an example of a euphemism.)

alacrity

cheerful promptness

The empty auditorium was the result of <u>a lack</u> of <u>alacrity</u> among the sleep-deprived students.

alias

a false name
"Your real name was <u>all I asked</u> for; why did you give me an <u>alias</u>?" the reporter said.

alimentary

supplying nourishment
When Watson asked, "What's a ten-letter word meaning 'supplying nourishment'?" Sherlock replied, "<u>Alimentary</u>, my dear Watson."

allay

to soothe; to make more bearable (see ALLEVIATE)
Note: This is one of a countless number of SAT words with this meaning.

He <u>allayed</u> his parents' fears by getting <u>all As</u> on his report card.

alleged

stated without proof
It was <u>alleged</u> that he died by falling off <u>a ledge</u>.

alleviate

to make more bearable
(see APPEASE)
Note: Think of Aleve, the pain med.

<u>A leaf he ate</u> successfully <u>alleviated</u> his hunger.

allude

to refer indirectly

allusion

a reference to something
<u>A lewd</u> person <u>alludes</u> to lecherous behavior.

altercation

a violent dispute
An <u>altercation</u> broke out when, at the <u>altar, Kate</u> said to her groom, "I don't."

amass

to collect; to get a bunch of
By publishing this book, we hope to <u>amass</u> <u>a mass</u> of perfect scores for our readers.

ambivalent	having mixed feelings or contradictory ideas about someone or something Amber was ambivalent about giving up chocolate for Lent.
ameliorate	to improve a bad situation Amelia rated her social life as having been ameliorated since last year.
amity	peaceful relations; friendship *Note:* The root "ami-" means "friend," as in "amiable." There was amity between the students at M.I.T. and their math professors.
amorphous	shapeless *Note:* This word is decodable if you know all the pieces: "a" = not (see ATYPICAL) "morph" = shape, form + "ous" = having the qualities of ————————————— amorphous = not having the qualities of shape If you take too much morphine, you'll feel like an amorphous blob.
antipathy	hatred; aversion; dislike *Note:* This word is also decodable: "anti" = against + "pathy" = feeling ————————————— antipathy = feeling against By this time you should be developing a strong antipathy to studying these words and their ridiculous definitions. Take a break. Put the book down and get a soda or a bottle of vitamin-enhanced water. Then return to your work refreshed and ready to continue.
apathetic	indifferent; showing lack of interest
apathy	indifference; lack of interest

Note: Another decodable word:

$$"a" = not$$
$$+ "pathy" = feeling$$
$$\overline{\text{apathy} = \text{not feeling}}$$

It's a pathetic thing to be apathetic.

"They found the cure for apathy, but no one showed any interest in it."—George Carlin

apex	**tip; peak; summit; way up there**

Note: This word is likely to be found in the analogy section. Its opposites are words such as nadir and bottom.

The ape exercised by jumping off the apex of the monkey house.

appease	**to soothe; placate (think: apeace; see ASSUAGE)**

He appeased his parents by eating a piece of slimy okra.

fishhead	**the head of a fish**

Just checking to see if you're still awake.

arbitrary	**chosen at random or without apparent reason**

If a college rejects you, just assume its admissions process is arbitrary.

arbitration	**settlement of a conflict by a third party**

The warring princes of Arbit turned to the Impartial Wizard for arbitration to settle which of the two was handsomer and finally bring harmony to the Arbit nation.

ardor	**heat; passion; zeal**

With ardor my prom date shouted, "Come in! And if you have to, break down our door."

Who's that running away with Ardor?

Ardor

assuage	to ease; pacify (see APPEASE) Buying <u>a suede</u> fringed jacket might <u>assuage</u> Donna's compulsive desire to shop.
astute	shrewd; wise; observing <u>A stu</u>dent must be <u>astute</u> to outwit the Evil Testing Serpent.
attribute	**(n.) a characteristic, usually a good one** **(v.) to explain by indicating a cause** In her article on Chris Evans, the reporter <u>attributed</u> the actor's physical <u>attributes</u> to exercise and a high-protein diet.
atypical	not typical *Note:* The prefix "a-" usually means "not." For example, *amoral* means "not moral," *asexual* means "not sexual," *apolitical* means "not into politics," and, as we have seen, *amorphous* means "not shaped." Although Stewart was in every other respect <u>a typical</u> boy, his blue skin was <u>atypical</u> for an earthling.
audacity	boldness Their <u>audacity</u> was evident when they published their <u>odd SAT</u> book.
august	majestic; awe-inspiring When Cleopatra saw <u>Augustus</u> in all his finery, she said, "<u>Aw</u>, <u>Gus</u>, you look <u>august</u>."
austerity	severity; strictness His <u>austerity</u> is actually a rarity; sev<u>erity</u> is not his specialty.
averse	opposed; unwilling I was <u>averse</u> to writing <u>a verse</u> So at the teacher I did curse And put mounds of coleslaw in her purse. *Note:* It's easy to confuse <u>averse</u> with <u>adverse</u>. You use <u>averse</u> when you want to say that a person or thing is opposed to

something else. For example: *Eggbert was <u>averse</u> to eating Frisbees.* (Note that *to* usually follows <u>averse</u>.)

You use <u>adverse</u> when you want to say that something else is opposed to a person or thing. For example: *Eggbert received <u>adverse</u> criticism for not eating Frisbees; Eggbert had to eat the Frisbee under <u>adverse</u> conditions.*

In the first example Eggbert is <u>averse</u> to eating, whereas in the second and third examples the criticism and the conditions are <u>adverse</u> to Eggbert.

It is helpful to make up a story using as many of the vocabulary words as possible from the list you have just learned. We have written some sample stories, but you should write your own, too. Here is our first one.

An Adventurous Aardvark

The <u>audacious</u> <u>aardvark</u> was rooting around in the grass for some lunch with which to <u>assuage</u> his hunger when his <u>adroit</u> friend Bob the baboon waddled up with <u>alacrity</u>. "Hey, man," Bob said, beginning an <u>altercation</u>. "Why do you <u>abase</u> yourself in that <u>atypical</u> way? I <u>advocate</u> the use of a knife and fork." *

"You are a moron," the <u>aardvark</u> replied politely. "It would be more <u>aesthetically</u> pleasing were I to eat that way, but the use of utensils would be too <u>affected</u> for a simple <u>aardvark</u>. In addition, I am <u>averse</u> to such an idea because it might <u>alleviate</u> my <u>acne</u>, which looks good on me."

"That has to be the <u>apex</u> of stupidity," Bob said, <u>aghast</u>. "And while we're on the subject of your appearance, I must ask why you are so <u>apathetic</u> about your hygiene. At least you could <u>ameliorate</u> your looks and odor by taking a bath."

"Never <u>allude</u> to my <u>alleged</u> <u>antipathy</u> to cleanliness again," the <u>aardvark</u> said with <u>austerity</u>. "May I remind you that you still pick lice out of strangers' hair."

Sensing that the conversation had gone awry, Bob's <u>audacity</u> <u>abated</u> and he too began to <u>amass</u> a pile of grubs from the grass.

*I personally prefer sporks because, you know, functionality. But to each her own.
—Samantha

B

begrudge — to envy, to resent

To <u>be</u> holding a <u>grudge</u> for so long against me means that you must <u>begrudge</u> my happy life.

beguile — trick

"The [Evil Testing] Serpent <u>beguiled</u> me and I did eat the apple."

belated — delayed; late

We sent a <u>belated</u> birthday present and in return got a month-old piece of ice-cream cake.

benevolent — kind

Superman may be the <u>benevolent</u> protector of the world, but have you ever noticed that he wears his underpants outside his tights?

berate — to scold severely

If you don't study for the SAT, your parents will <u>berate</u> you. If you don't do A work, your teachers will <u>berate</u> (<u>B-rate</u>) you.

bereft — lacking something needed

He felt sad and <u>bereft</u> just thinking about how she didn't love him; now he would <u>be left</u> without her.

bombastic — grandiloquent (wordy, pompous) in speech or writing

At the end of his long, boring, <u>bombastic</u> speech, the self-satisfied tyrant received a <u>bomb basket</u> as a farewell gift.

brevity — briefness

When Janet had a 20-page paper due, but wanted to go out, her friends suggested, "You can write your paper with great <u>brevity</u> and <u>brave a D</u>."

burgeon — to grow; sprout; flourish

Madonna's career <u>burgeoned</u> as soon as she changed the title of her unsuccessful song "Like a <u>Burgeon</u>."

A Bolivian Bacchanal

The burly buccaneers brutishly threw Bill and me out of the helicopter <u>bereft</u> of any parachute, and the <u>brevity</u> of our flight and our brutal landing were not what was promised in our blond travel agent's <u>bombastic</u> brochure.

We barreled through the trees of the Bolivian forest until we hit the ground with a bang.

"Yo," said Bill, brandishing a machete. "What say we bust our way out of this place?"

But before I could respond, we were captured by a band of natives about to perform a <u>belated</u> human sacrifice to the fish goddess.

"Yo," said Bill, his fear <u>burgeoning</u>. "I should <u>berate</u> you for <u>beguiling</u> me into going on this blighted vacation."

Then the ax fell and the bacchanalian rituals honoring the <u>benevolent</u> fish goddess began.

C

callous

unfeeling; unsympathetic
Brian complained of the <u>callus</u> on his big toe, but Meg remained <u>callous</u>.
If you don't like that sentence, don't <u>call us</u>; we're <u>callous</u>.

candor

frankness; candidness
"Speaking with complete <u>candor</u>, Hansel," said the wicked witch, "I have chopped Gretel up and <u>canned her</u>."

capitulate

to surrender (see RECAPITULATE, which does not mean resurrender)
After a ten-day siege, the king had no choice but to <u>capitulate</u> to the invading forces.

capricious

unpredictable; following whim
The album charts were <u>capricious</u>; one week Katy Perry was on top—but the next week Taylor Swift took over.

captious	fault-finding "What?! You're only in the Cs? And your room's still messy, and you haven't cooked us dinner," said the captious review-book authors.
cathartic	**cleansing; allowing a release of tension or emotion** Manek's method of preparing for the SAT is cathartic (see page 343).
caustic	**burning; characterized by a bitter wit** When she saw the dead mouse that her cat had hidden in her bed, she said caustically, "Having a cat has its costs. Ick!" *Note:* Being sarcastic and being caustic often go hand in hand, so relate them in your memory via the nonword *sarcaustic*.
censor	**(v.) to remove inappropriate stuff** **(n.) someone who censors things** When Alex sensed her secret mission was in danger, she grew angry and screamed, "Motherf— **CENSORED**
censure	**to criticize; blame** When someone starts to criticize you, you can sense you're being censured.
chagrin	**embarrassment** She grinned and blushed with chagrin.
chaos	**state of utter confusion** "We don't want to cause chaos," we told the customs official. "So just okay us for passage!"

circumspect — prudent; cautious

Note: This is one of those easily decodable words:

"circum" = around (as in <u>circ</u>le)

+ "spect" = look (as in in<u>spect</u> and <u>spect</u>acles)

circumspect = look around (which suggests being cautious)

"<u>Search 'em, inspector</u>," ordered the <u>circumspect</u> detective.

clemency — mildness of temper—especially leniency toward an enemy or in sentencing a criminal

Because Roger <u>Clemens</u> was accused of using steroids, it now remains to be seen if he'll be shown <u>clemency</u> and be voted into the Hall of Fame anyway.

The following three "cog" words all have to do with thinking:

cogent — clear; logical; well thought out

The two men (<u>co-gents</u>) on the debate team gave a <u>cogent</u> argument.

cogitate — to think about deeply and carefully (see RUMINATE)

A good time to <u>cogitate</u> about dairy products is while eating <u>cottage</u> cheese.

cognizant — fully informed and aware; conscious

When the factory repairman becomes <u>cognizant</u> that the <u>cog isn't</u> working, he will fix the gear.

commensurate — equal; proportionate

You don't think that this pile of gold is <u>commensurate</u> with that one? Well, <u>come measure it</u>.

commiserate — to sympathize; be miserable together

Note: Decode:

"co" = together

+ "miserate" = be miserable

commiserate = be miserable together

He <u>commiserated</u> with his friend at Clown College, who also got 200s.

comport

to behave in a particular way
Note: The root *-port* means "carry," as in the words *im<u>port</u>* (carry in), *ex<u>port</u>* (carry out), and *trans<u>port</u>* (carry across). In this context, <u>comport</u> has to do with how you carry yourself.

<u>Comport</u> yourself in a <u>comfort</u>able way.

compunction

strong uneasiness caused by guilt
(see REMORSE, CONTRITION)
I felt <u>compunction</u> about <u>punc</u>turing your tires with Japanese throwing stars, but I went ahead and did it anyway.

concurrent

at the same time
Note: This is another decodable word:

      "con" = together (see CONVOKE)

  + "current" = at this time

    concurrent = at a time together

John Adams's and Thomas Jefferson's deaths were <u>concurrent</u>; they both died on July 4, 1826.

conjecture

statement made without adequate evidence
"<u>Can Jack sure</u>ly reach that conclusion?" I asked. "Or is it only a <u>conjecture</u>?"

consenus

majority opinion
Collectively, we came to a <u>consensus</u> that the zombies <u>can't sense us</u> if we slather ourselves in peanut butter.

contrition

remorse; repentance; bitter regret felt owing to wrongdoing
When <u>Trish</u> broke the priceless gorilla sculpture, she was overcome with <u>contrition</u>.

convey

communicate; relate
Conner <u>conveyed</u> his sadness to Connie when she left him for a con man.

convoke	to call together; to cause to assemble

Note: Decode:

$$\frac{\begin{array}{l}\text{"con"} = \text{together}\\ + \text{"voc"} = \text{call (}\underline{\text{voi}}\text{ce)}\end{array}}{\text{convoke} = \text{call together}}$$

The mayor <u>convoke</u>s a town meeting so that the citizens <u>can</u> <u>voc</u>alize their grievances.

corporal	of the body; bodily

<u>Corporal</u> Thomas gave me <u>corporal</u> punishment because I saluted him with my foot instead of my hand.

corroborate	to testify in agreement

Do you have any witnesses who can <u>corroborate</u> that this is the restaurant where Bonnie and Clyde (<u>co-robbers</u>) <u>ate</u>?

covert	concealed; secret (see OVERT)

When the press finds out about the CIA's <u>covert</u> operations, the CIA tries to <u>cover it</u> up.

crass	uncultured

"Is it <u>crass</u> to scratch an <u>ass</u>?" the cow asked the donkey.

credulity	gullibility

His <u>credulity</u> led him to think that the preposterous alibi was <u>cred</u>ible. I found it too in<u>cred</u>ible to believe.

crestfallen	dejected

"I'm sorry I dropped the toothpaste," he said, <u>crestfallen</u>.

I can't believe I dropped it!

Crestfallen

criterion	**a standard to judge something by; a rule (singular form of *criteria*)** An established <u>criterion</u> for a dramatic actor is the ability to laugh or <u>cry tears on</u> cue.
crux	**main point; central issue; heart of the matter** *Note:* <u>Crux</u> is the Latin word for "cross," as you can tell from the word <u>crucifix</u>, and a cross is always made when two lines meet in the center. "The <u>crux</u> of our work is to <u>crucify</u> <u>crooks</u>," explained the Roman policeman.
cull	**to select; weed out** <u>Col</u>lege admissions officers <u>cull</u> the best applications from the pile.

A Cryptic Crime	It was one of those steamy nights when the sky is lousy with stars. I was <u>culling</u> the blue M&M's from the M&M's stash in the office of the Sure-Lock Homes Locksmith and Detective Agency. Suddenly, my <u>cogitations</u> were interrupted by a cacophonous sound and a cataclysmic vibration that reverberated through my office. I shouted words that have to be <u>censored,</u> then stepped with <u>circumspection</u> into the hall and found a <u>chaotic</u> scene: a man lying contorted at the bottom of the stairs. Blood was gushing through a wound in his side.
	
	    "Golly, are you okay?" I asked.
	
	    He replied <u>caustically</u>, "Sure, I'm just swell. And how was your day?"
	
	    "Peachy," I said.
	
	    At that he bellowed, "You <u>callous</u> idiot! Can't you see I've been shot? Get me to a hospital!"
	
	    "You don't have to be so <u>captious</u>. Let me <u>cogitate</u>!"
	
	    At that moment a lady walked into the office. She <u>comported</u> herself calmly and without <u>compunction</u>. She pointed at the wounded man and said, "We were in my apartment; he got up

to answer the door, and suddenly I heard a cacophonous sound and a cataclysmic vibration that must have reverberated in your office."

Just then my assistant, Watt, entered. He said, handing me the phone, "My kid wants to know what sort of tree he should plant in our garden. What do you think, Sure-Lock?"

"A lemon tree, my dear Watt's son," I said.

Then Watt became <u>cognizant</u> of the situation. He said, "What is that?"

"It's a plant with little yellow fruit and . . ."

He interrupted me, "No, that body on the floor."

"Oh golly, I forgot. We should get him to a hospital."

We all lifted the body <u>concurrently</u> and put it in my car.

When we arrived at the hospital, the doctor informed us that the man was dead.

"Golly, that's too bad," I said with <u>contrition</u>.

It was time for me to get to the bottom of this crime. <u>Convoking</u> the small crowd, I asked the dame, "Who was that man?"

"My husband," she replied, <u>crestfallen</u>.

"Aha! Well, let's get to the <u>crux</u> of this situation. Did you kill your husband?"

"How dare you <u>censure</u> me like that. What a crazy <u>conjecture</u>!"

I repeated, "Did you kill him?"

With <u>chagrin</u>, she <u>capitulated</u>. "Well, only a little, but Watt will <u>corroborate</u> that. He cajoled me into it."

"Watt! All the time I thought you were on the side of the law and you were really <u>covertly</u> planning this crime! I will bring you both to justice without <u>clemency</u>. Your sentence will include <u>corporal</u> punishment <u>commensurate</u> with the seriousness of the crime."

D

daunt to intimidate; frighten

dauntless bold, unable to be daunted

The <u>dauntless</u> mouse <u>daunted</u> the lion with his .357 Magnum.

dearth	scarcity (see PAUCITY); this word has nothing to do with the word *death*.
	Because of <u>Darth</u> Vader, there was a <u>dearth</u> of laughter on the Death Star.
debase	to lower in quality or value; adulterate (note the similarity to ABASE)
	The birds at <u>de base</u> of the statue <u>debased</u> it with excrement.
decoy	a lure or bait
	The <u>coy</u> duck disguised himself as a wooden <u>decoy</u>, but the hunters shot at him anyway.
defenestration	the act of throwing something out the window
	Note: It's highly unlikely that this word will be on the SAT, but it's the kind of word everyone should know anyway. You could use it if you ever witness the <u>defenestration</u> of a proctor.
delude	to deceive
	<u>De lewd</u> dude <u>deluded</u> himself into thinking he was deliriously attractive.
demur	to object mildly
demure	reserved; modest
	The <u>demure</u> poodle <u>demurred</u> at the Saint Bernard's drooling in public.
deplete	to lessen the supply or content of
	She <u>de-pleated</u> the skirt by ironing it, thus <u>depleting</u> her stock of pleated skirts.
desultory	aimless; disconnected; rambling; haphazard
	"That's why I love pepper," said Uri, finishing his <u>desultory</u> speech extolling the merits of salt. "<u>De salt, Uri</u>!" yelled his debate teacher.

Hey! What happened to all the folds in these skirts?

Deplete

deter	to prevent or discourage from happening Nothing could <u>deter</u> Mike Trout from hitting a home run for the Angels.
devoid	completely lacking; void; empty; without <u>Avoid</u> diving into swimming pools that are <u>devoid</u> of water; you could hurt yourself and that would suck.
dexterous	adroit or skillful in the use of hands or body Houdini was <u>dexterous</u>; he could escape from a straitjacket. Are you remembering to do the mnemonic thing? Picture yourself watching nine acrobats wearing banners across their chests that say *dexterous*. Each contorts into the shape of a letter to spell out the word *dexterous*. They are all named *Dexter*, except for one, who is named *Poindexter*. You lean over to your friend and say, "Wow, are they *dexterous*! I've never seen anyone so *dexterous*. I love *dexterous* people!" Then she looks at you like you're an idiot.
discern	to detect by the use of the senses The watchman <u>dis-earned</u> his pay by not <u>discerning</u> the thieves.
discord	lack of harmony "I won't use <u>dis chord</u> 'cause it would create <u>discord</u>," said Mozart.
disparage	to belittle; to reduce in esteem "<u>Dis porridge</u> is too hot," Goldilocks <u>disparaged</u>.
disseminate	to dispense objects, such as seeds, newspapers; to distribute While making his stock boy walk the plank, the captain explained, "<u>Dis seaman ate</u> all of the supplies that he was supposed to <u>disseminate</u>."
distraught	anxious; worried; <u>distressed</u> Snow White became <u>distraught</u> when the dwarfs drank booze and fought.

distribution	the frequency with which something appears in a given region or across a certain period of time The <u>distribution</u> of lions across the savanna kept the rest of the animal kingdom in check.
divers	several
diverse	distinct; varied; differing William Shakespeare's <u>divers verses</u> were about <u>diverse</u> subjects.
doleful	sad; mournful You will be <u>Dole-full</u> and sick if you eat 98 cans of pineapple chunks.
drastic	severe If your swimsuit strap breaks, you are in <u>drastic</u> need of elastic.
dynamic	energetic; vigorous; forceful The <u>dynamic</u> duo fell into the Joker's <u>dynamite</u> trap.

And on to a story:

The Distraught Dogcatcher

Dan was <u>distraught</u>. He knew he'd soon have to declare his candidacy for local dogcatcher. He knew he was <u>devoid</u> of charisma and not a <u>dynamic</u> speaker. He wasn't even <u>dexterous</u> at catching canines. Doubtless, he would <u>debase</u> himself by speaking like a fool.

Trying to appear <u>dauntless</u>, he shambled forward, but alas he demonstrated a <u>dearth</u> of enthusiasm.

"Ahem," he began, but was <u>deterred</u> from continuing when he noticed that a devious Great Dane was rapidly <u>depleting</u> his audience by devouring them. Feeling that this devastation might detract from his speech, Dan's thoughts were thrown into sudden <u>discord</u>, and he felt a <u>drastic</u> need to <u>defenestrate</u> himself. Using himself as a <u>decoy</u> to get the beast's attention, he <u>demurred</u>, "Ummm . . . please stop!" People <u>discerned</u> his foolishness.

   Later that day, a supporter <u>disparaged</u> Dan's speech. "It was rather <u>desultory</u>. <u>Divers</u> <u>diverse</u> rumors have been <u>disseminated</u> that he is depraved. We'll have trouble <u>deluding</u> the public into believing the contrary."

E

edify
to enlighten; educate
<u>Ed defi</u>ed the edict against education by trying to <u>edify</u> his pupils.

efface
to erase; rub out
Be sure to completely <u>efface</u> any answer circle you wish to change.

elation
exhilaration; joy
The jolly mountaineers found <u>elation</u> on high <u>elevations</u>.

empirical
based on experience rather than theory
I have <u>empirical</u> evidence to suggest my second <u>empire</u> will flourish; my first was wildly successful.

emulate
to imitate closely
When the tornado began, Dorothy called out, "Aunty <u>Em</u>, <u>you're late</u>. <u>Emulate</u> Toto and hurry up."

epitaph
memorial text carved on a tombstone
I read the <u>epitaph</u>, "Here lies a politician and an honest man," and wondered how they could fit two people in one grave.

epitome
something that perfectly represents an entire class of things; embodiment (pronounced "eh-pit'-oh-me")
"You're the <u>epitome</u> of stupidity," she screeched after I spilled bologna dip all over her dress.

equivocal
capable of two interpretations; ambiguous
Note: This word is decodable, too.

"equi" = equal

+ "vocal" = voice

_____

equivocal = giving equal voice to two sides

"A good meal from this cook is a rare treat" is an <u>equivocal</u> statement.

erode

to diminish or destroy by small amounts

When a <u>road erodes</u>, there are potholes all over the place.

erudite

scholarly

<u>Erudite</u> people say things like "<u>Ere you diet</u>, would you partake of the torte?" instead of "Want some cake?"

eschew

avoid; shun

"<u>Eschew</u>!" he sneezed loudly. "Gesundheit," she replied, while <u>eschewing</u> the globules of his sneeze juice.

Ew, GROSS! I'm not going near that guy!

Eschew Eschew

Eschew

esoteric

known only by a few people

Now you are one of the few people who knows this <u>esoteric</u> word.

eulogy

praiseful speech at a funeral

In Santa's <u>eulogy</u>, the priest explained that Santa had died of high cholesterol because of all those <u>Yule logs he</u> ate.

euphemism

nice way of saying something unpleasant

"Moved on to the next world" is a <u>euphemism</u> for "kicked the bucket," which is a <u>euphemism</u> for "died."

exact

On the SAT, the Serpent will use the secondary definition of this word, which is: to demand

The Stamp Act <u>exacted</u> from the colonists <u>taxes</u> they could not afford to pay. So they "<u>X</u>'d" the <u>act</u>.

exigent	urgent; requiring immediate attention It is <u>exigent</u> that I find a sexy gent to escort me to the prom. **excessively demanding; excessively exacting** I made <u>exigent</u> demands on my fairy godmother to find me a debonair prom date and a diaphanous dress.
Essay on Eggplant	I want to know which <u>erudite</u> vegetable maker invented eggplant. If he is dead, I will <u>efface</u> the <u>epitaph</u> from his tombstone. If he is alive, I will ensure he will not be <u>eulogized</u> when he dies. Eggplant is the <u>epitome</u> of bad vegetables and its destruction is <u>exigent</u>. I <u>eschew</u> eating it. This is an <u>exacting</u> demand, but would someone please <u>edify</u> me, without being <u>esoteric</u> or <u>equivocal</u>, as to one good thing about eggplant? It is mushy, it has seeds, it makes my tongue itch, and it has a dopey name. I wish all the soil on the world's eggplant farms would <u>erode</u>. Oh, and get this—when eggplants fertilize each other, the round ones with lots of seeds are the female ones and the long, narrow ones are the males. (No <u>euphemism</u> can soften this picture.) And they do it in public, in front of all the other vegetables. What would happen if humans <u>emulated</u> this behavior? The end.

F

fabricate	**to make something; to invent or make up something (often in order to deceive)** When Michael couldn't remove the stain from the <u>fabric</u>, he <u>ate</u> it and <u>fabricated</u> a story that aliens stole it.
facet	**side or aspect; face of something (e.g., gemstones)** "<u>Face it</u>! One of the <u>facets</u> of being a jeweler is sometimes selling flawed <u>facets</u>!"
facetious	**joking or jesting** She's so <u>facetious</u> that you should not take what she says at <u>face</u> value.

fallacious | false; wrong; incorrect
They used to castigate people who made <u>fallacious</u> statements. (Well, that was a long time ago.)

fatuous | inane; foolish; fatheaded
Eating 30 pounds of chocolate a day is a <u>fatuous</u> idea.

fawning | groveling; overly admiring
The hunter who killed Bambi's mother should have come back and made a <u>fawning</u> plea for forgiveness.

feasible | workable; plausible; possible
Homer's idea of opening a hair salon for bald people was not <u>feasible</u>—who would pay the $30 <u>fee</u>? D'oh!

That is an INCREDIBLE outfit!

the hat with the earflaps! VERY "IN"!

and the red checks are so "you"!

fervor | passion
I will fight a ferocious ferret and get its <u>fur for</u> you if it will prove the <u>fervor</u> of my love for you.

Fawning

fictitious | false; not genuine
Books of <u>fiction</u> have <u>fictitious</u> plots.

fluctuation | irregular variation
At the terrifying sight of the nasty sentence completion question, his heartbeat <u>fluctuated</u> wildly.

foment | to stir up; agitate; incite (think: when you stir something up it <u>foams</u>)
When your <u>foe</u> warned you not to <u>foment</u> the army against him, your <u>foe meant</u> he was afraid of getting his butt kicked.

forbearance | patience
He played dead with <u>forbearance</u> until the <u>four bears</u> got <u>antsy</u> and went away.

forte

strong point (think: forts are strong; pronounced "fort" or "for·tay")

His forte was sneaking into the fort that was just before Fort B.

frugal

sparing in expense; stingy; miserly

They told me that I was frugal because I bought a plastic bugle.

futile

completely ineffective

The one-armed floor layer felt his work was futile because he could lay only a few tiles a day.

Fred the Fish Thief

Freddy had a flaw. He stole fish, sometimes with fervor and sometimes with forbearance, but he never fluctuated from his forte. One day his mother, returning from the garden, said facetiously, "Freddy, is it feasible that you'll foment a fish odor if you continue to flaunt your fish stealing habits?"

Freddy frowned. "That is a fatuous as well as fallacious suggestion," he fulminated. "This facet of my abilities is not futile, as it provides fish for our otherwise frugal dinner. You should fawn over me."

The preceding story is fictitious, fabricated by the authors.

G

genre

category

It's hard to place *Up Your Score* in a specific genre. It's an SAT prep book, but also an epic narrative, an investigative report, and a monumental literary work.

germane

relevant; appropriate

"Germany is not germane to our discussion today," said the history professor. "Today we shall discuss last night's rerun of *The Bachelorette*."

gestate

to transform and grow, like a baby inside the womb

Mama Butterfly asked the <u>gestating</u> caterpillar if it wanted something to eat, but it said, "No, I <u>just ate</u>."

gesticulation

gesture; signal

Note: Somehow <u>gesticulation</u> seems as though it ought to have obscene connotations, and we would certainly tell you if it did, but it doesn't. You can make up an obscene mnemonic device, if that helps.

Igor <u>gesticulated</u> for Dick to hurry and enter the lab, saying, "<u>Yes, Dick, you're late</u> for your brain transplant."

gibberish

rapid, incomprehensible, or nonsensical speaking; drivel

The Lewis Carroll poem "Jabberwocky," which begins "'Twas brillig, and the slithy toves . . . ," is written in <u>gibberish</u>.

grandiose

excessively impressive; <u>grand</u>

Jay Leno has a <u>grandiose</u> chin.

graphic

vivid; explicit

In another sequel to his dinosaur movie, Steven Spielberg left out the prehistoric beasts and kept all the violence, titling the film <u>Graphic</u> *Park*.

gratuitous

unnecessary or unwarranted

Adding <u>gratuitous</u> sex and violence to this book has been the best thing about writing it.

Lesser-Known Adventures of the Three Billy Goats Gruff

The three Billy Goats Gruff met in the green grass near the bridge.

"I'm really scared of that gruesome troll," Billy Goat 1 said, <u>gesticulating</u> toward the bridge.

"I heard her gourmet appetite includes a grisly taste for goats' hooves!" BG 2 added nervously. "I really don't like <u>gratuitous</u> violence."

"Cowards!" BG 3 gibed. "I don't listen to non<u>germane</u> <u>gibberish</u> that only gullible fools like you would believe. I bet that troll is really a cool gal. Watch me cross that bridge!"

"You have a <u>grandiose</u> opinion of yourself, but you're really pretty dumb. So long, bud," Goat 1 replied, anticipating the <u>graphic</u> goat-mutilation horror that soon followed.

hackneyed

overused; trite
The plot of the movie *The Texas Chainsaw Massacre* was <u>hackneyed</u>. It was just another horror movie about an axe murderer who <u>hacked knees</u> off.

hallowed

holy; sacred
I was hanging out in the cemetery, but I didn't know I was on hollowed <u>hallowed</u> ground until I fell into a grave.

harbinger

forerunner; something that signals the approach of something; omen
Note: Some words have only one sentence in which they are ever used. The sentence for *harbinger* is: "The robin is the harbinger of spring."

haughty

proud; vain; arrogant
He thinks he's <u>hot. He</u> shouldn't be so <u>haughty</u>.

hierarchy

social pecking order
As Heather moved <u>higher</u> up the <u>high</u> school <u>hierarchy</u>, she realized

Oh great! All the really cool animals get to take the higher ark!

Hierarchy

that popularity was not all it's cracked up to be. (This sentence was based on an after-school special.)

The Homily

Just in case you don't know, a "homily" is a sermon.
—Samantha

The handsome young priest was preparing his sermon, and he needed advice from the hairy old pastor.

"I gotta give a good talk so I can move up in the church <u>hierarchy</u>," he explained. "Can you help me?"

"You speak on <u>hallowed</u> ground," the pastor began, "so be not <u>haughty</u>. A good public response to your sermon will be a <u>harbinger</u> of your advancement." The priest worked all night, searching for <u>hackneyed</u> expressions and heartwarming verses. But when dawn came he just said, "Oh, the heck with it."

iconoclast	**destroyer of tradition** When the pope decided that celibacy should no longer be required of the clergy, protesters outside his window yelled "Down with the <u>iconoclast</u>" while the pope screamed, "<u>I cannot last</u>."
ignominious **ignominy**	**characterized by ignominy** **dishonor; disgrace** They suffered an <u>ignominious</u> defeat. He couldn't bear the <u>ignominy</u> of getting a 600 on the SAT.
imbue	**to make wet; to saturate; to inspire** If you <u>imbibe</u> the meanings of all these words, you will be <u>imbued</u> with wisdom.
imminent	**about to occur; impending** *Note:* Don't confuse imminent with <u>eminent</u>, which means "famous." <u>I'm in entertainment and my curtain call is imminent</u>.
immutable	*Note:* The best way to learn this word is to learn the root <u>mut</u>, which means "change." Then you can decode <u>immutable</u> to mean "not changeable." You will also realize that <u>mutable</u> =

"changeable," <u>mutation</u> = "a change," and trans<u>mute</u> = "to change from one form to another."

"An anvil falling on your head would hurt" is one of the <u>immutable</u> laws of physics.

impale — to pierce with a sharp stake or point
The <u>imp paled</u> when we took a spike and <u>impaled</u> the mushroom he was sitting on.

impasse — dead end (think: impassable)
If you are trying to get into a building and your security <u>pass</u> isn't working, you have reached an <u>impasse</u>.

impassive — without emotion; expressionless
"It looks as if I've reached an <u>impasse</u>," Bart muttered <u>impassively</u> as he slammed into the brick wall on his skateboard.

impeccable — flawless and faultless; not capable of sin
Woody is not an <u>impeccable</u> woodpecker; he is always making mistakes.

impending — about to take place (see IMMINENT)
The dwarf cowered behind Snow White, sensing <u>imp-ending</u> doom.

imperious — domineering
The <u>emperor</u> was <u>imperious</u>.

impropriety — not <u>proper</u>; not displaying <u>propriety</u>
Howard Stern was fined by the FCC for his <u>impropriety</u>.

Here are two words that are sure to confuse you:

impugn — to attack as false; criticize

impunity — <u>immunity</u> from <u>punishment</u>

Impending

"You will not have <u>impunity</u> if you <u>impugn</u> my character with such impudence," Samantha shouted when she was rejected from the improv comedy troupe.

incessant

nonstop; ceaseless

Her <u>incessant</u> chatter forced me to throw her into a cesspool.

inchoate

incomplete; formless

His plan to trek to Saudi Arabia was <u>inchoate</u>; he was still only <u>in Kuwait</u>.

incite

to arouse; instigate

As soon as Drake came back <u>in sight</u>, his groupies' cheering <u>incited</u> the crowd to <u>ignite</u> their lighters and demand an encore.

incontrovertible

indisputable

"The evidence is <u>incontrovertible</u>," the lawyer concluded. "The sunburn on your bald head proves that you drive a <u>convertible</u>."

indomitable

unconquerable; impossible to <u>dominate</u>

He was the best <u>domin</u>oes player around; he was virtually <u>indomitable</u>.

inept

incompetent

The <u>inept</u> astronomy student thought that unicorns live on <u>Neptune</u>.

infer

to conclude based on facts

It can be <u>inferred</u> that people dressed <u>in fur</u> are not animal-rights activists.

Two more words that will confuse you:

ingenious

original; resourceful

ingenuous

showing childlike simplicity; innocent

Remember these words this way: <u>Ingenious</u> has an <u>i</u>, like <u>genius</u>, and it also expresses the main qualities of <u>genius</u>.

Baby <u>geniuses</u> frequently discover <u>ingenious</u> ideas in <u>ingenuous</u> ways. (It also helps if you know that <u>disingenuous</u> means "crafty," not innocent or straightforward.)

innate

belonging to someone from birth; inherent
The malice <u>in Nate</u> is <u>innate</u>. He's been nasty since birth.

insatiable

impossible to satisfy
You must develop an <u>insatiable</u> desire to learn more and more vocabulary words.

inscrutable

enigmatic; difficult to understand
The Swedish furniture manufacturer's instructions on how to <u>unscrew</u> the <u>table</u> were <u>inscrutable</u>.

insipid

lacking excitement; vapid
The <u>insipid</u> innkeeper stayed <u>in, sipped</u> wine, and slept.

intangible

not perceptible to the touch; impalpable
You can't touch the <u>tangent</u> of $\pi/2$; it's <u>intangible</u>.

intrinsic

natural; innate; inherent
I have an <u>intrinsic</u> love of travel, but I always get <u>train-sick</u>.

Five Irascible Fools

Samantha, Larry, Manek, Michael, and Paul were traveling incognito in the indigo-colored bus. They had reached an <u>impasse</u> in their <u>indomitable</u> attempts to think of sentences for the I's.

"Hey, Manek, do you have any <u>ingenious</u> ideas for 'inscrutable,' you <u>inept</u> fool?" Larry inquired.

Manek's face remained <u>impassive</u>. "You know you're just <u>inciting</u> me to anger with your <u>insipid</u> questions. If you continue this <u>impropriety</u>, I'll become irritated."

"Are we to <u>infer</u> that you are questioning Larry's <u>impeccable</u> integrity by implying that he acted in an idiotic manner?" Paul interjected <u>ingenuously</u>. "I'm sure he couldn't stand the <u>ignominy</u>."

"If you all don't shut up, I'll be forced to <u>impale</u> you," Samantha shouted.

"Our <u>incontrovertibly</u> <u>insatiable</u> desire to help students is failing!" Larry added.

"But what, ho!" Manek exclaimed. "I believe our destination is <u>imminent</u>."

So the bus stopped and they got off, continuing to argue <u>incessantly</u>.

J

There are no important words that start with J. ✱

✱Tell that to the 12,789 words in that section of the dictionary.
—Samantha

K

The only important word that starts with K is "kiosk," and you already know what that is. Or if you don't, go to your nearest kiosk and buy the pamphlet "Kiosks Unlimited: A Guide to Everything Kiosk."

L

labyrinth

complicated maze or winding series of corridors
You'd be a<u>maze</u>d at how easily the <u>lab</u>oratory rats get lost in the <u>labyrinth</u>.

laconic

not saying much; brief; terse; concise; succinct
This sentence is <u>laconic</u>.
There is a Greek story about the war between Laconia and Athens. The Athenians threatened the Laconians by sending a letter to them that said something like, "If we defeat you we will burn your houses, pillage your villages, maul your women and children, etc. . . . ." The <u>Laconians</u> sent back the <u>laconic</u> reply, "If."

lambaste

to thrash, maul, beat, whip, or bludgeon with big things and other fun stuff; to scold sharply or rebuke

"Baste that lamb or I'll lambaste you!" the cook yelled to his assistant.

Ow, not so hard

Lambaste

languid lacking energy; weak
languish to lose strength; waste away
languor sluggishness

Note: As you will notice, a lot of L words mean "lazy and lacking energy."

No doubt learning all this language is giving you so much anguish that you're starting to languish.

lassitude listlessness; a state of exhaustion or weakness

The ship's crew was in such a state of lassitude that they sailed to the wrong latitude.

latent potential but not yet displayed

He had a latent talent for playing the harmonica, but he didn't discover it until late in his life.

Note: Latent is often used in the phrase *latent talent,* which is a handy memory aid because the two words have the exact same letters.

laud (v.) to praise (think: "Praise be the Laud!")
(n.) praise

laudatory (adj.) praiseful

The students stuck in the loud auditorium did not have any laudatory comments at the end of the pep rally.

lethargy sluggishness; indifference

Are you overcome by lethargy from all this studying? Well, it's time to wake up, so:

STOP STUDYING!

1. Go to the nearest store.

2. Buy four cups of coffee and a six-pack
of Red Bull.

3. Rapidly consume everything you just bought.

4. Go back to work (and relax!).

liability	**someone or something that poses a potential problem; something that someone is legally responsible for** Lionel's constant lying was a <u>liability</u> for the Honesty Committee; once, he even <u>lied</u> about his <u>ability</u> to tell the truth.
limacine	**pertaining to or resembling a slug** This word won't be on the test, but it's a useful insult.
loathe	**to hate** "Pick up some bread at the store, okay?" she asked. "No, I'll buy tortillas," he replied. "You know I <u>loathe</u> <u>loaves</u>!"
lugubrious	**mournful or sad** When Lou the undertaker's friends died, he was too <u>lugubrious</u> to bury them. Finally, they got so tired of waiting to be buried that they came back to life and said, "<u>Lou, go bury us</u>."
An Open and Frank Note from the Authors	You're probably looking forward to a great story. Well, you won't find one here, but not because we were too lazy and <u>languid</u>. We actually did write a pretty lively one, but instead of <u>lauding</u> it, the editor <u>loathed</u> it. After she read it, she <u>lambasted</u> us with lethal cans of lima beans (we suspect they were obtained through larceny). This made us a bit <u>lugubrious</u>, but we were willing to come up with a new story. But when she <u>laconically</u> called us "<u>limacine</u> idiots," we left, suddenly overcome by our <u>latent</u> <u>lethargy</u> and <u>languor</u>. So, in protest, we didn't do an L story. Humblest apologies. We hope you'll forgive us.

M

macabre — gross; ghastly; suggestive of horrible death and decay

"This macabre story is about a psychotic farmer who chokes people with corn on the cob."

The root "mal-" means "bad." The next few words all begin with "mal-":

malaise — a feeling of illness or depression

After I ate the jar of mayonnaise, I had a feeling of malaise that made me lazy.

malice — the desire to do bad to others; spite

malicious — having malice

The Queen of Hearts felt malice toward Alice.

malign — to say bad things about; slander

He maligned me by saying that I couldn't remember my lines.

malignancy — a malevolent and malicious act (also, a malignant tumor)

In an act of extreme malignancy, the bully was trying to break my leg. Suddenly, the doorbell rang. I said to him, "Get off my leg'n see who's at the door."

maneuver — a skillful or clever move

The captain used a tricky sailing maneuver to rescue the man overboard. The grateful man said, "Man, you very clever."

meander — to wander around aimlessly

Me and her meandered down the path.

melancholy — sadness; depression; pensiveness

When he finds out that she can't elope, he'll be melancholy.

meticulous — extremely careful and precise

He was so meticulous that he used the metric system to measure the diameter of his navel lint.

Don't be sad, we can still get married

we just can't elope

Melancholy

minuscule | very tiny
Minuscule students go to minischools.

misnomer | an inappropriate or wrong name
"My name is Mrs. Troller!" screamed the teacher. "To call me Miss Gnomer is a misnomer!"

mitigate | to make less severe
The robber's escape was foiled when he was met at the gate by cops. His sentence was mitigated, however, when he offered the cops donuts.

modicum | little bit
When Lady Gaga was just a child, she began to show a modicum of talent, and instead of calling her mother, she would sing "Muduh, come!"

monotonous | always at the same pitch; boring; repetitious
This word is easy if you break it up into its parts:

"mono" = the same, one

"tone" = sound

+ "ous" = having the qualities of

---

monotonous = having the same sound

The concerto played on the one-keyed piano was monotonous.

moo | low, deep sound made by a cow
In a low, deep voice, the cow said, "Moo."

mordant | bitingly sarcastic or nasty
She mordantly told him that he needed more dental adhesive.

morose | sullen; depressed

If you love learning vocabulary words, you will be <u>morose</u> when you get to the word *overt* because after it there are no <u>more Os</u>.

myriad

many; a lot; a very large amount
<u>Mary had</u> only one little lamb, not <u>myriad</u> lambs.

Manek's Problems

In a small maritime village, there lived a <u>morose</u> review book author named Manek. Most of the citizens loved him because he was <u>meticulously</u> clean, but there was a <u>minuscule</u>-brained gang in town (led by Michael) who <u>maliciously</u> <u>maligned</u> him. "Hey, Manek," they would yell. "You smell worse than a <u>moo</u>-cow. Yeah, Manek is a <u>misnomer</u>: You should be called <u>moo</u>-nek!"

Manek bore the gang no <u>malice</u>, though he wished he could, through some ingenious <u>maneuver</u>, <u>meander</u> through the town's <u>myriad</u> streets without these <u>monotonous</u> insults. He grew <u>melancholy</u> and suffered from a great <u>malaise</u> as he <u>morosely</u> contemplated their <u>malignancy</u>.

There, that story wasn't so <u>macabre,</u> was it?

N

nadir

absolute lowest point
Note: The word *zenith* is the opposite of *nadir*. If you ever get these two confused, just remember that no one would name their brand of TV "Nadir."

Nadine knew their relationship had reached its <u>nadir</u> when she asked her husband to watch the Super Bowl with her and he said, "<u>Nay, dear</u>."

naive

lacking in worldly wisdom or experience
After God expelled them from Eden, Adam said, "The time is <u>nigh, Eve</u>. We can no longer be <u>naive</u>."

nascent

coming into being; emerging
Your <u>nascent</u> vocabulary will cause <u>an ascent</u> in your verbal score.

nemesis	vengeful enemy In the book of Genesis, the Serpent is Eve's <u>nemesis</u>.
neologism	a newly coined word, phrase, or expression *Note:* Decode this word. <div align="center">"neo" = new + "logism" = idea, word ——————————— neologism = new word</div>Whoever made up the word <u>neologism</u> created a <u>neologism</u>.
neophyte	beginner The <u>neophyte</u> boxer was <u>new</u> to <u>fight</u>ing.
nexus	bond or link between things A <u>nexus</u> is a bond that con<u>nects us</u>.
nonchalant	appearing casual, cool, indifferent, chilled out Because the hare considered the race against the tortoise a <u>nonchallenge</u>, he was <u>nonchalant</u> about it and ended up losing.
nonplussed	perplexed; baffled She had expected to get an A-<u>plus</u> on the test; when she received an A-minus, she was <u>nonplussed</u>.
normative	normal; typical; adhering to the status quo **(often refers to behavior)** Ms. Smith couldn't <u>ignore Matt if</u> he screamed, so he screamed for lollipops all the time, even though this was not <u>normative</u> behavior for a seventeen-year-old.
notorious	famous for something bad; infamous The nefarious note-person was <u>notorious</u> for leaving nasty <u>notes</u> on people's doors.
novel	On the SAT this won't refer to a literary genre. It will mean new; unusual; different Years ago there was <u>no Vel</u>cro. Then someone had the <u>novel</u> idea of inventing it.

Novice

novice	**beginner; person new to something** He was a <u>novice</u> when it came to carpentry—he had <u>no vise</u>.
nuance	**subtle variation in color, meaning, or some other quality** I could tell by the subtle <u>nuance</u> in her voice that my <u>new aunt</u> thought I was being a <u>nuisance</u>.

A Villain's Death

The nefarious villain had reached the <u>nadir</u> of his <u>notorious</u> career. He had run into his <u>nemesis,</u> Nice Ned, the sheriff, after stealing some counterfeit cash (he often didn't notice the <u>nuances</u> of forged bills). Now he lay dying in the desert from two fatal earlobe wounds.

Looking back, he recalled his <u>nascent</u> life as an outlaw. He had started as a <u>naive novice</u> in New York, but when the city fumes got to him, he headed west, where a <u>novel</u> future awaited him. In later years, no longer a <u>neophyte</u>, his <u>nonchalant</u> attitude had left him <u>nonplussed</u>. Now nearly dead, he wanted to establish a <u>nexus</u> with his lost youth, but it was too late.

O

obdurate	**stubbornly resistant to changing one's mind** I can't en<u>dure it</u> when I try to reason with you because you're <u>obdurate</u>.
obsolete	**out of style; outdated** In the age of iPhones and streaming, the compact disc is becoming <u>obsolete</u>.
obtuse	You may remember that in math an angle is called obtuse if it is greater than 90 degrees. However, the meaning that would be on the SAT Reading Test is **stupid, thick-headed** (think: an <u>obtuse</u> angle is "thick" and so is an <u>obtuse</u> person). *Note:* An acute angle is less than 90 degrees and an acute person is sharp-minded—the opposite of <u>obtuse</u>.

The <u>obtuse</u> man could not draw an <u>obtuse</u> angle.

odious | **offensive; hateful**
The drug dealer was <u>odious</u>—he was trying to <u>"O.D." us</u>.

omnipotent | **all-powerful**
Note: This word is totally decodable:

"omni" = all

+ "potent" = powerful

_____

omnipotent = all-powerful

Lex Luthor desires to be the <u>omnipotent</u> ruler of the Earth, but Superman always defeats him.

omniscient | **all-knowing**
Note: Also decodable:

"omni" = all

+ "scient" = knowledge, knowing

_____

omniscient = all-knowing

He read every old issue of *Omni* science magazine in the hope that he would become <u>omniscient</u>.

onerous | **burdensome**
Would you <u>honor us</u> by helping us carry this <u>onerous</u> box of lead?

opulent | **rich**
<u>Opulent</u> Oprah always wore <u>opals</u>— and diamonds and rubies and emeralds and . . .

orifice | **small hole, opening, or vent; often refers to the mouth, nostrils, and other bodily openings**
"I've had a hard day at the <u>orifice</u>," said the dentist.

HARD DAY AT THE
Orifice

oscillate	to swing back and forth "His behavior <u>oscillated</u>," the babysitter reported. "He would be d<u>ocile eight</u> hours and then go crazy!"
ostensible	apparent; seeming (but usually not really) The <u>ostensible</u> reason that <u>Austin is able</u> to bench-press 300 pounds is his daily workout routine. The real reason is anabolic steroids.
ostentatious	showy; pretentious Glittering Emerald City is <u>Oz-tentatious</u>.
overt	open and observable; not hidden (see COVERT) Meg <u>overtly</u> knocked <u>over</u> Teddy's crystal toothbrush holder in order to attract attention.

A Fairy Tale

I went to the king, seeking to marry his daughter, but he was <u>obdurate</u> in his refusal. <u>Odiously</u>, he kicked me out of the <u>opulent</u> palace. I went away, determined to raise an army and assault his <u>omnipotent</u> forces. However, my battalion was blown to oblivion.

I then went to see <u>Omniscient</u> Olga, an old one-eyed witch who dealt in the occult and <u>oscillated</u> between sanity and insanity. ✱ When I arrived at the <u>orifice</u> that led to her cave, she looked at me with her one eye as though I was <u>obtuse</u> to visit her. She advised me to go and be of service to the king, to offer to carry out every <u>onerous</u> task, <u>ostensibly</u> out of the kindness of my heart, but really to penetrate the castle and elope with the princess.

I made my way to the royal city. As I approached the gate, however, a guard cast me out of the kingdom. Heartbroken, I went to seek my fortune selling doorknobs to nomads.

✱I feel you, Olga.
—Samantha

P

palatable	acceptable to the taste; sufficiently good to be edible (think: plate-able) The cannibal found his <u>pal edible</u> and quite <u>palatable</u>.
palliate	to moderate the severity of, abate

"He looks pale; he ate something poisonous," the doctor said. "We'll have to palliate the poison with an antidote."

pallid	**having an extremely pale complexion** He was so pallid that even his eyes had pale lids.
palpable	**capable of being touched or felt (see TANGIBLE); real** I pinched my pal Pablo to see if he was palpable.
paragon	**model or example of perfection** Batman and Robin were a pair of goners, but Robin, that paragon of digital dexterity, managed to reach his utility belt and foil the Riddler's evil trap.
pathos	**quality in something that makes you pity it; feeling of sympathy or pity (remember "pathy" = feeling)** Feel pathos for me as I wander down this path oh so pitiful.
paucity	**smallness in number; scarcity (see DEARTH)** Remember, never name your pet store "Paw City." The poor city has a paucity of rich people.
pedagogue	**schoolteacher or educator; boring, dry teacher** The teacher was such a pedagogue that Peter gagged at the thought of listening to another one of her boring lectures.
pedestrian	You already know that this means a person traveling on foot. However, when it's used on the SAT it means **commonplace; ordinary.** Compared to being a neurosurgeon, being a pediatrician is pedestrian.
penchant	**strong liking; inclination** Baseball teams have a penchant for pennants.
pensive	**engaged in deep, often sad, thought** After much deep, often sad, thought, William Penn decided to call his new state Pensiveania.

WELCOME TO PENSIVE-ANIA

Pensive

perfunctory	done routinely, carelessly, and listlessly If you are studying in a <u>perfunctory</u> manner, it's time for a break. Put on some funk music and let it permeate your room. But you can't do that because you don't know what *permeate* means yet. So you'd better forget the break and continue studying.
permeable	capable of being <u>permeated</u>
permeate	to spread or flow through Your hair must be <u>permeable</u> to Pantene if you want a <u>perm</u>.
perspicacious	perceptive; understanding If you look at things from all <u>perspec</u>tives, you are <u>perspicacious</u>.
petulant	unreasonably irritable or ill-tempered That <u>pet you lent</u> me barked and snapped and was generally <u>petulant</u>. I'm giving it back.
philanthropy	improvement of the world through charity; love of humanity in general We did not write this book out of a penchant for pecuniary gain. Instead, <u>philanthropy</u> was our motive.
pithy	concise and meaningful <u>Pyth</u>agoras approached this triangle from the right angle, when he came up with his <u>pithy Pyth</u>agorean theorem: $a^2 + b^2 = c^2$.
	Note: The root "plac-" in the next two words means "calm."
placate	to appease, pacify, or calm 7 tried to <u>placate</u> gossip-starved 8 by telling her that 9 had 6 with 5, but instead of appeasing her, the news seemed to <u>plague 8</u>.
placid	calm; composed; undisturbed "<u>Pla</u>!" <u>Sid</u> said, spitting out a mouthful of water. "This lake is calm and <u>placid</u>, but it tastes disgusting."
plaintive	sad; see MELANCHOLY (think: com<u>plain</u>) When she realized that the judge was going to rule against her, the <u>plaintiff</u> became <u>plaintive</u>.

plethora	superabundance; <u>plenty</u>; excess (opposite of DEARTH) In case you haven't noticed yet, there is a <u>plethora</u> of terrible puns in this book.
politic	shrewd; clever <u>Politic</u>ians must be <u>politic</u> in order to win votes.
posthumous	**continuing or done after one's death** *Note:* Decode: "post" = after + "humus" = earth ———————————— posthumous = after earth Suppose the five of us died of "pun"icillin poisoning. Our book would have to be published <u>posthumously</u>.
postulate	**to assume; to claim, often without much evidence or proof** Peter <u>postulated</u> that the mailman would arrive on time, but as usual, the <u>post</u> came <u>too late</u>.
pragmatic	**practical (think: "pragtical")** The Craftmatic adjustable bed is <u>pragmatic</u> because it is <u>prag</u>tically auto<u>matic</u>.
precocious	**characterized by unusually early development** The high school basketball coach hoped that there would be some <u>precocious</u> basketball players in our elementary school, so he <u>precoached us</u>.
precursor	**predecessor; what came before** Although Mickey might disagree, many would say that the <u>precursor</u> to the mouse was the computer keyboard.

You mean you have to type in all your commands? What about the "mouse"?

This is before all that

Precursor

presage	to give an indication or warning of something that will happen in the future

> "pre" = before
>
> + "sage" = a smart person who tells people things
>
> ---
>
> presage = tell before

When the economists <u>presaged</u> that the economy was going to get worse, Michelle watched the <u>prez age</u>.

prevalent	commonly occurring or existing

Before knights were <u>prevalent</u>, the world was in its <u>pre-valiant</u> period.

profuse	abundant; overflowing

Our <u>prof used</u> <u>profuse</u> amounts of <u>profane</u> language. Then he was fired.

proliferate	to increase or spread rapidly

The <u>prolife</u> movement <u>proliferated</u> on the conservative campus.

prolific	producing lots of offspring or fruit; fertile; producing lots of work or results

The guy who writes CliffsNotes is <u>pro-Cliff-ic</u>; he's got hundreds of titles in print.

prosaic	lacking excitement or imagination; dull

The sad artist thought her artwork was <u>prosaic</u>. At whatever angle she studied it, she still thought her <u>mosaic</u> of giant artichokes was lacking.

Petulant Peanuts

Philip DePance and his coworker, Peanuts Burnes, were on a lunch break from the <u>philanthropic</u> firm of "<u>Paucity</u> to <u>Plethora</u>."

"I'm parched," said Phil. "Let's start this meal!"

They ordered fruit after the waiter <u>perfunctorily</u> told them that the banana trees were <u>prolific</u> at this time of year, and they were brought spotted bananas that seemed <u>palatable</u> enough.

*A plethora
of P words!*
— Samantha

But soon Phil turned <u>pallid</u>. "My nose is detecting something putrid," he said.

"Eww!" Peanuts added. "It's the bananas! I knew those spots <u>presaged</u> something."

"Waiter," Phil called. "We are <u>petulant</u> already because of problems at <u>Paucity</u> to <u>Plethora</u> and, to make a long story <u>pithy</u>, we do not have a <u>penchant</u> for rotten banana stench <u>permeating</u> the room. Please dispose of the offending fruit before the odor <u>proliferates</u> further!"

"I don't smell anything," the waiter replied.

"We will not be <u>placated</u> until we have <u>palpable</u> proof that the <u>prevalent</u> filth is gone!" said Peanuts in the fashion of a true <u>pedagogue</u>.

<u>Plaintively</u>, full of <u>pathos</u>, the waiter smashed the bananas and took them away. "Even <u>posthumously</u>, my <u>precursor</u> still makes me look like the <u>paragon</u> of poor service! These bananas were planted by him!" he muttered as he stalked off.

"Well, I feel better, Peanuts. We could work here!" Phil said, once again <u>placid</u>.

Q

qualm

doubt; uneasiness; sudden pang of sickness or faintness

The model had some <u>qualms</u> when the photographer asked her to pose atop a volcano in Guam.

qualitative
quantitative

having to do with a <u>quality</u>

capable of being expressed as, or having to do with, a number or <u>quantity</u>

But what if I rain and no one's even planned a picnic?

THE **Qualm** BEFORE THE STORM

"I did really well on my history exam" is a <u>qualitative</u> description of how you did on the history exam.

"I got a 96 on my history exam" is a <u>quantitative</u> description of how you did on the history exam.

quandary   state of uncertainty; dilemma
He was in a <u>quandary</u> about whether to do his laundry; he
liked the grunge look, but his clothes were beginning to smell.

quarantine   isolate because of a disease
We had to │ quarantine │ this word so that it wouldn't infect
its neighbors and make them queasy.

quixotic   **having the same foolish, impractical, romantic idealism as
Don Quixote (Really, this isn't a pun.)**
Nestlé's CEO had the <u>quixotic</u> notion of making <u>Quik exotic</u> by
offering flavors like sun-dried tomato.

quorum   **minimum number of people who have to be at a meeting in
order for the meeting to be official**
(It sounds like a video game, doesn't it?)
Before the council can begin the boredom, it's required that
they have a <u>quorum</u>.

**A Quick Meeting
of Minds**

"<u>Quorum</u>, <u>quorum</u>, we must have a <u>quorum</u>!" shouted the
leader.

"Why?" asked an idiot. "<u>Qualitatively</u> speaking, it's quicker
to quantify the quarks in a quarter."

"We need a <u>quantitative</u> estimate of how many quacks are
here."

"Yes, it is a bit of a <u>quandary</u>," spoke another idiot. "I know,
why don't we vote on whether or not to begin the meeting?"

"I have <u>qualms</u> about doing that," said the first idiot.

"Quiet, you idiots, or you'll be <u>quarantined</u>!" quoth the
leader. "Now then. I have a plan. You may think me somewhat
<u>quixotic</u>, but I truly believe that if we burst forth with enough

clever quotations, we might be recognized as not being quite so stupid as we really are. And with that thought in mind, I'd like to close this meeting of the village idiots."

R

rampant	unrestrained

The <u>ram pant</u>ed after it ran <u>rampant</u> around the field for two days.

rationalize	**to make rational; justify**

It is impossible to <u>rationalize</u> the senseless crime of cat juggling.

raze	**to tear down; demolish**

The striking cereal workers used an enormous <u>razor</u> to <u>raze</u> the <u>raisin</u> bran factory.

Raze

recalcitrant	**stubborn**

I adamantly and obdurately refuse to admit that I am <u>recalcitrant</u>.

recapitulate	**to repeat, or state again, in a form that is much briefer than the manner in which it was initially stated**

Now we are going to <u>recapitulate</u> the above definition: to repeat concisely.

Think: When a sportscaster <u>recaps</u> the game, she gives a brief summary of what has happened.

reciprocal	**mutual**

We have a <u>reciprocal</u> agreement not to spit watermelon seeds at each other.

recondite	obscure; abstruse
	If this story weren't so <u>recondite</u>, I <u>reckon I'd</u> understand it.
	concealed; hidden from sight
	He kept his pet condor <u>recondite</u> for fear that his environmentalist sister would set it free.
rectify	to correct; set right
	Tim had to visit the proctologist to <u>rectify</u> <u>rec</u>urrent <u>rec</u>tal problems.
recumbent	**lying down**
	With both legs broken and his th<u>umb bent</u>, he spent most of the day <u>recumbent</u>.
redress	**to set right; remedy; rectify**
	When Cinderella arrived at the ball wearing only a slip and glass slippers, the prince suggested it was time to <u>redress</u> the situation.
redundant	**repetitious; done over and over many times; repeatedly repetitive**
	The above definition is <u>redundant</u>.
refute	**to disprove**
	"<u>Ref, you'd</u> better listen up while I <u>refute</u> your call," said the irate player. "That ball was in."
reiterate	**to repeat**
	Note: <u>Iterate</u> also means <u>repeat</u>.
	I would like to <u>reiterate</u> my accusation—you are a noodlehead.
relative	**only understood in relation to something else; not independent**
	<u>Relative</u> to the larger human population, my <u>relatives</u> are imbeciles.
relevant	**having significant importance**
	Peanuts are <u>relevant</u> to an <u>elephant</u>'s development.
remorse	**bitter regret; guilt**
remorseless	**having no <u>remorse</u>**

When the <u>remorseless</u> spy catcher took away our telegraph machine for the second time, we were <u>re-Morse-less</u>.

reticent   **silent; restrained in behavior**
Scarlett said to Rhett, "Why are you so <u>reticent</u>?" He did not respond. "Is it because I didn't write you a letter?" she asked. He nodded. "But <u>Rhett, I sent</u> you a postcard."

retrograde   **moving backward to an earlier, usually inferior, position**
After receiving an A <u>grade</u> in history first semester, Michael's C– <u>grade</u> second semester was <u>retrograde</u>.

rhubarb   This won't be on the test, but try repeating it five times quickly out loud.

Retrograde

ruminate   **to chew cud (this definition won't be on the SAT); to think a lot about; cogitate**
Note: The definitions are related. "To think a lot about something" is kind of like "chewing something over in your mind." Also, when cows are chewing their cud, they look like they're thinking.

The physicist went into the laboratory <u>room 'n' ate</u> cupcakes while <u>ruminating</u> about how to put the filling inside Twinkies.

A Romance of Sorts   He was <u>recumbent</u> on his bed, <u>ruminating</u> on his affair with the countess. She had abandoned him and then <u>redressed</u> their relationship by returning. Now that she was <u>reciprocating</u> his love, he was once again the happiest man in the realm. Or was he?

There was a rap on the door. "Darling," she said, entering. He frowned as she kissed him, and she laughed. "Really. Don't be such a <u>recalcitrant</u> child. You're being altogether too <u>reticent</u>." She kissed him again.

He refused to smile. She reclined next to him. "I'm sorry I left you. I had to. I needed room. . . ." She began <u>recapitulating</u> the <u>relevant</u> parts of the <u>recondite</u> explanation she had given when she left. He did not respond.

Suddenly, there was an explosion on the street below. The countess strode to the window.

"It's the army. They're on a rampage." A group of soldiers began to batter the front door. "Let's escape via the roof." They raced over rooftops, with the soldiers running <u>rampant</u> through the streets below. "<u>Remorseless</u> rogues," she muttered. "They'll change their tune later when they have to <u>rectify</u> all the damage they're doing."

"Undoubtedly, they've <u>rationalized</u> their behavior by saying it was the only route open for them," he replied.

"I can't <u>refute</u> that," she said.

The outskirts of town were quiet. They slipped into a restaurant. "Now listen here," he scolded, sipping his red wine. "I want some assurance that you won't run off again and leave me ruing the day I met you."

"Whatever are you ranting about?" she retorted.

He <u>reiterated</u> his request, becoming riled.

She laughed. "Darling, you're being ridiculous as well as <u>redundant</u>. It's such a bore, really. Let's just enjoy our <u>rhubarb</u> soup."

S

saga   **long adventure story**

Titanic is the <u>soggy saga</u> of a boatload of beautiful people hitting a really big ice cube.

scrutiny   inspection; study; careful searching

An inspection of Canadian police is a <u>scrutiny</u> of the Mounties.

sedition   **conduct or language inciting rebellion against authority**

Karl Marx's publisher rejected Marx's first manuscript of *The Communist Manifesto*, saying, "Thi<u>s edition</u> does not contain enough <u>sedition</u>."

sequester   **to separate, set apart, isolate**

Tired of having his SAT studies interrupted, Larry hired a boat and went on a <u>sea quest</u> for a desert island where he could <u>sequester</u> himself for a semester.

shiftless   **lazy; showing lack of motivation; incompetent**

The <u>shiftless</u> secretary couldn't type capital letters. (Get it?)

simultaneous   **happening at the same time**

I will now attempt to rub cheese on my chest while <u>simultaneously</u> drinking salsa through a straw and juggling ostrich eggs.

sinister   **foreboding of evil**

Note: Sinister means "left" in Latin. In ancient times the left side was considered unlucky—the side from which evil would approach. This notion survives today in phrases such as *right-hand man* and *left-handed compliment.*

Six <u>sinister</u> sisters scared seven silly senators. (Say this ten times fast.)

skeptical   **doubting; disbelieving**

You think you can <u>escape tickle</u> torture? I'm <u>skeptical</u>.

somber	dark; dull; gloomy The remorseful b<u>omber</u> was <u>somber</u> when he realized what he had done.
stagnant **stagnate**	not moving or flowing; motionless, <u>stat</u>ionary to be <u>stagnant</u> The air in SAT testing halls is often <u>stagnant</u>, which perhaps explains why the proctors look stale and crusty.
static	On the SAT, this probably would not refer to the fuzzy noise you hear when you get too far away from a radio station's signal nor to the effect produced when you rub a balloon across your head. Instead, it will probably mean having no motion; at rest; <u>stat</u>ionary. The contents of our <u>attic</u> are <u>static</u>; they haven't changed in years.
stinkhorn	Look up this word in an *American Heritage Dictionary*, New College Edition (the first edition). The picture is the most phallic image you will ever see in a venerable reference book.
stipulate	to specify a condition of an agreement Steven <u>stipulates</u> that he will pull only five of the wagons; you, however, must <u>still pull eight</u>.
submission	the act of yielding to the authority of another The submarine captain demanded the <u>submission</u> of the sailors on the <u>sub mission</u>.
subvert	to overthrow or undermine the power of The prizewinning poet was accused of trying to <u>subvert</u> his poetry when he started writing his verses on submarine sandwiches.
suffrage	right to vote; franchise Before 1920, women <u>suffered</u> from a lack of <u>suffrage</u>. But the <u>suffragettes</u> changed all that and now women can rock the vote along with men.

Following are three superior words beginning with "super-."

superfluous | **beyond what's necessary; extra**

<u>Super</u>man once <u>flew us</u> home without his cape. This suggests that his cape is just a <u>superfluous</u> item and not something he needs in order to fly.

superlative | **most; of the highest order; surpassing all others**

We're going to be <u>super late</u> if the car breaks down, and Mom is going to be <u>superlatively</u> pissed off.

supersede | **to take the place of**

After Farmer Clark planted the new tomato <u>super seed</u>, it completely <u>superseded</u> the regular seeds.

Boy, did I get left in the dust!

NEW SUPER SEED

OLD REGULAR SEED

Supersede

sweat gland | **small secretory gland in the skin that excretes water and body salts**

Are you awake?

A Shocking Courtroom Saga

My <u>sweat glands</u> were working overtime in the <u>stagnant</u> air of the courtroom as I unscrupulously questioned the <u>sinister</u> defendant on trial for <u>sedition</u>. Although he proclaimed his innocence, the jury was obviously <u>skeptical</u>. When I <u>superseded</u> him on the courtroom floor, it was clear that the other lawyer's points were silly compared to my <u>superlative</u> arguments.

I was confident. All further speech was <u>superfluous</u>. So I said, "The State rests, Your Honor." I ran out to lunch, and the jury was <u>sequestered</u>.

Two hours later the jury was summoned, and I waited, expecting the word *guilty*. So I was surprised when I heard the word *not* as well. "I've been <u>subverted</u>!" I yelled. Then the bailiff hit me over the head and I <u>submissively</u> left the courthouse.

Now I cultivate <u>stinkhorns</u> and lead a much quieter, <u>static</u> life.

T

table

The SAT would not refer to the four-legged household object. Rather, the SAT definition would be "to remove from consideration."

The legislature <u>tabled</u> the amendment that would have made everyone eat their vege<u>tables</u>.

tact

skill in dealing with people in difficult situations
Think: good social <u>tact</u>ics
When at a funeral, it is not <u>tact</u>ful to say, "Darn, she owed me money."

tangible

existing materially; palpable; able to be touched
Compare with in<u>tangible</u>: Love, fear, and hope are in<u>tangible</u>. <u>Tang</u>erines, antelopes, and pencils are <u>tangible</u>.

tedious

boring; tiresome; trivial
The other team scored so many touchdowns that it became <u>tedious</u> to watch them <u>TD us</u>.

tenacity

persistence; tending to hold on firmly
The student took <u>ten SATs</u> with <u>tenacity</u> until she got a 1600.
It took her so many tries because she hadn't read *Up Your Score*.

tenet

principle or doctrine
The Ten Commandments are <u>ten eternal</u> <u>tenets</u>.

tepid

lukewarm; somewhat warm
(Did you ever try the one where you put a sleeping person's hand in <u>tepid</u> water and . . .)
Tom's tea was <u>tepid</u>, so he nuked it in the microwave.

terse

concise; free of superfluous words
This <u>verse</u> is <u>terse</u>.

thwart	**to prevent from taking place; challenge** "We must <u>thwart the wart</u>," the dermatologist decided.
tirade	**long and vehement speech** The department store owner gave the police a <u>tirade</u> when he discovered he had been the victim of a <u>tie raid</u>.
treachery	**betrayal of trust; traitorousness** When <u>Treach</u> left his rap group Naughty by Nature to embark on a solo career, the group called him <u>treacherous</u>.
triskaidekaphobia	**fear of the number 13** If you have <u>triskaidekaphobia</u>, you'll always skip questions numbered 13 on the SAT. (This word won't be on the test, but you should use it as often as possible.)
truncate	**to shorten by chopping off the end** The elephant's <u>trunk</u> was <u>truncated</u> when his friend <u>ate</u> his <u>trunk</u>.

Truncate

U

ubiquitous	**being or seeming to be everywhere at the same time; omnipresent** Take ten yellow Post-it notes and write *ubiquitous* on each one. Then stick them all over your house. The stickers will then be <u>ubiquitous</u>.
unassuming	**not pretentious; modest** Although they were rich enough to pay off the federal deficit, they were <u>unassuming</u> and lived in a tent.

unruly	difficult to govern; impossible to discipline They were used to living without <u>rules</u>, so they were <u>unruly</u>.
unscrupulous	unprincipled; lacking ethical values After the church robbery, the minister lamented, "It takes an <u>unscrupulous</u> criminal to <u>unscrew</u> the seats and leave us <u>pewless</u>."
unwitting	unaware; not knowing Whitman <u>unwittingly</u> let the priceless thoroughbred escape by leaving the barn door unlatched.
upshot	outcome; result *Note:* This word was originally an archery term. The last shot of an archery tournament was called the <u>upshot</u>, and it often determined the result or outcome of the tournament. Bart was hit in the rear by an <u>upshot</u> at the archery tournament. The <u>upshot</u> of this was that he had to take the SAT standing <u>up</u>.
usurp	to illegally seize the power or rights from another Yusef <u>usurped</u> Boris's position by staging a coup.
utilitarian	useful; practical Uma wanted to book a vacation, but paying her <u>utility</u> bill was a more <u>utilitarian</u> use of her paycheck.

Tutu Story	"Do you think Congress will <u>table</u> the discussion about the new river reeds?" the turtle asked.
	    There was an almost <u>tangible</u> silence. Then a grumpy tortoise put an ice cube in his tea and said, "That's a touchy subject here. We're all upset about our senator's <u>unscrupulous</u> <u>treachery</u> in supporting the bill. He has no <u>tact</u>."
	    "We're going to try to <u>thwart</u> him," the talkative tadpole in the tutu said <u>tersely</u>. "If that bill passes, I'll <u>truncate</u> his term with allegations of <u>unscrupulousness</u>. We must not forsake our <u>tenets</u>."

Her words caught me unawares. The tadpole had seemed to me to be polite and <u>unassuming,</u> but instead she was an <u>unruly</u> youth with a penchant for <u>tirades.</u>

Craziness was <u>ubiquitous.</u>

V

vacillate — to waver from one side to the other; oscillate
While the skier <u>vacillated</u> about whether to use Vaseline or ChapStick, his lips got chapped.

vacuity — emptiness; vacuum
The scientists were amazed by the utter <u>vacuity</u> in the proctor's brain—there was not a trace of brain matter anywhere.

vehement — with ardor; energetically or violently forceful
The <u>vehement</u> protesters put down their signs for a moment and freshened their breath <u>via mints.</u>

ver- — **The motto of Harvard is "Veritas" and the motto of Yale is "Lux et veritas."** These two schools may be knocking down your door once you get your 1600, so you might as well know that *veritas* is Latin for "truth." (*Lux* means "light.") When you see the root "ver-" in an SAT word, that word probably has something to do with truth.

"La verdad" means "the truth" for those of us in Spanish class.
—Samantha

Examples:
veracity—truthfulness; accuracy
verification—proof that something is true
verisimilar—appearing to be true or possible
verisimilitude—quality of being verisimilar
veritable—unquestionable; actual; true
verity—statement or belief considered to be the permanent truth
vermicide—anything used to kill worms (Well, it doesn't always work.)

verbose	excessively wordy

Note: This word has nothing to do with truth.

They wrote and transcribed and copied down on paper and composed and thought of and typed a sentence that would be <u>verbose</u> because it had excessive <u>verb</u>s.

vex	to irritate or bother
vexation	the act of vexing

His <u>vexing</u> habit of reciting vocabulary words during sexual activity ruined his sex life.

vilify	to slander; defame

Think: make vile

Senator Joe McCarthy's <u>vill</u>ainous lies <u>vilified</u> many innocent people.

Although the next two words have the same first six letters and are related, they are not at all synonymous.

vindicate	to clear of blame or suspicion

The lawyers will <u>vindicate</u> their client by displaying evidence they ha<u>ve, indicating</u> that he didn't mean to steal the adult diapers from the grocery store.

vindictive	vengeful

The <u>vindictive</u> Wicked Witch of the West wanted to kill Dorothy to avenge the death of the Wicked Witch of the East.

vocabulary	the bane of our existence, according to anyone who has made it all the way to the Vs

voracious	eager to consume mounds of food

We were so <u>voracious</u> that we even ate the Tupperware.

Vulcan | pointy-eared alien, devoid of warmth and emotion, who thinks logically
Come on! Don't fall asleep. Only two more pages to go.

vulnerable | unprotected
The Evil Testing Serpent is <u>vulnerable</u> to the tricks in *Up Your Score*.

whim | capricious, freakish idea
On a <u>whim</u>, the tournament directors decided to let the <u>wimp</u> play at <u>Wim</u>bledon.

wistful | yearning; <u>wishful</u> with a hint of sadness
As he thought of his lost love, William <u>whistled</u> a <u>wistful</u> melody and drank a bottle of her perfume.

wow | of or pertaining to golly-gee-whillikers

wrath | anger; rage
Elmer Fudd is full of <u>wrath</u> at that <u>wrath</u>cally wabbit that keeps eating his garden.

Sorry, there are no SAT words that begin with X.

yummy | delicious
Well, we didn't want to cop out for two letters in a row!

An Avuncular Vendetta (or I'm Hungry, You Vile Worm) | My uncle's <u>verbose</u>, <u>vacuous</u> speeches terrified and bored his enemies. Certain <u>vindictive</u> individuals have attempted to <u>vilify</u> his reputation by insisting that he was a <u>vulnerable</u> wimp, but he has always managed to <u>vindicate</u> himself by <u>vehemently</u> <u>verifying</u> the <u>veracity</u> of his claims of courage.

Anyway, one day while my uncle was <u>vacillating</u> over a choice of beverages, Victor Ventura burst in on him, extremely vexed. "I consider you a vile swine, and in the future I will not hesitate to spray you with vermicide," he said.

"Pray tell," said my uncle, "what is the cause of your vexation?"

"I came here with a voracious appetite," replied Victor, "and on a whim you denied me any food, you wretched worm."

"Wow," said my uncle wistfully, "you may as well spare me your wrath, because I don't have anything yummy to offer you."

Z

zeal

enthusiasm

zealous

full of zeal

The zealous seal spun the ball with zeal.

zenith

peak; summit; acme (see NADIR, zenith's antonym)

If the Zenith company could invent a TV that would change channels automatically whenever a show started getting stupid, that would be the zenith of television technology.

zest

gusto; happy and vivacious enjoyment

If you use Zest soap, you will feel full of zest for the rest of the day. You will also feel clean.

zyzzyva

any of various tropical weevils of the genus *Zyzzyva*, often destructive to plants

Who cares about zyzzyvas? You are done with the word list. Congratulations! Think of all the words you know now that you didn't know before. Good work. You are going to rock the Reading Test.

A Final Poem

A zany, zealous
Zyzzyva
Zestfully
Zigzagged up to the
Zenith.

CHAPTER 4

The Writing and Language Test

Embracing Your Inner Grammaniac

KNOW YOUR ENEMY

*This is a normal, accepted thing in college. It is the only reason I go out.
—Samantha

Are you an Alpha Grammarian? Do you like to stand around at parties, correcting people as they speak? * Do you pore over newspaper articles and advertisements, circling dangling modifiers? Do you get into heated arguments over whether or not to use the Oxford comma? If you've answered yes to any of these questions, then this section may be old news for you.

But if, like 99.9 percent of the population, you answered no, then we have some work to do.

On the Writing and Language Test, you will wield your pencil like a flask of holy water against the vampires of bad writing. As usual, the Evil Testing Serpent has some tricks up its sleeve, but with our guidance and some dedicated studying time, you will emerge victorious and with your blood (mostly) undrained.

The Nuts and Bolts

*Prose means "not poetry." They don't want us to be entertained with rhyme or rhythm.
—Samantha

The Writing and Language Test makes up 100–400 points of your all-important Evidence-Based Reading and Writing Test score, which is graded on a scale of 200–800 points. You will have 35 minutes to answer 44 questions.

For years, your teachers have been forced to read your mistake-ridden essays, circling error after error after error after error. Well, the Writing and Language Test is their revenge. It features four prose * passages that are filled with an average of 11 intentional mistakes per passage. The mistakes run the gamut from basic grammatical errors to poorly structured arguments to stylistic problems. Remember that the Writing and Language Test no longer includes the Essay, which is tested and scored separately now and is (nominally) optional. It is explained in detail in Chapter 6.

The passages in the Writing and Language Test come in three different forms. Each test will include **one nonfiction narrative** (for example, "The Time I Saw a Turtle"), which will usually be a first-person essay in which the author shares an experience. There will be either **one or two passages in an argument format** (for example, "Toothpaste Should Come in Fruit

Flavors"), where the author uses persuasive writing to defend an opinion. And there will be **one or two passages in an informative/explanatory format** (for example, "Stars Are Made of Stuff"), which seeks to educate readers about a given topic and does not try to promote the author's opinion.

The Writing and Language Test passages fall under four different topic areas. Each test features a passage about a topic in **history/social studies** and another one about a **science** topic, just like the Reading Test. The science passage will probably be in informative/explanatory form, and will definitely include an infographic that will come up in a question. The history/social studies passages could be informative/explanatory, but they might also be written as an argument, or there might be one of each.

The other two passages are about subject areas that you'll see only on the Writing and Language Test—**careers** and something related to "the **humanities**."

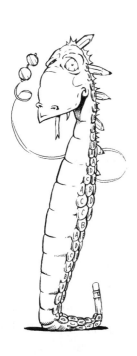

Every test includes a passage about a particular career (usually in the informative/explanatory form). The writer's attitude toward the given career is likely to be positive. Whether the passage is about sanitation workers, civil engineers, or doll makers, it will contain a glowing analysis of what these jobs contribute to society and how good the employment prospects in this field are. This passage is also likely to feature an infographic.

You'll also find a passage that's humanities-oriented. It will be about something that history and social studies don't cover—painting, sculpture, theater, puppeteering. It could appear as an informational piece, like a short biography of, who knows, perhaps the peerless and sadly forgotten puppeteer Sergey Obraztsov. It could also be a personal narrative about something in the arts. It could be about *any* art, not necessarily puppeteering, even though this is the best and truest art form.

As with all passages on the SAT, previous knowledge of the subjects is not assumed, and a close analysis of the passages' content is not the goal. You will need to understand the content

of the passage in order to answer all of the questions, but this part of the SAT is primarily focused on your knowledge of the "rules" of good writing.

Those "rules" are the "**Standard English Conventions**": sentence structure, grammar, word choice, punctuation, and which fork to use for salad. These will make up 45 percent of the questions. The other 55 percent of the questions on the Writing and Language Test are about the "**Expression of Ideas**," which is a fancy term for questions that ask you to choose the best ways to revise the passage to make it more accurate, clear, and persuasive. Many of these "Expression of Ideas" questions, as you will see, will ask about the evidence and rhetoric being used in the passage. If any of this makes you feel panicked, take a deep breath and relax. You don't have to be an aspiring novelist like Manek to rock the test.

In this chapter, we break it down by question type. First up is "Standard English Conventions," where we will guide you through the 12 Commandments of Grammar and their attendant questions. We will also review punctuation, from the simple period to the terribly complex comma. We will then go over many different kinds of "Expression of Ideas" questions. Finally, we will test you on all this with a sample Writing passage. By the end, you will have the knowledge and confidence you need to totally annihilate the Writing and Language Test.

But before we delve into all of that, a general tip: With each passage you read, imagine you are peer-editing a friend's essay. Your friend has a lot of great ideas, but she just needs some help with the execution. Perhaps the idea of helping out a friend will make this part of the SAT seem more tolerable and less, well, SAT-like.

STANDARD ENGLISH CONVENTIONS

Here's a fun game: Try to think up a more boring-sounding category than "Standard English Conventions." (We couldn't.)

Okay, so these questions won't be the most exciting, but on the brighter side, they also don't have to be that difficult. If you master some fundamental grammar and punctuation rules, you'll be able to easily spot writing errors in the passages and revise them with confidence. You'll also be able to write more clearly, which is not a terrible life skill to add to your résumé. And it's good to feel confident on these questions because the other kind of question, "Expression of Ideas," can be a little tricky (but more on that later).

First, let's lay out some grammar basics.

A Grammar Refresher

It has probably been a while since you studied grammar. Now is a good moment to bring all those terms you learned in middle school flooding back to mind.

NOUN

Word that denotes a person, place, thing, idea (joy), quality (stickiness), or act (drooling). Excellent nouns include: wicket, catamaran, sledge, viscosity.

PRONOUN

As Homer Simpson defined it when he was studying for his high school diploma, "A noun that has lost its amateur status." Actually, a word that takes the place of a noun. For example: The Evil Testing Serpent is evil. It is cruel. *It* is a pronoun because *it* takes the place of Serpent. Some other terrific pronouns: I, me, you, he, him, they, them, she, her, we, us.

Pronouns are important, especially in Harry Potter when they're referring to Volde— Never mind.
—Samantha

VERB

Word that expresses action (jump) or a state of being (be). A verb tells what's happening in the sentence. The two best verbs: ransack and crinkle.

SUBJECT

Noun or pronoun that "does" the action of the verb in the sentence. For example: He shadowboxed. *He* is the subject because *he* is the thing that shadowboxed.

OBJECT

Noun or pronoun that the verb acts on. For example: He tickled me. *Me* is the object because *me* is the thing that got tickled.

PREPOSITION

Words like *to, at, in, up, over, under, after, of.* They go with objects. For example, in the phrase "in the house," *in* is a preposition and *house* is the object. The fanciest preposition: *atop.*

SINGULAR

Having to do with a single thing or single unit. For example: one lone noodle.

PLURAL

Having to do with more than one thing. For example: oodles of noodles.

The 12 Commandments of Grammar

Behold! The sacred rules of grammar outlined below will illustrate the most common concepts on the Writing Test. If any of these rules are violated, you must correct them and cast these mistakes into the blackest abyss.

COMMANDMENT 1: THY VERBS SHALT ALWAYS AGREE WITH THY SUBJECTS.

Subject and verb must agree in number. In other words, if the subject is singular, the verb should be singular; if the subject is plural, the verb should be plural. So isolate the subject and the verb and make sure they match.

Example 1:

The proctor, as well as the students, were overcome by the tedious ticking of the timer and fell asleep. *

Isolate: subject: proctor (singular)
　　　　verb: were overcome (plural)

Don't let this example become real life. Sleep (and the occasional energy drink) is your friend.
　　　　—Samantha

Combine: "The proctor were overcome."

This should sound wrong to you. *Proctor* is singular, so the verb should be singular—*was overcome.* Don't be tempted by the plural word *students*; it is set off by a pair of commas, so it's not part of the subject.

Correct: The proctor, as well as the students, was overcome by the tedious ticking of the timer and fell asleep.

Three expressions that are similar to the *as well as* in the previous example are: *in addition to, along with,* and *together with.* When you see one of these expressions on the test, chances are the Serpent is trying to make you think that the subject is plural.

Example 2:
The anguish of the students have been a source of pleasure to the College Board. ✱

Isolate: subject: anguish (singular)
        verb: have been (plural)

Combine: "The anguish have been a source of pleasure."

This should sound wrong to you. Don't get confused by the plural word *students*, because it isn't the subject. *Students*, in this sentence, is an object. You can tell because it comes after a preposition: *of.* Whenever a word comes after a preposition, it is an object, not a subject.

Correct: The anguish of the students has been a source of pleasure to the College Board.

Example 3:
Let's do this as an SAT-style question.

Each of the streets <u>were painted green</u>.

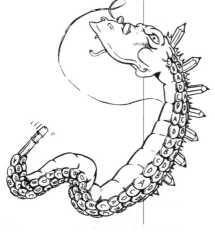

✱ What was the source of pleasure? Not the students, of course, but their <u>anguish</u>.
        —Samantha

Of the following, which best replaces the underlined portion?
A) NO CHANGE
B) were painting green.
C) was painted green.
D) was painting green.

Isolate: subject: each (singular)
       verb: were (plural)

Combine: "Each were painted green."

This one is a little trickier. You have to realize that the subject of the sentence is *Each* and not *of the streets.* (*Streets* is an object of the preposition *of.*) Anytime you see "of the _____," the word that goes in the blank is an object, not a subject. Although *streets* is plural, the subject of the sentence, *Each*, is singular. If you replace the "of the _____" part of the sentence with the word *one*, it is easier to see why the subject is singular: "Each one was painted green" sounds much better than "Each one were painted green." Answer choice C, then, is correct.

There are 13 singular subjects like *each* that you should memorize: *each, every, either, neither, one, no one, everyone, everybody, someone, somebody, anyone, anybody,* and *nobody.* ✱ Whenever you see one of these words as the subject of a sentence on the test, pay careful attention to whether the verb is singular. For example:

Incorrect: Neither of the streets were painted green.

Correct: Neither of the streets was painted green.

Again, it helps to replace the "of the _____" part of the sentence with the word *one*: "Neither one was painted green" should sound better to you than "Neither one were painted green."

Incorrect: Either this street or that street were painted green.

✱ *Ten bonus points to anyone who can make a mnemonic device for these. My best one so far is ONANASEENEEE.*
    —Samantha

Correct: Either this street or that street was painted green.

Incorrect: One of the streets were painted green.

Correct: One of the streets was painted green.

COMMANDMENT 2: THY PRONOUNS SHALT ALWAYS AGREE WITH THY NOUNS.

Singular subjects take singular pronouns; plural subjects take plural pronouns. Remember that list of singular subjects that you just memorized (*each, every, either, neither, one, no one, everyone, everybody, someone, somebody, anyone, anybody,* and *nobody*)? If you don't, then shame on you. It was literally eleven sentences ago. Anyway, each of these words takes a singular pronoun. Whenever one of the words on the list is the subject, the pronoun that refers to that word has to be singular. This is a hard rule to "hear" because so many people break this rule that we're used to hearing it the wrong way.

Example 1:
Not one of the boys read their SAT study guide.

Isolate: subject: one (singular)
pronoun: their (plural)

This sentence doesn't sound awful to most people, but it's wrong. The subject *one* is singular, but the pronoun *their* is plural. (*Boys* is plural, but it's an object. You can tell it's an object because of the "of the _____" construction.) The correct pronoun would be *his*.

Correct: Not one of the boys read his SAT study guide.

Example 2:
Each of the girls ate their lunch.

Isolate: subject: Each (singular)
pronoun: their (plural)

Each is singular, but *their* is plural. Try replacing the *of the girls* part of the sentence with *one* and you should see why the pronoun *her* sounds better than *their*.

Correct: Each of the girls ate her lunch. (Again, think "each one.")

There are also some pronouns that can go either way. These are *some, any, none, all,* and *most.* They can be either singular or plural, depending on the subject. You can remember them easily by combining them into one ridiculous word that sounds like "suminnynunallmost." *

*This word will not be on the SAT.
—Samantha

COMMANDMENT 3: THOU SHALT USE SUBJECTIVE AND OBJECTIVE PRONOUNS CORRECTLY.

You must know when to use the words in the column on the left and when to use the words in the column on the right:

Subjects	Objects
I	me
he	him
she	her
they	them
we	us
who	whom

The words on the left are subjects. They are used to describe the person who is doing the action in a sentence. The words on the right are objects. They receive the action that the subject does. This sounds like an easy distinction, right? In fact, we mess this up ALL THE TIME.

Example 1:

Julio and me were down by the schoolyard.

Always simplify these sentences. Does "Me was in the schoolyard" sound right? No. "I was in the schoolyard."

Correct: Julio and I were down by the schoolyard.

Example 2:
The SAT writing section was easy for Huey and he because they had read *Up Your Score.*

"The SAT writing section was easy for he" should sound wrong to you. If it doesn't sound wrong, then recognize that the word *he* represents an object in the sentence and therefore should be *him.*

Correct: The SAT writing section was easy for Huey and him because they had read *Up Your Score.*

Example 3:
Let's do an SAT-style question.

The dog and <u>him are eating pizza.</u>

The underlined portion would be be replaced by which of the following options?
A) NO CHANGE
B) him ate pizza.
C) he eats pizza.
D) he are eating pizza.

Does "Him is eating pizza" sound right? No. "He is eating pizza." Choice D is correct: The dog and he are eating pizza. We're jealous! ✻

COMMANDMENT 4: THOU SHALT USE PRONOUNS CONSISTENTLY.

This is a simple rule, once you've learned it. If you start off a sentence using the pronoun *you,* you need to use *you* throughout. If you start off using *one,* you need to use *one* throughout. And so forth.

Example:
The more you study for the SAT, the more one thinks about moving to Mongolia.

✻If there is a double subject (more than one person/place/ thing) completing an action, cross out the one that's not the pronoun and then read the sentence. You'll be able to tell if it's right or wrong.
—Samantha

This sentence starts with the pronoun *you*, and then ends with the pronoun *one*. This is inconsistent. If there are ever two different pronouns in a sentence, they should refer to different subjects/objects. (Example: The more he watches TV, the more she yells at him for being lazy.)

However, in this sentence, *you* and *one* refer to the same person. It does not make sense that there are two pronouns in reference to the same subject. It should be either:

The more you study for the SAT, the more you think about moving to Mongolia.

or:

The more one studies for the SAT, the more one thinks about moving to Mongolia.

COMMANDMENT 5: ENSURE THAT THY TENSE MAKES SENSE.

The time of action needs to make sense across a sentence. Look for key "time words" such as *when, while, as, after,* and *so forth,* and read the sentence aloud to make sure the time line checks out.

Example 1:
After he ate the newt and brushed his teeth, I will kiss him.

The problem here is that the verbs *ate* and *brushed* happened in the past, whereas *will kiss* is going to happen in the future. Change it to either:

After he eats the newt and brushes his teeth, I will kiss him.

or:

After he ate the newt and brushed his teeth, I kissed him.

Example 2:
While I was painting his feet, he had tickled me.

Underline your verbs and make sure they match. (Underlining is my favorite pastime.)
—Samantha

Presumably, he interrupted the feet painting with his tickling, so the sentence should read:

While I was painting his feet, he tickled me.

This makes the sentence consistent. Never mind that it's weird—consistency is all that matters here. So, as the people in these sentences carry on with their mildly deviant activities, just go through and make sure everything is done in the proper time sequence.

COMMANDMENT 6: THOU SHALT NOT REPLACE AN ADVERB WITH AN ADJECTIVE, NOR AN ADJECTIVE WITH AN ADVERB.

Remember the difference between an adjective and an adverb? If not, your sixth-grade teacher will hunt you down and banish you from recess. The College Board likes to mix these two up.

Adjectives describe nouns. An adjective will always make grammatical sense in the phrase the _____ wombat. (Example: the lascivious wombat)

Adverbs describe verbs or adjectives or other adverbs. They usually, but not always, end in "-ly." An adverb will always make grammatical sense in the sentence:

The wombat did it _____ . (Example: The wombat did it lasciviously.)

Example 1:
I ran slow.

The word *slow* is an adjective. You can tell because it makes sense in the phrase "the slow wombat." However, in Example 1, it is being used to describe the verb *ran*. This is impossible. Adjectives describe only nouns. Adverbs describe verbs. Use *slowly*, the adverb, instead.

Correct: I ran slowly.

Example 2:

Poindexter juggles good.

Poindexter has problems. The word *good* is an adjective, but it's being used to describe the word *juggles*, which is a verb. Again, you have to use the adverb.

Correct: Poindexter juggles well. (Notice that *well* is an adverb even though it does not end in "-ly.")

Example 3:

Let's do an SAT example.

I hate lumpy fish on <u>soporific afternoons</u>.

The underlined portion above is best replaced with?

A) NO CHANGE
B) soporifically afternoons.
C) soporific after noons.
D) DELETE underlined portion

The answer is A. The sentence is grammatically correct, not to mention worthy of analysis from a psychological perspective. If you immediately jumped on this sentence and tried to correct it, it means you're too tense. Relax. Go eat some frozen yogurt.

This is also as good a time as any to tell you that it is totally possible for an underlined portion to be correct. This is devious, because the mere fact that it is underlined will make you want to change it. Don't worry: If it sounds correct to you, it probably is!

Another tricky aspect of adjectives and adverbs is that they can be turned into *comparative* and *superlative* versions of themselves. Take the adjective *juicy*. If you're talking about only one object, you would use *juicy*: "This salamander is juicy." If you're comparing two objects, you would use *juicier*: "This salamander is juicier than that newt." If you're comparing more than two objects, you would use the superlative *juiciest*: "Of the three lizards, the gecko is juiciest."

Example 4:

Dan is the older of the four athletes.

Since there are more than two objects being compared, we can't use *older*.

Correct: Dan is the oldest of the four athletes.

COMMANDMENT 7: THY CONSTRUCTIONS SHALT ALWAYS BE PARALLEL.

Ideas that are parallel (related) should be expressed in the same way.

Example 1:

Michael likes spitting, drooling, and to slurp.

Spit, *drool*, and *slurp* are parallel activities. They should be expressed in the same way:

Correct: Michael likes spitting, drooling, and slurping.

Correct: Michael likes to spit, to drool, and to slurp.

Correct: Michael likes to spit, drool, and slurp.

Michael, you're disgusting! Stay away from us!

Example 2:

Paul likes spitting and drooling but not to slurp.

Even though Paul doesn't like slurping, it should still be parallel with spitting and drooling, which he does like. (Why, we do not know.)

Correct: Paul likes spitting and drooling but not slurping.

Example 3:

Let's do this SAT-style.

> The juicer chops vegetables, squeezes oranges, <u>and proctors can be liquefied with it.</u>

> The underlined portion above should be
> replaced with:
> A) NO CHANGE
> B) and liquefies proctors.
> C) and proctor liquefaction.
> D) and proctors can liquefy themselves with it.

Chopping vegetables, squeezing oranges, and liquefying proctors are all parallel actions. They should be expressed in the same way. The correct answer is B: The juicer chops vegetables, squeezes oranges, and liquefies proctors.

COMMANDMENT 8: THOU SHALT NOT ALLOW THY SENTENCES TO RUN ON, NOR SHALT THOU FRAGMENT THEM.

A **run-on sentence** is usually two complete sentences that are incorrectly joined by a comma instead of separated by a period or a semicolon.

Example 1:

Samantha ate the mysterious object, it was a noodle.

The two independent clauses in this run-on sentence could be broken into two sentences:

1. Samantha ate the mysterious object.
2. It was a noodle.

They could also be combined into one sentence using a semicolon: Samantha ate the mysterious object; it was a noodle.

Sentence fragments are parts of sentences, usually verb-less, that are made up to look like real sentences. They are usually placed next to real sentences into which they should be incorporated.

Example 2:
All the kids had rashes on their bodies. Especially those with uranium lunch boxes.

In this example, the first sentence is complete, but the second is a fragment. The two could be combined like this:

All the kids had rashes on their bodies, especially those with uranium lunch boxes.

These errors involve punctuation, and as such we will discuss them in a bit more detail in the punctuation section that starts on page 178.

COMMANDMENT 9: THOU SHALT NEVER LET THY MODIFIERS DANGLE.

Dangling modifier is a fancy grammatical term for a simple concept. Here are some sentences with dangling modifiers.

Example 1:
Taking the test, his copy of *Up Your Score* was in his pocket.

This sentence does not mean what the person who wrote it wanted it to mean. This sentence implies that the copy of *Up Your Score* was taking the test. (This book can do many things, but it cannot take the test all by itself.) Whenever a sentence begins with a phrase like "Taking the test," which is supposed to modify (that is, describe) a word in the sentence, the word that it modifies must be in the sentence, and it must come right after the modifying phrase.

Correct: Taking the test, he had his copy of *Up Your Score* in his pocket.

The sentence can also be corrected another way.

Whenever there's a modifier, it has to modify the first noun that comes after it. (On the real, though, I wish my copy of <u>Up Your Score</u> could have taken the test for me.)
—Samantha

Correct: While he was taking the test, his copy of *Up Your Score* was in his pocket.

Whenever you see a sentence with an "-ing" word in a phrase at the beginning, be on the lookout for a dangling modifier.

Example 2:

Let's do this one SAT-style:

> Conscientious about proper grammar, <u>dangling modifiers were always on Bertha's mind</u>.

> Which of the following would best replace the underlined portion above:
> A) NO CHANGE
> B) dangling modifiers was always on Bertha's mind.
> C) Bertha's dangling modifiers were always on her mind.
> D) Bertha always had dangling modifiers on her mind.

Were the dangling modifiers conscientious about proper grammar? No, Bertha was. So she should come right after the comma.

The correct answer is D: Conscientious about proper grammar, Bertha always had dangling modifiers on her mind.

(This example is an exception to the rule about dangling modifiers having an "-ing" word at the beginning.)

Example 3:

Parachuting over the Emerald City, the ant gasped in awe.

Was the ant parachuting? Hell, yes—so the sentence is correct.

A tip for connector words: Look through the options in the answer choices and label them as either positive (+) or negative (−), positive meaning they support the original idea and negative meaning they oppose the original idea. Then read the next clause of the sentence to see what its relationship to the original clause is.
—Samantha

COMMANDMENT 10: THOU SHALT USE THE LOGICAL CONNECTOR WORD.

"Connector words" are *and, but, however, also,* etc. These words link up clauses to show their direction and logic. If you misuse a connector word, the logic of the sentence will seem a little off.

Example 1:

Some sentences may initially seem grammatically <u>correct, and do not say what</u> the writer wants them to say.

Which of the following best replaces the underlined portion above?
A) NO CHANGE
B) correct, and do not say that which
C) correct, but do not say what
D) correct, with the exception that

The correct answer is C. One would expect that if the sentences seemed grammatically correct, they would say what the author wanted them to say. But they don't. The connector word *but* indicates that the part of the sentence after the comma contradicts what you would expect after reading the first part of the sentence.

Example 2:

Students compare the SAT to a bed of nails, <u>as does a charging rhinoceros.</u>

Which of the following best replaces the underlined portion above?
A) NO CHANGE
B) just as a charging rhinoceros.
C) as is a charging rhinoceros.
D) or to a charging rhinoceros.

The correct answer is D. The original sentence literally says that the rhinoceros, along with students, compares the SAT to a bed of nails. Unless the author believes that rhinoceroses think about the SAT in this way, * the right answer is definitely D: Students compare the SAT to a bed of nails *or to* a charging rhinoceros.

> ** I believe that they would if they could.*
> *—Samantha*

COMMANDMENT 11: THOU SHALT USE THE CORRECT WORDS, NOT WORDS THAT SORT OF SOUND SIMILAR TO THE CORRECT WORDS.

Sometimes the College Board will deliberately mess up an expression to try to fool you. The only way to prepare for this type of question is by becoming familiar with standard, formal English and being able to hear or see which words or phrases just sound or look wrong. Okay, so this is not really a grammatical rule, but it most definitely is something to watch out for.

Example 1:

Since it's a beautiful day, I'd just assume walk.

The expression is "just as soon," but it sounds a lot like "just assume." You have to really look at the sentence, not just hear it in your head, to answer these questions.

Correct: Since it's a beautiful day, I'd just as soon walk.

Example 2:

If it had been raining, I would of stayed inside.

The expression is "would have" but it is often confused with "would of." *

Correct: If it had been raining, I would have stayed inside.

COMMANDMENT 12: THOU SHALT COMPARE LIKE THINGS.

This is another rule that we mess up in speech all the time and

> **THIS IS IMPORTANT!! I am SO tired of seeing "I would of studied/gone to the movies/eaten that rhubarb pie" as I scroll through my Twitter feed.*
> *—Samantha*

that the Serpent loves to test. When we compare two things, they need to be the same *type* of thing.

Example 1:

My mother's salary is higher than Jane's mother.

Your mother's salary is higher than Jane's mother's salary, not higher than Jane's mother. How could a salary be higher than a person?

Correct: My mother's salary is higher than Jane's mother's.

Example 2:

Harry raised more cows than Jim's ranch.

This above sentence is comparing Harry with Jim's ranch. The writer of the sentence should instead compare Harry with Jim. That would be more logical.

Correct: Harry raised more cows than Jim did.

BONUS COMMANDMENT: THOU SHALT ALSO WATCH OUT FOR THESE ASSORTED ERRORS.

- *Either* goes with *or*; *neither* goes with *nor*.
- When referring to a country, don't use *they*; use *it*.

Example:

The United States is the richest country in the world. They have the highest GNP.

Correct: It has the highest GNP.

- Use the word *fewer* if you can count what you're describing; if not, use the word *less*. *

Example:

Now that there are fewer elephants milling around, there is less dust being kicked into the air.

* I got fewer points on my SAT because I knew less of the information in this helpful book.

—Samantha

A Punctuation Refresher

Perhaps the SAT will one day test students' use of emoji.

—Samantha

The SAT Writing and Language Test is going to throw a number of punctuation errors at you, so let's review the punctuation rules we learned in middle school.

Before we begin, we need to get straight on one concept: independent and dependent clauses. An independent clause is like an adult and can walk around on its own, making sense wherever it goes. A dependent clause, like a child or a Chihuahua, cannot go anywhere without an independent clause.

Independent clause: Your tie is the color of vomit.

Dependent clause: Because I vomited on it.

That first clause makes total sense on its own. The second needs to be conjoined to an independent clause in order to make sense. Are we cool with that? Good, because that is all we need to know before talking about punctuation.

PERIODS: STRAIGHTFORWARD AND SIMPLE

What does a period do? It ends the sentence. Don't put it in the middle of a sentence. Put it at the end.

Example 1:

Incorrect: I've got mustard. All over my pants again.

Correct: I've got mustard all over my pants again.

That wrong period creates the sentence fragments that you saw in Grammar Commandment 8.

You don't need another example, do you? Really? Fine, here you go.

Example 2:

Incorrect: Over the course of this chapter. I've developed a terrible dependency on examples.

Correct: Over the course of this chapter, I've developed a terrible dependency on examples.

That last example also involved commas. Don't worry, we're going to get to commas. But first . . .

SEMICOLONS: SLIGHTLY LESS SIMPLE, BUT STILL PRETTY SIMPLE

Here's how a grammarian would define the semicolon: A semicolon connects two independent clauses.

Example:

Incorrect: We're sick and tired of blueberry pie, we've been eating it for weeks.

Correct: We're sick and tired of blueberry pie; we've been eating it for weeks.

But wait! Isn't that just like a period?!?! Excellent question. A grammarian would say that a semicolon differs from a period in that it connects closely linked ideas. But that is a totally subjective judgment. So remember this: The Testing Serpent does not test the difference between the semicolon and the period. For the sake of this test, they are exactly the same.

COLONS: A BIT THORNIER THAN SEMICOLONS, BUT NOT GROUNDS FOR FREAKING OUT

Just like the colon in our bodies, the grammatical colon has a few jobs. It always follows an independent clause, and it can introduce a list, an explanation, or an explanatory quotation.

Example 1: Introducing a list.
There are a few things I will not eat: pigeons, haggis, fish eyes, and salad.

Example 2: Introducing an explanation.
And here's the reason why: These are all gross foods.

Example 3: Introducing an explanatory quote.

I live by the following mantra: "Do not digest that which disgusts!"

There are two ways the Serpent will try to trick you with colons. Most often, it will use a comma instead of a colon. Like so:

Incorrect: I brought everything to the beach, my sunblock, my sun hat, my novel, my couch and bed, my dinette set, and my refrigerator.

Correct: I brought everything to the beach: my sunblock, my sun hat, my novel, my couch and bed, my dinette set, and my refrigerator.

This is rarer, but sometimes the Serpent will use a dependent clause before the colon. This is a no-no.

Incorrect: Of course: I was the envy of Brighton Beach.

Correct: Of course, I was the envy of Brighton Beach.

THE APOSTROPHES: NOW THINGS ARE GETTING TOUGH

The apostrophe plays a couple of roles—it swaps in for the missing letters in a contraction and indicates possession. Let's start with possession.

Example 1:
Incorrect: That is Jeremys bread.

Correct: That is Jeremy's bread.

Now let's add in a contraction:

Example 2:
Correct: But I did not know it was Jeremy's bread.

Also correct: But I didn't know it was Jeremy's bread.

Example 3:

Correct: That is no excuse! Jeremy's name is written in Sharpie right on the loaf!

Also correct: That's no excuse! Jeremy's name is written in Sharpie right on the loaf!

CONTRACTIONS: OMG!

The Evil Testing Serpent will—and we mean *will*—test you on the two difficult contractions.

Its vs. *It's*

Remember: *It's* is a contraction of *it is*. The possessive *Its* has no apostrophe. ✳

Incorrect: Its no sin to eat another person's bread, right?

Correct: It's no sin to eat another person's bread, right?

Their vs. *They're*

They're is a contraction of *they are*. *Their* is possessive.

Incorrect: If people take each other's bread, their going straight to hell.

Correct: If people take each other's bread, they're going straight to hell.

COMMAS: DEAR LORD, NO, RUN FOR THE HILLS!

Commas are a pain in the neck. You know this, we know this, and most importantly, the Serpent knows this. We've already seen commas crop up in our examples. They are by far the most commonly tested punctuation mark.

Commas do a lot of things. They separate asides, they separate elements in a list, they link independent clauses with conjunctions such as *and, but, so,* and they link independent and dependent clauses.

✳ *I didn't know this until I was sixteen. I know adults who still do not know this.*
—Samantha

The face being breathtaking and divine has nothing to do with it being itchy, so the clause is nonessential.
— Samantha

Here is a comma separating an aside:

Incorrect: My face which has been called "breathtaking" and "divine" by a number of reputable sources is very itchy.

Correct: My face, which has been called "breathtaking" and "divine" by a number of reputable sources, is very itchy.

What we are calling "asides" are technically called nonrestrictive clauses, which just means "information that is not essential to the sentence." One tricky rule to remember with commas is that a restrictive clause, or information that is necessary to the meaning of the sentence, is *not* separated by commas. Check it out.

Incorrect: People, who are easily nauseated, should not try Paul's cooking.

Correct: People who are easily nauseated should not try Paul's cooking.

That phrase "who are easily nauseated" seems like it might be an aside. But if we take it out, the sentence drastically changes its meaning ("People should not try my cooking"). So we do not use commas! Nor do we eat Paul's cooking!

Next, here is a comma separating the elements in a list:

Incorrect: I enjoy French films, French cheese and crackers.

Correct: I enjoy French films, French cheese, and crackers.

Read this sentence aloud. Do you pause after "cheese"? Yes. Use a comma.
— Samantha

The comma before the last element in that list is called the serial comma. (It's also known as the Oxford comma.) Some people use it, and some people don't. The SAT does! And it uses it for a good reason. In the above sentence, the first, wrong sentence could mean French cheese and French crackers, because there is no comma. The second sentence makes it clear that crackers are their own element of the list.

Next, here is a comma linking two independent clauses with a conjunction.

The comma is by far the most commonly tested punctuation mark on the SAT. Know your commas!

Incorrect: I went to the moon but it was already jam-packed with astronauts.

Correct: I went to the moon, but it was already jam-packed with astronauts.

Here is a comma linking a dependent clause with an independent clause.

Incorrect: Hoping to make foie gras I fed my goose way more food than is recommended.

Also incorrect: Hoping to make foie gras. I fed my goose way more food than is recommended.

Correct: Hoping to make foie gras, I fed my goose way more food than is recommended. ✳

Do you recognize those first two errors? That's right, those are the run-ons and sentence fragments from Commandment 8. Why did we repeat ourselves? Because the Serpent will test this, so it bears repeating.

✳ *Foie gras is my mother's favorite food. This one's for you, Mom.*
—Samantha

BONUS PUNCTUATION MARKS: DASHES AND PARENTHESES

Congratulations! You've been so diligent about reading these punctuation rules that you've earned two more. Dashes and parentheses are basically the same: They both separate an aside that is even more of an aside than the asides that commas separate. We're talking extremely aside. Like this:

Correct: Queen Elizabeth—whose name rhymes with Shmeen Murpipzalik, sort of—is the longest-reigning monarch of the U.K. ever.

Also correct: Queen Elizabeth (whose name rhymes with Shmeen Murpipzalik, sort of) is the longest-reigning monarch of the U.K. ever.

But here's a question: Is it wrong to use commas instead of dashes or parentheses? No. This is just a style choice. So the SAT will not test the difference among use of commas, dashes, and parentheses. More likely, it will give you an error like this:

Incorrect: (Queen Victoria used to be the longest-reigning monarch of the U.K.), but now she's the second-longest-reigning monarch of the U.K.

Correct: Queen Victoria used to be the longest-reigning monarch of the U.K., but now she's the second-longest-reigning monarch. of the U.K.

In other words, parentheses or a dash can always be replaced by a comma without breaking any International Grammar Laws, but the opposite is not true. We cannot replace any old comma with dashes or parentheses.

And that's it! Now on to some weightier ideas!

EXPRESSION OF IDEAS

After the Evil Testing Serpent crafted all the "Standard English Conventions" questions, it still felt like there was something missing. So from the dark, grimy recesses of its serpenty mind it conjured up another question category, christening it with the vaguest of names: "Expression of Ideas." What does it mean? Well, these questions will focus on everything beyond grammar. . . . Namely, the development of an argument, the organization of a passage, and the use of effective language. Again, imagine you are peer-editing a friend's paper, and you've already caught all of the basic grammar mistakes (good job!). Now, you have to actually *improve the quality of the writing.* ✱

If this sounds subjective, that's because it is. Although there are hard and fast grammar rules, "Expression of Ideas" is murkier territory—two different people could have two different yet equally viable approaches to editing the same essay. However, don't fret—we happen to know just what the Serpent is looking for, and we're going to show you how to jump through all of its hoops one concept at a time, with sample questions along the way.

✱ *Gasp!*
—*Samantha*

How to Build an Argument

Remember how we said in the Reading Test chapter that the Serpent is totally evidence-crazy now? Well, its madness persists in the Writing Test. Many questions are going to ask you to identify the best piece of evidence to support an author's argument. Check this:

> The U.S. economy faces a dangerous new threat. Netflix binge-watching has a debilitating effect on the productivity of the American workforce. A study of one Fortune 500 company found that 40 percent of employees who had watched the entire second season of *Stranger Things* after its midnight release chose to not go to work after they finished the final episode at about 1:00 p.m. Those who showed up late to the office compiled 80 percent fewer spreadsheet entries than their daily average. The nationwide effect of binge-watching on productivity is not yet known, but it's not looking good.

Which of the following pieces of evidence could be cited in the passage to support the author's argument?

A) Netflix, Inc., has been targeted by the anti-streaming activist group Get Off Your Couch in a number of pending lawsuits.

B) Americans in suburban communities spend 28 percent more time watching Netflix than those in large cities. *

C) A 2017 poll of Netflix subscribers found that *Stranger Things* was binge-watched at a 21 percent greater rate than *Orange Is the New Black*, another Netflix Original Series.

D) 120 million Americans binge-watched at least half of a TV season in 2017, a 74 percent increase from the previous year.

*Untrue. I've lived in both a suburb and a city. Watching Netflix for unhealthy amounts of time is universal.
—Samantha

The answer is D. This choice gives the reader more information about the general increase in binge-watching, which is more relevant to the argument being made in the paragraph—increased binge-watching leads to less work—than the fact that Netflix is being sued (choice A), or that more binge-watching occurs in some places rather than others (choice B) or that some shows are more binge-watched than others (choice C).

Similarly, some questions will ask you whether an argument can be improved by adding or removing a particular sentence.

Archaeologists have been conducting excavations of Egypt's Great Pyramids and their surroundings for centuries, but they continue to make new discoveries each year. In 2016, an archaeological dig near the three enormous pyramids uncovered what is believed to be the predecessor of the selfie stick. <u>The pyramids are made of limestone blocks.</u> The team uncovered several three-foot rods of sycamore wood, each attached to a small mirror of polished bronze.* With the invention of photography still thousands of years away, the Romans must have simply viewed themselves and their companions in the bronze mirror, and tried to capture a mental picture of their visit to this ancient wonder of the world.

1 The writer is considering deleting the underlined sentence. Should the sentence be kept or deleted? *

A) Kept, because it strongly relates to the passage's primary topic.

B) Kept, because it sets up the following sentence.

C) Deleted, because it doesn't relate to the passage's primary topic.

D) Deleted, because it repeats information already provided in this paragraph.

*These can get tough. Before you read the answer choices, pick a side—and then choose the right reason for your decision.
—Samantha

The correct answer is C. The fact that the pyramids are made of limestone blocks has nothing to do with the topic of the passage, the ancient selfie stick. If a sentence blurs the focus of a passage, it should be cut.

2 The author considered adding the following sentence at the *: "The sticks are believed to have been used by Roman tourists in the first century CE." Should the author make this addition here?

A) Yes, because it provides a relevant piece of information that deepens readers' understanding of ancient selfie sticks.

B) Yes, because it provides an interesting counterpoint to the passage's primary argument.

C) No, because it provides distracting information unrelated to the passage.

D) No, because it conflicts with the following sentence.

The correct answer is A. The proposed sentence offers relevant information about the selfie stick and deepens readers' understanding of the topic, and thus would make a valuable addition.

Basically, sentences should be added or kept if they feel *relevant* to the topic of the passage and provide new information or perspective. A sentence should be deleted if it digresses randomly from the topic of the passage or if it just repeats information the passage already provides. *

Some questions will ask you to rearrange the structure of the passage in order to give it a more logical, natural flow. Often, a sentence will be out of place, and you'll be asked to choose its correct position in the paragraph. For example:

*Randomness and redundancy: the Serpent's most prized pitfalls.
—Samantha

What Goes Where?

[1] <u>Scientists believe that these craters are the result of asteroid collisions.</u> [2] Some people think that our moon looks like Swiss cheese because it has so many craters. [3] Asteroids are more likely to hit the moon than Earth because the moon has a much thinner atmosphere. [4] Asteroids usually completely burn due to atmospheric friction before they reach the surface of the Earth, but the moon has less protection and therefore more craters. [5] This is why it looks like Swiss cheese.

What is the best placement for sentence 1?
A) After sentence 2
B) After sentence 3
C) After sentence 4
D) Where it is now

It doesn't make sense to talk about explanations for the craters until the existence of the craters is introduced. But after sentence 2, the focus of the paragraph shifts from craters to the asteroids that cause them. Sentence 1 should be placed after the one that first mentions craters (sentence 2) but before the sentence introducing asteroids. So the correct answer is A. A big clue in sentence 1, you might have noticed, was the word *these*. The word must be referring to something just stated in a previous sentence. Keep an eagle eye out for clue words like that.

Though this was not the case in the above example, oftentimes the misplaced sentence will be a summary or introductory sentence stuck in the middle of the paragraph. Watch out for this as a red flag.

Anchovies: Supermarket Items or Superheroes?
[1] They claim that anchovies can increase heart health and reduce the risk of cancer. [2] <u>Nutritionists call</u>

anchovies a "miracle food." [3] They are a good source of omega 3 fatty acids, which have numerous proven health benefits. [4] One should try to incorporate anchovies into every meal, even breakfast. [5] Are their slimy texture and fishy taste hard for you to stomach? [6] That's why we at "Pan Academy" (pronounced "pahn," like the Spanish word for "bread") have created a delicious recipe for whole wheat anchovy pancakes. [7] Enjoy with maple syrup—but not too much of it because sugar is bad for your health. *

What is the best placement for sentence 2?
A) NO CHANGE
B) After sentence 3
C) After sentence 5
D) Before sentence 1

As it is, the beginning of the paragraph is obviously choppy and needs reorganization. Sentence 2 provides general introductory information that the other sentences elaborate on. As a rule of thumb, sentences that summarize or generalize other sentences in the paragraph should either be positioned first or last (more often first). In this case, it doesn't make sense to place sentence 2 at the end of the paragraph because the topic by then has been shifted from the health benefits of the fish to the pancake recipe. * Therefore, the most logical placement of sentence 2 is at the beginning of the paragraph, before sentence 1. (The correct answer is D.)

Other questions test your ability to identify good introductions, conclusions, and transitions.

Google is trying to gain a foothold in a variety of industries. With its latest venture, "G-Clown," Google hopes to revolutionize children's birthday party entertainment. With the G-Clown app, parents can

*You don't need this kind of negativity in your life.
—Samantha*

*Reasonably so. Pancake recipes are always more important.
—Samantha*

summon a troupe of acrobatic clowns that will appear at the party via drone within the hour. The convenience of this app is unrivaled. <u>Next</u>, Google's PartiMatch technology assures that, before they arrive, the clowns will be instructed to dress and behave in a way that will not frighten the party guests.

Which of the following words would best replace "Next"?
A) NO CHANGE
B) Afterward
C) Subsequently
D) Furthermore

These questions are very similar to our "connector word" problems earlier. The difference here is that we need to understand the context of the argument in order to pick the right answer. Here, the right answer is D. A, B, and C are all words that imply that PartiMatch, the creepiness reduction software, is used after the clowns arrive at the party, when the rest of the sentence states that it is used before this point. "Furthermore" fits with the author's intent to simply explain an additional feature of G-Clown, not to describe a chronological sequence.

Syntax Attack

Do you remember how to diagram a sentence? No? That's okay, neither do we. You won't have to diagram any sentences on the SAT, but you will need to think about sentences on a structural level in order to answer syntax questions. *Syntax* refers to the arrangement of the elements of a sentence. . . . In other words, the relationship among the subject, object, and predicate (verb).

Consider the following two sentences:
1. Spot was a bad dog; Spot bit me.
2. Spot was a bad dog; I was bitten by Spot.

Sentence 1 is the superior option for two reasons. First, if you start out talking about the dog, you should stick to talking about the dog. "Spot bit me" most logically supplements "Spot was a bad dog." Furthermore, in sentence 2, the second clause ("I was bitten by Spot") uses the passive voice and emphasizes the recipient of the action ("I"). Both sentences are grammatically correct, but sentence 1 is better because its syntax is more logical and consistent from clause to clause.

A note about passive/active voice: Go ahead and cross off any answer-choice written in passive voice, especially if another clause in the sentence is in active voice. Sentences with passive verbs and active verbs jumbled together can get really confusing and won't sound good to your inner ear. The passive voice should be used only when you specifically want to emphasize the recipient of an action, often to imply that it has little control over its fate (e.g., "The man was struck by lightning").

Here's a practice question with wacky syntax:

The University of Kentucky men's basketball team was dominant in the 2014–2015 season. <u>That season, every team that Kentucky played was defeated, except for the Wisconsin Badgers, who won in the Final Four.</u>

The author is considering changing the second sentence. Which of the following would best replace this sentence?

A) NO CHANGE

B) Kentucky beat every team it played that season, except for Wisconsin, to whom it lost in the Final Four.

C) The only time that they were defeated that season, Wisconsin beat Kentucky.

D) In the Final Four, Wisconsin beat Kentucky, who was not defeated by any other team it played that season.

The correct choice is B. As we mentioned, in general, the active voice ("Kentucky **beat** every team") is preferable to the passive voice ("every team that Kentucky played **was defeated**"). Choice B is the only option that consistently uses the active voice. It is also the sentence with the most specificity; it says exactly when and to whom Kentucky lost.

Lastly, you want to be sure that your pronouns are not vague. If a pronoun could plausibly refer to two nouns, then it is vague. Try this out:

> The Space Marine and the alien both fired their guns at the same time, <u>but only he survived.</u>
>
> Which of the following would best replace the underlined portion?
> A) NO CHANGE
> B) and only he survived.
> C) but only the Space Marine survived.
> D) but survival was enjoyed only by the Space Marine.

The error is that the pronoun *he* could refer plausibly to either the Space Marine or the alien.* We need to choose, then, between answer choices C and D. D sounds terrible, so our answer is C.

*I've got my bets on the Space Marine.
—Samantha*

Precision and Concision

Not quite satisfied with your mastery of syntax, the Serpent has also decided to test your understanding of *precision* and *concision*. Precision questions ask you to choose the best, most *precise* word to use in a given context. (You didn't think the Serpent had stopped obsessing over vocabulary in context, did you?) These questions require a careful assessment of the sentence to determine what word makes the most sense in this particular case.

Here is a modified **precision question** from the College Board:

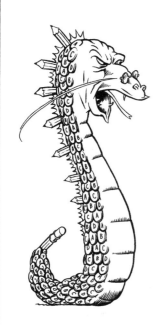

Taylor Swift's first albums included many radio-friendly country hits. But her fourth album, *Red*, featured songs with more electronic sounds and mainstream pop influences. Her next one, *1989*, marked a complete <u>vacancy</u> from country music; even her Southern accent disappeared.

Which of the following words would best replace "vacancy"?
A) NO CHANGE
B) evacuation
C) blank space
D) departure

D is the best choice. While two words like *departure* and *evacuation* might seem similar out of context, in the context of this particular sentence *departure* more precisely articulates the idea that T-Swift ditched country music to become a global pop superstar. (The College Board sample that we based this question on describes a landscape painter whom you have probably never heard of, nor care about. Unfortunately, SAT passages are more likely to be about landscape painters than pop stars.)

Concision questions ask you to choose the most efficient, least redundant way of expressing an idea. Oftentimes an author of an SAT passage will repeat herself unnecessarily at some point. Case in point:

Vin Diesel's new contract gives him the lead role in <u>ten *Fast and Furious* films to be released in the upcoming future</u>.
A) NO CHANGE
B) ten *Fast and Furious* films in the upcoming future.
C) ten *Fast and Furious* films yet to be released in the future.
D) ten forthcoming *Fast and Furious* films.

"Fast and Furious": a tale of a student who realizes she has eleven reading comprehension questions left and only four minutes and twenty-nine seconds to answer them.

—Samantha

Besides D, all of the options express the idea that the movies are "yet to be released" multiple times. So D is the most succinct (and correct!) answer.

Style and Tone

*Read the passage. Do not lick the passage.
—Samantha

You will also encounter questions asking which, if any, revision will make a sentence fit better with the style and tone of the essay. These questions require that you read the passage thoroughly to get a sense of its flavor. Is it formal or informal? Funny or serious? Drenched in academic words, or easy to read? Trust your gut instinct here.

Whistling is quite singular among the methods of musical expression. Many people are awed by beautiful violin and saxophone solos because mastery of these instruments requires innate talent, technical skill, and countless hours of practice—not to mention the confidence necessary for performing onstage. But whistling seems kind of simple to most people and anyone can do it without a whole lot of training. Consequently, it remains an underappreciated art.

Which version of the underlined sentence is the best fit for this paragraph?
A) NO CHANGE
B) But whistling is easy, so easy that even my sister Sue can do it, and she can't do anything right.
C) By contrast, whistling is considered unrefined and easy to master.
D) Whistling, on the other hand, is for punks and losers and deadbeats who have nothing better to do.

The correct answer is C. The informal style of the underlined sentence—as well as choices B and D—clashes with the more formal style that the author employs throughout the rest of the paragraph. Choice C is an appropriately formal version of the original sentence. C also expresses the idea most succinctly and with an economy of words. Thus, C is the best choice.

INFORMATIONAL GRAPHICS

Finally, the Testing Serpent likes to stick a couple of informational graphics into the Writing and Language Test passages because having them on the Reading Test just isn't enough. The graphics on the Writing and Language Test are similar to those on the Reading Test in that they are really just dressed-up data analysis questions. In the Writing and Language Test, rather than ask about the graphic itself, they will often ask you to fix the passage's incorrect interpretation of the graphic. Here's an example in which the author misunderstood the data shown in the graph.

Snowplow drivers perform an essential function in the United States: clearing the roads of snow and ice so Americans can still be safe and productive through the winter months. However, employment prospects for snowplow drivers vary widely by region. <u>While 25 percent of Buffalo's workforce was employed as snowplow drivers in 2017, only 5 percent of Atlanta's employed citizens drove snowplows for a living that year.</u>

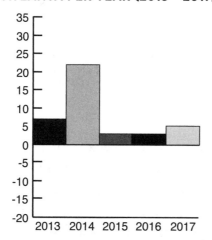

PERCENTAGE INCREASE IN SNOWPLOW EMPLOYMENT IN ATLANTA PER YEAR (2013 – 2017)

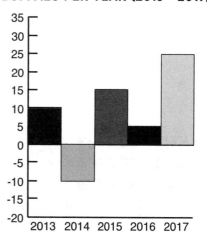

PERCENTAGE INCREASE IN SNOWPLOW EMPLOYMENT IN BUFFALO PER YEAR (2013 – 2017)

Which choice replaces the underlined sentence with accurate information from the graph?

A) NO CHANGE

B) Although the number of snowplowing jobs increased by 25 percent in Buffalo in 2017, Atlanta only saw a 5 percent increase in these jobs.

C) Although 25 percent of snowplow job applicants were offered positions in Buffalo in 2017, only 5 percent of applicants for these jobs were accepted in Atlanta.

D) Buffalo and Atlanta saw equal increases in snowplow jobs in 2017.

Even though Buffalo could probably use that many snowplow drivers, common sense tells you that there's no way that a quarter of Buffalo's jobs are in plowing, or that 5 percent of Atlantans push snow around in the wintertime. The title of the graph tells you that it shows the percent *increase* in snow-plowing jobs from 2013 to 2017. Choices A, C, and D miss the idea that the graph measures the increase in percent rather than in total numbers. Choice B is the only answer that recognizes this and includes accurate information.

LET'S PUT THIS ALL TOGETHER AND PRACTICE!

Now, the moment you've all been waiting for: It's time to put everything you've learned to the test with a sample passage. But first, a suggestion about the **procedure you should follow** when doing Writing and Language sentence correction questions (which make up most of the test):

1. Read the whole sentence, not just the underlined part. Often the underlined part is grammatically correct by itself but is wrong in the context of the whole sentence.

2. Even if you think that the original sentence is correct, plug in each fragment and read out each version of the sentence in your head to make sure there isn't a better option.

3. If you still think that the original sentence is correct, then pick NO CHANGE.

4. If you decide that the sentence is wrong, look for the choice that will make it right. If you run through the different options per step 2, you should find one that just sounds right.

5. If you are completely stumped and can't figure out the answer, choose the shortest one. English is a relatively efficient language. Good writing often involves short, to-the-point sentences that don't go on for ever and ever talking about all sorts of things, and getting redundant, and being just generally too long, when they could be short but aren't because they're long, in fact much longer than they have to be (like this sentence). So choosing the shortest answer works on an extraordinary percentage of questions. Take a look at this question:

Mr. Howe's class has organized a special program for our school: the purpose being to help us increase our understanding of Japanese culture.

A) NO CHANGE

B) school and the purpose is to

C) school, the purpose is to

D) school to

The answer is the shortest: D.

Makes sense? Now let's try out these tips on the following sample passage.

What are those weird looking numbers in the passage? The ones in the black boxes correlate to the questions that follow. The ones in the brackets indicate the sentences involved in the "best order" questions.
—Samantha

Perfect Planning?

When we think of dinner parties, we think of friendship, home-cooked food, and relaxation. What we don't think **1** about, massive planning, expense, timing, stress. Unfortunately, you cannot have the former without the latter. **2**

Though there have always been private-party planners, the field did not come into **3** it's own until the 21st century. Planners Incorporated was founded in New York City in 2004, Dinner's Ready in Chicago in 2009, **4** and the creation in Dallas of Cook 4 You in 2012. Now, in 2017, the industry altogether employs more than 30,000 **5** professionals, sending chefs, servers, and cleaners into American homes every night of the year.

6 **JOBS ADDED TO LABOR MARKET IN 2017 (OUT OF A TOTAL OF 150,000)**

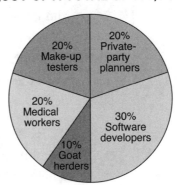

[1] But some argue that there are downsides to the popular practice of hiring out one's evening soirees. **7** At some point, you might as well just go to a restaurant. [2] The central appeal of a dinner party, they say, is that you are partaking of the host's creativity and effort. [3] What's more, the introduction of chefs, waiters, and cleaning staff cuts down on the intimacy.

Ultimately, however, there is no fighting the future. As long as people are willing to pay for extra help, extra help will make itself available. When the Romans needed help fighting the Gauls, **8** however, many militias volunteered their services. Those who want to maintain the age-old practice of planning, shopping, setting tables, cooking, serving, and cleaning **9** they're more than welcome to do so.

1 Which of the following would best replace the underlined portion?

A) NO CHANGE

B) about: massive planning

C) about; massive planning

D) about. Massive planning

2 Which of the following sentences, if added, would provide the best transition to the second paragraph?

A) You need to buy a paper calendar or a calendar app in order to schedule all the tasks necessary to plan a successful party.

B) The history of party planning is more interesting than you would think.

C) Perhaps this is the reason why private-party planning has become a rich, new field of employment.

D) It is enough to turn someone off hosting forever.

3 Which of the following would best replace the underlined portion?

A) NO CHANGE

B) its own

C) their own

D) they're own

For the questions on replacing the underlined portion, "No Change" will always be Choice A. Finally, some consistency.

—Samantha

4 Which of the following would best replace the underlined portion?

A) NO CHANGE

B) and the Dallas creation of Cook 4 You in 2012.

C) and the 2012 creation of Dallas's Cook 4 You.

D) and Cook 4 You in Dallas in 2012.

5 Which of the following would best replace the underlined portion?

A) NO CHANGE

B) professionals, sends

C) professionals, sent

D) professionals, even now sending

6 Does the graph illustrate the claim that 30,000 professionals work in the private-party planning industry in 2017?

A) Yes, because 20 percent of 150,000 workers is 30,000 workers in the field.

B) Yes, because the 20 percent of new jobs in the medical field means that these workers cannot also work in the private-party planning industry.

C) No, because 20 percent of 150,000 workers is less than the number of workers in the private-party planning industry.

D) No, because the 30,000 private-party planners represented in the graph represent only new workers, rather than the total of all workers in the field.

7 The underlined sentence would best be placed

A) where it is now.

B) after sentence 1.

C) after sentence 3.

D) it should be deleted.

8 Which of the following would best replace the underlined portion?

A) NO CHANGE

B) for example

C) nevertheless

D) regardless

9 Which of the following would best replace the underlined portion?

A) NO CHANGE

B) their

C) is

D) are

Answers: 1) B. 2) C. 3) B. 4) D. 5) A. 6) D. 7) C. 8) B. 9) D.

PITHY PARTING WISDOM

Congratulations on making it through another chapter. You're getting there!

We know you're getting sick of hearing this, but one of the best things you can do to prepare for this section is to take as many Writing and Language Tests as you can get your hands on. By the time you are done, you will have seen every type of question the Serpent can throw at you, and you are less likely to be surprised.

The other secret tool is your *ear*. If you grew up speaking English as a first, second, or even third language, then you have been hearing the conventions of English for a long time. The best way to tap into that experience, however, is less through your eyes than through your ears. Read the passage out loud (or whisper-read, if you don't want to become the least popular kid in the testing center). After you've picked your answer, read it again. This is called the "ear test," and it is one of your most effective weapons for taking on this section.

Finally, your absolute best preparation, for this test and also the Reading Test and the optional (not optional) Essay, is to read challenging writing. We know we've made this point before, but it bears repeating. Not only is reading quality writing one of the most effective ways to boost your awareness of the conventions of English, it is also the most pleasurable.

Oh, also be careful of the writing on Twitter, Facebook, Instagram, etc. The grammar used on those social networking services is enough to make any self-respecting English teacher implode.

CHAPTER 5

The Math Test

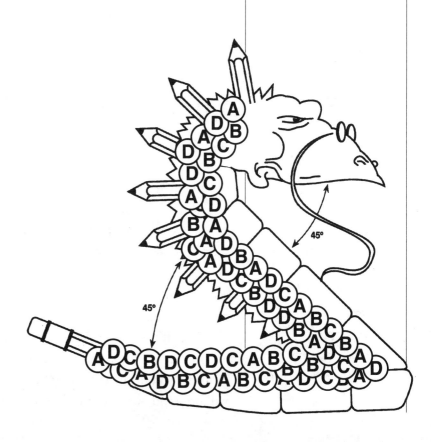

WELCOME TO MATH

For many, the Math Test is scarier than the Evidence-Based Reading and Writing Test (despite that test's daunting name). Why is that? One theory is that most of us read and write all the time, whereas most of us are not solving equations all the time. Math feels more *foreign*. That's one theory, at any rate. Another theory is that math was invented by vampires and ghouls.

The Math Test's difficulty is a result of *unfamiliarity*. If we say "addition," you say "No prob, Bob." If we say "inverse proportionality," you scream in terror. But if you can get comfortable with the concepts, the Serpent loses 97 percent of its power. That's the goal of this chapter, to introduce you, or *re*introduce you, to most of the concepts included on the Math Test.

We are *not* going to reteach the basics like addition and subtraction. If you need a refresher on arithmetic, we recommend you go talk to your math teacher. Direct contact with a good teacher is far more useful than anything we can tell you, but be sure to wear rubber gloves. What we *will* do is show you the concepts that are most often included on the test and some test-savvy ways to tackle those types of questions.

BEFORE WE BEGIN

We are going to discuss some relatively advanced subjects, especially those in the Passport to Advanced Math* section. If you are shooting for a high math score, we recommend that you learn the material in these sections, especially if your day-to-day math experience is limited to grocery shopping. You will learn helpful vocabulary and be able to recognize tricky problems immediately on the test so if—despite our expert guidance—you do happen to decide they're impossible, you can skip them without wasting time. (Of course you'll need to fill in an answer choice for every question. For more on guessing and math, see page 324.)

One thing to look out for is vocabulary. "What?!" you say. "*More* vocab?" Yup. Sorry. One of the Serpent's oldest tricks is to throw you off by including the mathiest words available. We will help you out by putting tricky math words in **boldface type**.

*Why is it a "passport"? Because with it, you're going to be going places. Ha ha.
　　　　—Samantha

THE SHAPE OF THE TEST

Don't let the word "easier" make you too relaxed. I once missed the first problem of the math section because I thought 24 divided by 4 was 8.

—Samantha

HOW IS THIS DIFFERENT FROM THE OLD SAT?

The Math Test is broken down into two sections: one 55-minute section with a calculator, and one 25-minute section with no calculator. Again, there is no penalty for a wrong answer, so you MUST GUESS if you don't know the answer. Your raw score (the number you answered correctly) will be compared to all of the other raw scores on your test date to create your final score, which is out of 800. Additional subscores (namely Heart of Algebra, Problem Solving and Data Analysis, and Passport to Advanced Math) will be available, but that final score out of 800 is the number that matters to colleges, and hence to you.

Both sections of the test will begin with easier questions, then get harder.* All the questions will be pulled from four loosely defined content areas: the above-mentioned Problem Solving and Data Analysis (word problems and statistics and charts); Heart of Algebra (variables, equations, and their graphs); Passport to Advanced Math (quadratic and exponential equations, functions); and Additional Topics (geometry and coordinate geometry, plus a few scary leftovers like imaginary numbers and cosines). We have organized our math chapter to follow these groupings.

Those of you who have never seen an SAT before or have only seen one post–March 2016 can skip this part. Cruise right on over to Mental Math Tricks on the next page.

However, those of you who have already taken an SAT or PSAT before March 2016, or those of you who are regular subscribers to *History of Standardized Tests Magazine*, need to know that the current SAT Math Test is a *new test*. So what's new?

Well, there's the official answer, and then there's the real answer. The official answer is that not too much has changed in the Math Test. There is a larger focus on algebra, a few new topics (such as complex numbers and margins of error), and a new section in which calculators are forbidden. The real answer is that *a lot* has changed. There is a *much* greater focus on algebra (and less on geometry), statistics, and the interpretation of graphs and charts, as well as evaluating data samples and making inferences based on that data. A quick flip through a new Math Test will also reveal *a lot* more words. In the new word problems, the Testing Serpent is interested in creating *real-world* situations (think currency exchanges, bank loans, and toxicity reports) rather than the how-many-bus-routes-go-through-Sasparilla-type questions of yesteryear.

Also—and this is crucial—the new Math Test includes a section that is 55 minutes long. That is a *very* long time to spend on math. This will require a level of endurance that you have not yet experienced.

So, real talk: Is it harder?

Yes.

But this is not all bad news! Test-prep nerds like the *Up Your Score* authors have long been worried that the old SAT Math section was, in a sense, *too easy*. So many kids were getting strong scores on the old SAT Math section that it totally messed up the grading curve. On a recent test date, *one mistake* on a math section dropped you from a perfect 800 to a 740. That's right: 60 points off for *one* mistake. Three mistakes could land you in the high 600s. That should never be the case. The hope is that the difficulty of the new test will, in this bizarro way, allow you to get a higher score even if you make more mistakes. *

But here's our big point: The new SAT Math Test is very new. So read the following pages carefully.

*"Victory will only come through struggle."
—not Samantha*

MENTAL MATH TRICKS

It is definitely important to know how to use your calculator, but you should also know how to use your brain, for two reasons. For one, some arithmetic is just easier to do in your head than on a calculator. For example, what is 2/5 plus 1/5? You should be able to answer 3/5 faster than you could enter it into your calculator. (If you couldn't, then you should definitely read and then reread our section on fractions.) The other reason is that there is a brand-new, **no-calculator** portion of the test.

One great way to sharpen your mental knife is to learn/

relearn the concepts on the test (which we will do in a few pages). But *another* great way is to memorize the following tips and tricks.

MENTAL MATH TRICK 1: TENS AND ONES

The first trick is simple. If I say "What is 346 plus 211?" You can make your life easier by breaking down the 211 into 200 + 10 + 1, and then adding each separate piece. So 346 + 200 = 546, then 546 + 10 = 556, and finally 556 + 1 = 557. This trick breaks a complicated addition problem into a sequence of problems that are so easy they are almost *automatic*. They save you time and energy, and you are less likely to make a calculation mistake. The same goes for multiplication. "What is 56 times 14?" First, do 56 × 10 = 560, then do 56 × 4 = 224, then add them together to get the answer: 784. Perhaps that middle step (56 × 4) was too complicated to do in your head? Just break it down: 50 × 4 = 200, and 6 × 4 = 24. Add them together to get 224.

This might feel funky at first, but with a bit of practice, "Tens and Ones" can save you oodles of time and energy.

MENTAL MATH TRICK 2: KNOW YOUR PREMDAS

The easiest and most common mistake to make in mental math is to mess up your order of operations. It's possible you haven't reviewed your PEMDAS in years. Refresher—go in this order: Parentheses, Exponents, Multiplication and Division, Addition and Subtraction. Remember that when you're doing addition and subtraction, go left to right; ditto with multiplication and division. Here's a handy-dandy graphic for you to tattoo on your forearm:

$$\frac{(\text{PLEASE})^{\text{EXCUSE}} \cdot \text{MY}}{\text{DEAR}} \quad +\text{AUNT} -\text{SALLY}$$

A root is really just a type of exponent. That's why the "R" is often left out.
—Samantha

More helpfully, it should be PREMDAS because we shouldn't forget "R" for roots. Operations under root signs should be done at the same time as the exponents (move from left to right to decide which to do first). PREMDAS is precisely the kind of math concept you learned ages ago and *think* you know, but being hazy on this can *really* mess you up.

$$5 + \sqrt{4} \times 6 - 2 = ?$$

If you go from left to right, you get 40. If you follow PREMDAS, you get 15. Those are two different answers. The first is wrong, the second is right. The SAT *will* try to catch you on this.

MENTAL MATH TRICK 3: DIVIDING TRICKS

Division is one of the more annoying operations to do in your head. A few SAT problems will require that you determine whether a large number is divisible. For example, do you know if 32,571 is prime? To solve this, you could do a whole bunch of trial and error with your calculator. But this will take a while, and if no calculator is allowed, you're in trouble. So consider this chart a list of cheat codes to help you determine whether a large number is divisible, and by which numbers.

IT'S DIVISIBLE BY	IF	EXAMPLE
1	It is an integer.	Do you really need one?
2	It's an even number.	Hmm . . .
3	Its digits add up to a multiple of 3.	186. 1 + 8 + 6 = 15 15 = (3 × 5)
4	Its last two digits form (not "add up to") a number divisible by 4.	103,424 24 is divisible by 4 (24 ÷ 4 = 6)
5	It ends in 5 or 0.	5,746,893,765
6	It is divisible by 2 and 3.	522

IT'S DIVISIBLE BY	IF	EXAMPLE
7	There's a rule, but it's more complicated than it's worth.	
8	Its last three digits form a multiple of 8.	10,496,832 (832 ÷ 8 = 104)
9	Its digits add up to a multiple of 9.	34,164. 3 + 4 + 1 + 6 + 4 = 18 = (2 × 9)
10	It ends in 0.	1,600

Using these rules, you can see—at a glance—that 32,571 is *not* prime. It's divisible by nine!

Here's an example of the type of problem you might see on the No Calculator section.

What is the *least* positive integer divisible by the numbers 2, 3, 4, and 5?
A) 30
B) 40
C) 60
D) 120

Rather than do a bunch of math, just look at the answer choices. You can immediately tell that they're all divisible by 2 and 5 because they end in 0. You can use the 3 rule to cross out B and the 4 rule to cross out A. That leaves C and D, and because we want the smallest number, C is the answer.

Another arithmetic cheat: Check the last digits. If you're multiplying two large numbers, you can figure out what the last digit of the answer is without multiplying them completely. Multiply the end numbers together and take the last digit of this product. Let's try this out.

Pay attention to italics. In this case, two of the answer choices are divisible by 2, 3, 4, and 5—but the italicized word told you which to choose.
—Samantha

23 × 257 =
A) 5,911
B) 5,312
C) 4,517
D) 5,118

Without multiplying it out, let's do a last-digit check: 3×7 (the last two numbers) = 21; last digit = 1. Only choice A ends in 1, so the answer is A.

MENTAL MATH TRICK 4: KNOW YOUR SQUARES

We are going to talk about exponents and square roots at a later point in this chapter, but you should memorize the basic squares. We assume you know the squares of 1 through 10, but here's 11 through 20, plus 25. These will not only help you speed through problems that involve squares, but will also help you decode sophisticated-seeming problems.

Number	Square	Number	Square
11	121	17	289
12	144	18	324
13	169	19	361
14	196	20	400
15	225	25	625
16	256		

So if you see a problem involving the number 169, your "square-sense" should be tingling!

MENTAL MATH TRICK 5: KNOW YOUR MATH TERMS

As we mentioned, one way that the Evil Testing Serpent likes to overwhelm the mind and torture the soul is to stuff a problem full of math terms. You can save yourself a good deal of stress by making yourself familiar with some of the most commonly used terms.

Don't worry, we are going to address a few of these words (like *mean, factor, numerator,* and *denominator*) in more detail later on. But when you read a math problem, these words should stand out in **bold** in your mind (or <u>underlined</u>, or *italicized*, or <u>***all three***</u>) because each one must be considered when solving the problem.

Digits: 0, 1, 2, 3, 4, 5, 6, 7, 8, 9

Units Digit: the digit in the one's place (5,32**6**)

Integer: any number, including negatives and zero, that is not a decimal or a fraction

Consecutive: in order

Quotient: the result (answer) of a division problem

Product: the result (answer) of a multiplication problem

Prime: any number that can be divided only by 1 and itself. But remember, 2 is the first prime number, not 1!

Factor: the integers that can be divided into a number. For example, the factors of 18 are 1, 2, 3, 6, 9, 18. (Don't forget to include 1 and the number itself.)

Multiple: the answers you get when you multiply by a number. For example, the multiples of 6 are 0, 6, 12, 18, 24, 30, etc.

Numerator: the number in the top part of a fraction

Denominator: the number in the bottom part of a fraction

Area: the region inside a two-dimensional shape, such as a square or a circle

Volume: the space inside a three-dimensional shape, such as a box or a cylinder

Perimeter: the distance around the outside of a shape

Radius: the distance from the center to a point on the perimeter of a circle

Diameter: all the way across a circle through the center (twice the radius)

Chord: any segment connecting two points on a circle

Circumference: distance around the perimeter of a circle

Mean: average

Median: the middle number in a set of numbers arranged in order (3, 4, 4, **5**, 6, 7, 8)

Mode: the most frequently occurring number in a set of numbers (3, **4, 4**, 5, 6, 7, 8)

MENTAL MATH TRICK 6: TRANSLATE WORDS INTO OPERATIONS

In word problems (which most SAT problems are), certain English words usually refer to certain basic operations.

Of usually means multiply: ½ of *y* means ½ × *y*.

Exceeds by or *is greater than* usually means subtract (or add): *x* exceeds *y* by 7 means $x - y = 7$ (or $y + 7 = x$).

Total or *altogether* usually means addition: the total of *x* and *y* means $x + y$.

Each usually means multiply (or divide): 20 baskets, each with 12 eggs, means you have 20 × 12 eggs, or 240.

MENTAL MATH TRICK 7: NO CALCULATOR FOR FRACTIONS

This is less a trick than a warning. Before we tell you all about fractions, it's important to know that calculators are not great at handling fractions. On a non-graphing calculator, you have to first convert fractions to decimals, which is an added step. On a graphing calculator, you have to bracket your fractions in parentheses, which creates a ballroom-size room for error.

SOME ARITHMETIC REMINDERS

As we said, the SAT breaks down its math problems into four major categories, Problem Solving and Data Analysis, Heart of Algebra, Passport to Advanced Math, and Additional Topics. Before we get into those areas, we need to review two basic arithmetic concepts that are heavily involved in *all* of those areas: fractions and negative numbers.

Fractions and Their Meaning

Now, we know you've seen a lot of fractions in math class, and you know more or less how to work with them. But the SAT requires that you know what a fraction *means*. You need to understand that ⅗ not only means three-fifths, but also 3 divided by 5. You need to understand that miles/hour means miles divided by hours. If this feels a little iffy, then read this section carefully because this is one of the most important ideas on the Math SAT.

The following problem will illustrate why *three-fifths* and *3 divided by 5* are the same thing.

THE QUICHE PROBLEM

Rihanna, Madonna, Beyoncé, an accountant named Merle, and Sia are having breakfast together. They order three quiches, which they plan to divide equally. How much does each person get?

Step 1: Cut the first quiche into five equal pieces (i.e., into fifths) and give one piece to each person.

Step 2: Do the same thing to the second quiche.

A quiche (pronounced "keesh") is an eggy pie thing with cheese and ham or veggies. It's never pronounced "quickie."

—Samantha

Step 3: Do the same thing to the third quiche.

Now, as you can see, everyone has three slices of quiche. Each slice is a fifth of a quiche, so everyone has three-fifths (3/5) of a quiche. So three quiches were divided equally among five people to give each person 3/5 of a quiche.

This is what this problem was designed to demonstrate—that 3 divided by 5 and 3/5 are the same thing: three quiches divided by five people = 3/5 of a quiche per person. Read this paragraph over and over again until you understand it. Then go eat some quiche.

Complex Fractions

The Evil Testing Serpent loves testing your ability to work with fractions by creating problems that contain complex fractions. A complex fraction is a regular fraction divided by another regular fraction. Here are some complex fractions:

$$\frac{\frac{3}{5}}{\frac{7}{13}} \quad \text{or} \quad \frac{\frac{a}{b}}{\frac{c}{d}} \quad \text{or} \quad \frac{\frac{\text{miles}}{\text{hour}}}{\frac{\text{wombat}}{\text{person}}}$$

Because complex fractions are a pain in the neck, you want to turn them into regular fractions. There is a simple rule for simplifying complex fractions.

Simple Rule: Flip the bottom fraction and multiply it by the top fraction.

Simple? Well, actually it is. You just have to recognize each individual fraction. Label the complex fraction like this:

$$\text{upper} \left\{ \cfrac{\dfrac{\text{top of the upper}}{\text{bottom of the upper}}}{\underbrace{\dfrac{\text{top of the lower}}{\text{bottom of the lower}}}_{\text{lower}}} \right.$$

What the Simple Rule says is that you can simplify any complex fraction by flipping the bottom fraction and multiplying it by the top fraction. It works because when you divide you are really just multiplying by the reciprocal (*reciprocal* means "whatever it was, only flipped over"). This is what the Simple Rule looks like:

$$\frac{\dfrac{a}{b}}{\dfrac{c}{d}} = \frac{a}{b} \times \frac{d}{c} = \frac{ad}{bc}$$

> Basically, multiply the outsides together and then divide that by the insides.
> —Samantha

You may want to draw arrows:

$$\frac{\dfrac{a}{b}}{\dfrac{c}{d}}$$

Using real numbers:

$$\frac{\dfrac{2}{3}}{\dfrac{7}{6}} = \frac{2}{3} \times \frac{6}{7} = \frac{12}{21} = \frac{4}{7}$$

Here are some problems. Make each complex fraction into a simple (regular) fraction. Practice the Simple Rule.

1.
$$\frac{\dfrac{3}{5}}{\dfrac{4}{7}} = \ ?$$

You should immediately rewrite this as:

$$\frac{3 \ \times \ 7}{5 \ \times \ 4}$$

2.
$$\frac{\dfrac{kumquats}{person}}{\dfrac{brains}{oat\ bran}}$$

You should immediately rewrite this as:

$$\frac{kumquats \times oat\ bran}{person \times brains}$$

Word Fractions

Miles per hour is a way we measure speed. You've probably seen miles per hour written as a fraction: miles/hour. Using the quiche problem, we just confirmed that *fractions* mean "division." So *miles per hour* must mean "miles divided by hours." But what does that mean? How do you divide a mile by an hour? What does it mean to travel 400 miles divided by 8 hours? The following problem will attempt to answer all these questions.

THE ICE CREAM PROBLEM

After they finish their quiche, our group of megawatt songstresses (and Merle the accountant) drive to the nearest Coldstone Creamery. Unfortunately, the nearest Coldstone Creamery is 500 miles away. If it takes them 10 hours to get there, what was their average speed?

Answer: The key is to realize that if they drive 500 miles in 10 hours, then they have 500 miles to divide among 10 hours of driving. (It's just like having 3 quiches to divide among 5 people.) So rewrite it as:

$$\frac{500 \text{ miles}}{10 \text{ hours}} = \frac{50 \text{ miles}}{1 \text{ hour}} = 50 \text{ miles/hour}$$

Now you know why *miles per hour* is the same thing as miles/hour.

Units

Anything you can count or measure has a unit associated with it. *Pounds* are units, *miles* are units, *hours* are units, *miles/hour* are units, even *noodles* can be units if, like us, you spend your Saturday nights counting and measuring with noodles.

Knowing how to work with units is ridiculously helpful both for speed and understanding in many SAT math problems. The rule for working with units is that you can multiply and divide them just as you would numbers. For example, when you multiply (or divide) fractions containing units you can cancel units in the numerator with units in the denominator:

$$\frac{10 \text{ miles}}{1 \text{ hour}} \times 5 \text{ hours} = 50 \text{ miles}$$

$$\frac{10 \text{ pizzas}}{3 \text{ people}} \times 7 \text{ people} = \frac{70}{3} \text{ pizzas}$$

And you can divide using the Simple Rule:

$$\frac{\dfrac{5 \text{ pounds}}{\text{chicken}}}{\dfrac{3 \text{ chickens}}{10 \text{ McNuggets}}} = \frac{50 \,(\text{pounds} \times \text{McNuggets})}{3 \,(\text{chickens})^2}$$

After some practice, multiplying and dividing units will be as simple and as natural to you as multiplying and dividing numbers.

For a nerdy laugh, check out Wikipedia's "List of Humorous Units of Measurement." But don't convert miles into wiffles or beard-seconds on the SAT.

—Samantha

Quick tip:
If you multiply the 7/3 gallons/acres ratio by 2, you find that it takes 14 gallons to plow 6 acres. Now you know 16 gallons will plow something close to 6 acres.
—Samantha

We will now do a practice problem from a real SAT that shows the procedure for solving units problems.

A gasoline tank on a certain tractor holds 16 gallons. If the tractor requires 7 gallons to plow 3 acres, how many acres can the tractor plow with a tankful of gasoline?

A) $6\frac{6}{7}$ B) $7\frac{1}{6}$ C) $7\frac{1}{3}$ D) $10\frac{2}{3}$

There are two steps to all units problems:
1. Figure out what information is given.
2. Pick, from only three options, what to do with that information in order to get the correct unit in the answer.

Step 1: Figure out the information given.
  a. "7 gallons to plow 3 acres" = 7 gallons/3 acres
  b. "A gasoline tank holds 16 gallons" = 16 gallons
  c. "How many acres?" means . . . answer in *acres.*

Step 2: Do the right thing with the information given.

In all units problems, you have three options for what to do with the given information:
  1. Multiply the first thing × the second thing.
  2. Divide the first thing/the second thing.
  3. Divide the second thing/the first thing.

The great thing about units problems is that it is not necessary to understand what's going on in order to know which of the three options to use. You automatically know which one to choose because only one of the options will give you the answer in acres (the unit you want). Look at the three options:

1. $\dfrac{7 \text{ gallons}}{3 \text{ acres}} \times 16 \text{ gallons} = \dfrac{(16 \times 7) \text{ gallons}^2}{3 \text{ acres}}$

A fancy name for this process of multiplying fractions to get the right units is "dimensional analysis."

—Samantha

Nope! The answer has to be in terms of acres, not in terms of gallons²/acres.

2. $\dfrac{\dfrac{7 \text{ gallons}}{3 \text{ acres}}}{16 \text{ gallons}} = \dfrac{7 \text{ gallons}}{3 \text{ acres} \times 16 \text{ gallons}}$

Nope! We want acres in the numerator.

3. $\dfrac{16 \text{ gallons}}{\dfrac{7 \text{ gallons}}{3 \text{ acres}}} = \dfrac{16 \text{ gallons} \times 3 \text{ acres}}{7 \text{ gallons}} = 6\dfrac{6}{7} \text{ acres}$

Yes! This is the right answer. Notice that we didn't even have to figure out what the problem was all about; we just manipulated the information so that the answer would be in the correct unit.

AND NOW WE BREAK FOR A COMMERCIAL . . .

Don't you hate it when rabid elephants attack you and steal your pencils? I sure do. On the day of my test, I was carrying no fewer than four number 2 pencils when a tremendous elephant lunged out of a dark alley and grabbed my writing implements. Shucks!

That's why I now use Oxford Anti-Elephant Soap. It not only keeps those pesky pachyderms away, it also keeps my skin fresh and clean! Now, my life is elephant-free and perfect!

The point of this message is to remind you to bring enough number 2 pencils to the testing center. Also, we wanted to give you a break from reading about math. We hope you enjoyed it— now *get back to work!*

Negative Numbers

Another tricky concept that pops up in all sorts of problems is negativity. No, we don't mean the pessimistic-voice-in-your-head-foretelling-the-apocalypse type of negativity. We mean mathematical negativity.

The best way to think about negative numbers is to construct a mental (or real) number line, like this:

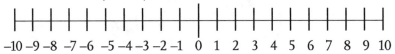

When you are adding or subtracting negative numbers, you should mentally (or actually) put your pencil on the starting number, then move to the right or left, depending on the situation. Let's try:

$$-7 + 3$$

We start on the first number (-7) and then move to the right three spaces, and land on our answer: -4.

$$5 - -4$$

This is when our number line really comes in handy. We start, as always, on our first number, 5, but now we have to determine whether we go right or left. The minus sign makes us think we should go left, but the negative sign on the four means we should go right four spaces to our answer: 9.

With multiplication and division of two numbers, just remember the rule: Different signs give you negative products; same signs give you positive products.

$$(+)7 \times -7 = -49$$

$$\frac{(+)16}{(+)4} = (+)4$$

$$\frac{-55}{(+)11} = -5$$

$$-6 \times -5 = (+)30$$

PROBLEM SOLVING AND DATA ANALYSIS

The first content area of the Math section is Problem Solving and Data Analysis. Vague, right? Don't worry, they just mean standard word problems involving ratios, probability, percentages, statistics (which really means mean, median, and mode), and interpreting graphs. Let's dig in!

Ratios and Proportions

A ratio is basically just a fraction, and a proportion is a way to compare two equal ratios. Here's an example of a proportion, written in two different ways (that mean the same thing):

$$\frac{x}{y} = \frac{4}{3}$$

$$x{:}y = 4{:}3$$

What this is saying is that when $x = 4$, $y = 3$. What happens if I double the x? Well, if we double our x, we have to do the exact same thing to y in order to maintain the proportion.

$$\frac{4}{3} = \frac{8}{6}$$

When you have to solve for a variable in a proportion, the simplest way is to use a very powerful tool with a very boring name: "cross multiplication." To cross multiply, you turn the two fractions into a simpler equation by multiplying diagonally across the equals sign. For example, if you have a proportion like:

$$\frac{4}{3} = \frac{9}{x}$$

You can solve for x by multiplying each denominator by the numerator on the opposite corner, and setting those two expressions equal to each other.

$$\frac{4}{3} \diagdown \frac{9}{x} \rightarrow 3 \times 9 = 4x \rightarrow 27 = 4x \quad \frac{27}{4} = \frac{4x}{4} \rightarrow x = \frac{27}{4}$$

Now let's take a look at a more difficult problem:

At the jelly bean factory, the ratio of watermelon jelly beans

> *This section of the Math Test requires fewer calculations and more common sense.*
> *—Samantha*

to popcorn jelly beans is 6:2. If 800 watermelon and popcorn jelly beans are manufactured per day, how many watermelon jelly beans are manufactured per day?

The first step is to try to ignore the thought of how disgusting watermelon jelly beans would taste when mixed with popcorn jelly beans. The second step is to think of the given ratio as a relationship of part to part. For every six watermelon jelly beans the factory makes, it makes two popcorn jelly beans. But with the information given, we need to make a new ratio of part to whole, and then set up a new proportion. To get the whole, we will add the two parts together: 6 + 2 = 8. Now what is the ratio of watermelon jelly beans to *all* jelly beans? 6:8, or 6/8. Let's use that new ratio to set up a new proportion and solve:

$$\frac{6}{8} = \frac{x}{800}$$

Cross multiplying and solving for *x* will tell us the total number of watermelon jelly beans: 600.

Probability

A probability problem is a ratio problem in disguise. When a problem asks what the chance is that a particular thing will happen, all it's really asking you to do is to set up a ratio like this:

$$\frac{\text{number of times the particular thing could happen}}{\text{number of times any of the things could happen}}$$

Here's an example:

If there are 12 pairs of boxer shorts and 36 pairs of briefs in a huge laundry bag, what is the probability that, at random, Bill will grab the boxer shorts?

Our "particular thing" here is grabbing a pair of boxer shorts, of which there are 12. "Any of the things" is the number of underwear total, which is 48.

$$\frac{12}{48} = .25$$

Bill has a 25% chance of grabbing a pair of boxers. Good luck, Bill!

On most probability problems, however, the SAT is going to ask for the probability of multiple events.

A deck of cards includes 10 blue cards, 10 green cards, and 10 black cards. What are the odds of drawing two black cards in a row, if no card is replaced once it is drawn?

We see that we are dealing with two events (drawing one card, *then* drawing another). The first event is easy.

$$\frac{10 \text{ (because there are 10 black cards)}}{30 \text{ (because there are 30 cards total)}}$$

The odds of our first event are ⅓. But our second event is trickier. Remember, if we have *already* drawn one black card, that changes our numerator and denominator.

$$\frac{9 \text{ (because there are 9 black cards left)}}{29 \text{ (because there are 29 cards left total)}}$$

Finally, we just multiply our two events together, then reduce our fraction to the lowest whole numbers:

$$\frac{10}{30} \times \frac{9}{29} = \frac{90}{870} = \frac{3}{29}$$

Percentages   Percentages are fraction problems in disguise because *percent* means *per hundred*. So 25% can also be read as 25/100. So if I ask for "25% of *y*," I am asking for 25/100 × *y* or if you're using a calculator: .25 × *y*.

We do the same thing for percentages greater than 100%. For instance, 250% means 250/100 or 2.5.

But there are more difficult percent questions, such as:

13 is 20% of what number?

Here we can set up an equivalency, like this:

Whenever I see a percent, I automatically think of the fraction it represents. 20% = 20/100 = 1/5. So, to solve 13 is 1/5 of what number, you just multiply 13x5 and— voilà—65.

—Samantha

$$\frac{\text{part}}{\text{whole}} = \frac{\text{percent}}{100}$$

Let's plug in our numbers. Be careful! Is 13 the *part* or the *whole*? If we are saying that 13 is a percent *of another number*, it must be the part.

$$\frac{13}{\text{whole}} = \frac{20}{100}$$

Cross multiply to find that our whole is 65.

PERCENT INCREASE AND DECREASE

A wig seller raises the price of a wig by 25% to a new price of $65. What was the original price?

When you solve this problem, don't fall into the trap of subtracting 65 by 25% of 65 (this is sure to be one of the answer choices you want to avoid). Instead, all you have to do is remember and apply the ironclad rule for these types of problems: The percent change expressed as a decimal (or, to say the same thing, divided by 100) equals the difference over the original:

$$\frac{\text{\% change}}{100} = \frac{\text{difference in price}}{\text{original}}$$

The difference in price is the new price minus the old price. Since the original price is the unknown (and what we're looking for), call that *x*, and solve:

$$.25 = \frac{65 - x}{x}$$

With some cross multiplication, you should get $x = 52$. So the original price is $52.

Here's a similar problem involving a decrease: A wig is sold at 20% off, and the discounted price is $48. What was the original price before the discount? Well, you apply the same ironclad rule, except this time the percent change is negative, because it's a decrease.

$$-.20 \ = \ \frac{48 - x}{x}$$

Cross multiply again to get $-.20x = 48 - x$, and solve for x to find the original price of $60.

EXPONENTIAL GROWTH

The main thing to recognize about exponential growth is that it's fast—the fastest growth you can imagine. You know at the beginning of those zombie movies where the research guy with crazy hair and glasses starts raving about how quickly the zombie-making virus is spreading through the world population? And the red dots on his screen start multiplying from one or two cities to dozens and then hundreds within a few seconds, and soon the whole world is red? That's exponential growth in a nutshell. Here's a sample graph of what exponential growth looks like. Notice that the curve starts off slowly and then explodes upward!

An exponential function will always involve putting the independent variable—usually time—into the exponent part of the function. For example, $f(x) = 2^x$ is a very simple exponential function. Try plugging in some values of x and you can see how quickly $f(x)$ rises to astronomical levels. However, most exponential growth problems on the SAT will involve financial situations, not astronomy. Behold:

If Jita invests $2,500 in a savings account that earns 2% interest per year, how much money will she have in three years?

There is a right way to do the problem, and a wrong way. The wrong way is to think: *Hmm, she's getting 2% per year, so I'll just multiply 2% times 3, and multiply the result by the original investment of $2,500.* This would be incorrect. And likely one of the answer choices will correspond to this method because the Serpent is hoping you will make this logical, but wrong, attempt.

To answer this correctly, you should memorize the **compound interest formula:**

$$A = P\left(1 + \frac{r}{n}\right)^{nt}$$

In this formula, A is the total amount accumulated, P is the principal or starting amount, r is the growth rate (expressed as a decimal), and t is the number of years invested. The n is a little more complicated. It's the number of times per year the interest is assessed. Since in our example, the interest is compounded per year, $n = 1$, this gives us:

$$A = 2{,}500\left(1 + \frac{.02}{1}\right)^{1\times3} = 2{,}500\,(1.02)^3 = 2{,}653.02$$

Note: When you do this on the calculator, make sure you evaluate the exponent part first, and then multiply by the 2,500 (using parentheses on a scientific calculator works best).

EXPONENTIAL DECAY

Just as things can grow very quickly, they can also shrink exponentially; this is called "decay." For example, a stock price that starts at $50 per share may drop by a certain percentage each year. If a $50 stock declines 20% per year, you can calculate its final value after 3 years, just as you calculated the growth of an investment over 3 years. You'll use the *exact same formula* as growth, with one important difference—the plus sign before the *r/n* part becomes a minus sign:

$$A = 50\left(1 - \frac{.20}{1}\right)^{1\times3} = 50\,(1 - .2)^3 = 50\,(.8)^3 = \$25.60$$

Exchange Rates

Problems involving exchange rates are also just ratio problems in disguise.

A student traveling in Moscow bought a sweater for 175 rubles. When she checked her bank account, she realized that this was equivalent to $65. What was the exchange rate of rubles per dollar, rounded to the nearest tenth?

A) .8   B) 1.1   C) 1.7   D) 2.7

To figure out a rate of exchange, set up an equivalency:

$$\frac{175 \text{ rubles}}{65 \text{ dollars}} = \frac{x \text{ rubles}}{1 \text{ dollar}}$$

Cross multiply to find out that there are 2.69 rubles per dollar, which rounds to 2.7, or D.

INTERPRETING GRAPHS

The SAT is obsessed with data and graphs, and there are many types of graphs that it can include in a problem. Depending on your familiarity with graphs, these might seem more or less frightening. But one thing is certain: Graph problems take time. So if you can familiarize yourself with these graph types now, then you'll save yourself oodles of time on test day.

Line Graphs

The first thing to do when you see a graph is to "tell the story of the graph." This means that first and foremost you need to **understand the axes**. Take a look.

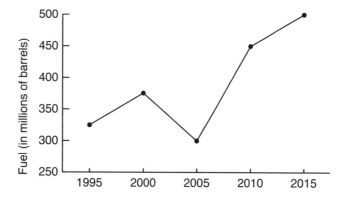

AMOUNT OF FUEL CONSUMED IN USA

What's the story here? The title of the graph is the first hint: We're talking about how much fuel the United States consumes. Our *x*-axis is time, our *y*-axis is the number of barrels. So in 1995, the United States consumed a bit more than 300 barrels, right? Be careful, the axis is labeled "Fuel (in millions of barrels)," so in 1995 the United States consumed a bit more than 300 *million* barrels. This climbed to about 370-ish million barrels in 2000, then declined, then rose again. Pretty straightforward, right? Line graphs are not terribly intimidating, once you know to look at the axes. But let's crank this up a notch.

Bar Graphs

Pro Tip: Beware! Graphs are often used for multiple problems! Whenever you see a graph of any type on the math section, there is a high likelihood that the next two or three problems will refer back to that same graph.

FUEL USE BY TYPE OF VEHICLE

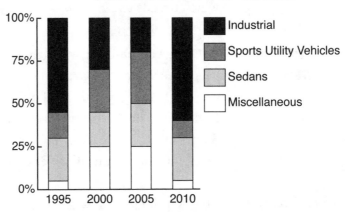

Slightly more terrifying, right? As we can see by the title, this graph breaks down the fuel use by vehicle type: industrial vehicles (like trucks, presumably), SUVs, sedans, and finally miscellaneous (like fuel-powered robot dinosaurs, presumably). The *x*-axis is still time, and still in intervals of five years. The *y*-axis is now percentage, and here is where bar graphs can be tricky. When we look at, for example, the amount of industrial fuel use in 1995, we see that the segment takes up a bit more than 50% of that year's bar. It does not matter *where* on the bar the industrial segment lies; all that matters is *how much of the bar* it takes up. SUVs, for example, seem to take up about 15% of that year's fuel. It doesn't matter *where* on the bar that 15% lies; all that matters is that it is 15%.

Let's combine the two graphs to answer this very typical SAT graph question:

> Between 2000 and 2005, by how many barrels
> did miscellaneous use decrease?

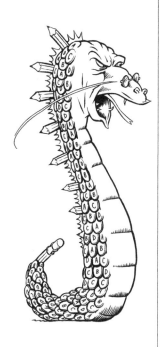

There are two helpful clues in this question, the word *miscellaneous* (which points us to the bar graph) and the word *barrel* (which points us to the line graph). So in 2000, we see that miscellaneous vehicles used about 25% of the total. But what was the total? Let's go to the line graph, where we can see that the total number of barrels in 2000 was about 375 million. Calculate .25 × 375 = 93.75. (Why did we not type 375,000,000? Because we can add those zeroes back on at the end and save our fingers from cramping.) In 2005, miscellaneous vehicles again used about 25% of the total, but the line graph shows us that the *total* has decreased to about 300 million. Let's calculate .25 × 300 = 75. So the decrease was 93.75 − 75 = 18.75. Now we can add on our zeroes to get our proper answer: 18,750,000 barrels.

Do you mind if we add one final layer of complexity? Of course you don't.

Circle Graphs

What's the story? The pie chart below breaks down the fuel use of the various types of miscellaneous vehicles by type, all in 2010. So in 2010, 33% of the fuel used by miscellaneous vehicles was used by Segways; 13% was used by Jet Skis, etc.

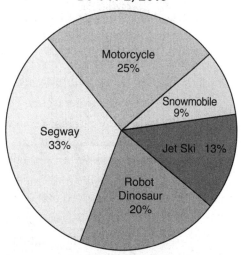

FUEL CONSUMED BY MISCELLANEOUS VEHICLES BY TYPE, 2010

How many barrels of fuel were consumed by motorcycles in 2010?

To answer this question, we need to use all three graphs. First off, how much fuel was used in 2010 total? Look at the line graph to find 450 million barrels. What percent of this was used by miscellaneous vehicles? The bar graph tells us that it is about 5%. So $.05 \times 450 = 22.5$ million barrels for miscellaneous vehicles. If motorcycles used 25% of that fuel, then $.25 \times 22.5 = 5.625$ million barrels.

Comprehension and Trend Questions

Graphs are not terribly difficult, once you get used to using multiple graphs at once. But the SAT might ask you questions to see if you really understand what the graph is and *is not* saying. Like this:

> In 2010, what was the most popular miscellaneous vehicle?
> A) Motorcycle
> B) Segway
> C) Snowmobile
> D) Not enough information to answer the question

At first glance, we might answer that clearly the Segway was the most popular, as it takes up the largest slice of the pie chart. But remember that the pie chart is saying that the Segway used the most fuel. Does this *necessarily* mean that the Segway was the most popular? No way! Perhaps Segways are just gigantic fuel-guzzlers, and relatively few Segways use more fuel than the more popular motorcycles. The real answer is D. None of the graphs tell us about popularity, so we cannot answer this question. Try this:

> Based on the graphs, what is the likeliest amount of fuel consumed, in barrels, in 2020?
> A) 400,000,000
> B) 450,000,000
> C) 500,000,000
> D) 550,000,000

This is a *prediction* problem, and these at first look impossible. Who knows about 2020?!? It's not on the graph! But the *trend* in the line graph is an increasing amount of fuel use. Even though there was a dip in 2005, the overall movement is toward greater fuel consumption. So if we used 500,000,000 barrels in 2015, the likeliest number in 2020 is the only answer that is higher: D.

Tables

NUMBERS OF PARTICIPANTS IN WEDNESDAY AFTER-SCHOOL ACTIVITIES				
	Freshmen	Sophomores	Juniors	Seniors
Sports	60	55	45	40
Drama/Theater	22	15	12	8
Newspaper	15	10	8	6
Watching TV	60	45	37	20
Contemplation	7	19	33	55

Just like in a line or bar graph, the title and axes of a table are necessary to tell the story of this table. Here, we are looking at the number of participants in Wednesday after-school activities. For example, 15 sophomores are involved in theater as their Wednesday after-school activity. Can we spot any trends in this table? For one, we see a decline in participation in every single activity except contemplation, in which more and more students enroll as they move toward graduation.

You might see an accompanying problem asking:

If a student is selected at random, what are the odds that he or she will be a junior and a theater participant?

To answer this type of problem, which is really a type of probability question, you need to first find the number of junior thespians (12), * then divide this by the total number of students participating in activities (572).

$$\frac{12}{572} = \frac{3}{143}$$

I wonder what has the seniors contemplating so much . . .
—Samantha

*Actors. Junior actors.
—Samantha

Scatterplots

Scatterplots are frightening graphs because they look at first like a chaos of data points. On the following two graphs, we see that the *x*-axis tells us a student's SAT score, and the *y*-axis tells us the number of hours they studied. Bob, for instance, studied about 75 hours and got a little more than 1300. Sounds fair. But Jermaine studied for less than 50 hours and got a perfect 1600, while poor Hildegard studied for 250 hours and got a 1200. Hildegard, you need to read *Up Your Score!*

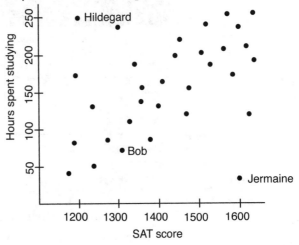

An SAT question might ask about the trend in a scatterplot. To answer this you need to draw a line where the points are most thickly clustered. (This is sometimes called the "line of best fit.") Like so:

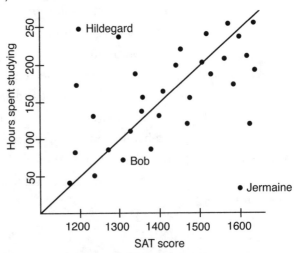

What that line says is that *in general*, the more someone studies, the better they will score. There may be outliers like Hildegard and Jermaine, but for the most part, studying more gets you results. (Not that we are trying to imply anything. It's just an example, we swear.)

STATISTICS

In typical Testing Serpent fashion, the SAT likes to use the horrible word *statistics* to cover some much-less-horrible math concepts. For example, the most common statistics problems are . . .

MEAN, MEDIAN, AND MODE

The *arithmetic mean* is the most commonly used average, and if you are asked to simply find the average, you should find the mean.

Arithmetic mean = $(a + b + c + d)/n$ where a, b, c, d are the numbers and n is the number of numbers being averaged. For example, the mean of 3, 5, 6, 7 is

$$(3 + 5 + 6 + 7) / 4 = 5.25$$

Notice that the denominator is 4 because there are four numbers in the group. Sometimes figuring out what n is can be tricky.

Manek got 75% of the questions correct on his first test, and 65% correct on his second. What does he need to score on his third test to have an average of 80% for the three tests?

To find the answer, let's say that the third test score is n.

$$\frac{75 + 65 + n}{3} = 80$$

$$140 + n = 240$$

$$n = 100$$

Median is the middle value of a group. It's the number that would be right in the middle of the list if you arranged the numbers from smallest to largest.

1, 4, 56, 59, 342, 697, 3455

The median of that group is 59. If the number of values is even (which would mean that there are two "middles"), then the median is the mean of these two middle values.

$$3, 8, 45, 67, 107, 156, 223, 1302$$

The median of that group is the mean of 67 and 107, or 87. (If you are given a list of numbers that is not in numerical order, put it in order before looking for the median.)

   Mode is the value or values that appears the greatest number of times. The mode of 3, 24, 95, 74, 74, 24, 56, 74, 61 is 74. The mode of 34, 46, 27, 1, 83, 46, 90, 63 is 46.

Standard Deviation

At least one problem on the SAT will include the term *standard deviation*. This refers to the amount of *dispersion* among a set of data. For example, let's say ten test takers received the following scores:

$$800, 950, 1100, 1120, 1200, 1200, 1280, 1350, 1400, 1500$$

Our mean, or average score, would be 1190. Let's plot those scores on a graph.

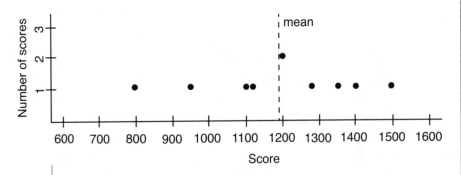

Now let's take another set of ten scores:

$$1130, 1140, 1150, 1170, 1180, 1200, 1210, 1230, 1240, 1250$$

If you calculate the mean, you will find that these scores have the same average: 1190. But if we plot the scores, we will see a very different graph.

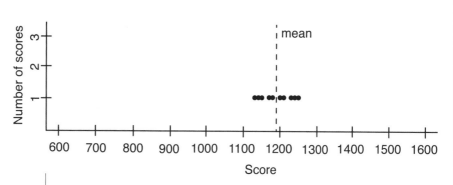

Though the *mean* is the same for both sets of data, the *standard deviation*, or distance between the mean and each score, is different. Now, there are ways to calculate the standard deviation, but our main concern for the SAT is to understand that for the first set of scores, the standard deviation is greater, or *spread wider* about the mean, while for the second set of scores, the standard deviation is less, or *grouped closer* to the mean.

Population Parameters, Margin of Error, and Valid Conclusions

A smaller number of SAT questions are going to wade into slightly murkier statistical waters. If you have not taken a statistics class, then you are about to learn some new terms. But don't worry, if you can grasp the basics, then you'll have no trouble with these SAT problems.

What do statisticians do? To put it as simply as possible: They look at groups of people (which they call **populations**), and record data about the stuff they do. For example, you could walk around your classroom, asking your fellow students how they scored on the SAT. Not only will this net you a bunch of new friends, but it will also get you a big ol' pile of data. * We could chart it like this:

And likely a couple of enemies. —Samantha

number of students	score range
2	800–1000
7	1000–1200
6	1200–1400
4	1400–1600

What's the story here? Two students scored between 800 and 1000, seven between 1000 and 1200, and so on. We can illustrate the table in this graph:

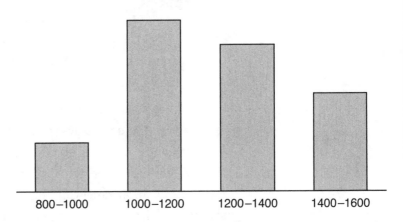

SAT SCORES IN OUR CLASS

800–1000	1000–1200	1200–1400	1400–1600

Looking at that graph, you might conclude that most kids scored between 1000 and 1200. But any statistician worth his Statistician Badge would take a look at that data and smirk. "This is terrible data, the group is too small, and it's not random. Those kids are all from the same neighborhood, in a similar socioeconomic class, have had the same level of education. If you want *real* data, you should pick 3,000 kids randomly from all across America." What that statistician just recommended, in stat-talk, is *enlarging the population parameter*. In general, a larger population parameter yields *more accurate* data.

Let's say we asked 3,000 American kids. Our table would look more like this:

number of students	score range
420	800–1000
1,057	1000–1200
1,072	1200–1400
458	1400–1600

Which we could graph like this:

SAT SCORES OF AMERICAN STUDENTS

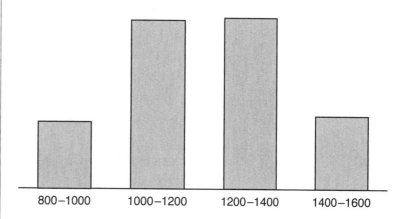

| 800–1000 | 1000–1200 | 1200–1400 | 1400–1600 |

What is important to a statistician is that the second bar graph is *better* than the first. It is better because it provides us with a more accurate depiction of reality, because we have taken into account a larger population. Another way to say this is that the second bar graph has a smaller **margin of error**. The SAT might test your understanding of this in the following way:

> A statistician is trying to determine the average time a high school swimmer can hold his breath underwater, so she asks 30 high school swimmers how many seconds they can hold their breath underwater. The mean (average) response is 55 seconds, with a margin of error of 10 seconds. Another statistician wants to replicate the study, but with a smaller margin of error. Which of the following would accomplish this:
>
> A) Ask 15 high school swimmers
> B) Ask 300 randomly selected people
> C) Ask 300 high school swimmers
> D) Ask 15 randomly selected people

Remember that a *larger* population size decreases our margin of error, so A and D are out. The initial study focused on high school swimmers, so answer choice B expands the population too widely. Our correct answer choice, then, is C.

The last tricky element of statistics is determining exactly which conclusions can and cannot be drawn from a set of data. Let's go back to the bar graph about American student test scores on the previous page. The SAT might throw this particularly devious question at you:

> Which of the following can best be inferred from the graph:
> A) It is easiest to achieve a score in the 1000–1400 range.
> B) Our education system does not prepare students adequately to achieve a score above 1400.
> C) Any student is most likely to score in the 1000–1400 range.
> D) Any student in America is most likely to score in the 1000–1400 range.

The problem with answer choice A is that the graph only records scores, not the ease with which those scores were attained. B might very well be true, but the graph itself does not explain *why* fewer students score above a 1400. The difference between C and D is that C refers to any student in the world, whereas D focuses on those in America. Remember that our data is all taken from American students, so D is the more valid conclusion.

Let's Review

Let's do some Problem Solving and Data Analysis questions.

1 The ratio of tattoos to nose rings in this room is 3 to 1. The number of nose rings is 12. How many tattoos are there in total?

Let's set it up.

a. $\dfrac{\text{tattoos}}{\text{nose rings}} = \dfrac{3}{1}$

b. Number of nose rings = 12

c. Replace the words *nose rings* in the first step with the number 12: $\dfrac{\text{tattoos}}{12} = \dfrac{3}{1}$

Now, solve for tattoos. Tattoos = 36.

Why? Because $\dfrac{36}{12} = \dfrac{3}{1}$, right? Or 36:12 = 3:1.

2 In the chart that follows, cruller prices recorded from all over the world are arranged by cruller length, as well as the line of best fit. Which of the following can be said about the data?
A) A 7-inch cruller will cost $9.
B) A 7-inch cruller is likely to cost $9.
C) A 5-inch cruller will cost $9.
D) A 5-inch cruller is likely to cost $9.

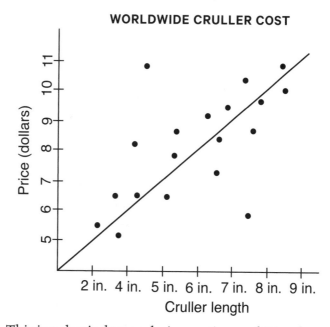

WORLDWIDE CRULLER COST

This is a classic data-analysis question, and it involves two steps. First, you need to be able to read the graph, then you need to determine whether the data is absolute or approximate. We can see from the answer choices that we are looking at the $9 mark. So go to $9 on the *y*-axis, then move to the right to see where it hits the line of best fit. It finds the line at approximately 7 inches on the *x*-axis. Now, will a 7-inch cruller *always* cost $9? No, this is the line of best fit; it is an approximation. Our answer is B.

	FRESHMAN	SOPHOMORE	JUNIOR	SENIOR	TOTAL
Spaghetti	6	4	3	2	15
Sushi	4	5	7	4	20
Salmon	8	5	4	3	20
Souvlaki	2	4	6	8	20
Total	20	18	20	17	75

3 A survey was given to a high school student body, in which they were asked to choose their favorite food that started with the letter *S* from a list of four options. They were allowed only one answer, and were mandated to answer. Which of the following is true?

A) Of juniors, 25% chose spaghetti.

B) Of the total number of freshmen, less than half chose salmon and souvlaki.

C) More than 30% of sophomores preferred salmon.

D) Juniors made up 10% more of the total number of students who chose souvlaki than sophomores.

Like the previous problem, this requires that we read some data, this time in the form of a chart rather than a scatterplot graph. We need to be careful that when we calculate percent, we are looking at the appropriate parts and totals. For answer choice A, 3 out of 20 juniors chose spaghetti, which is less than 25%. * For B, exactly half chose salmon or souvlaki, not less

They clearly haven't tried my roommate's mom's mom's mom's pasta recipe.

—Samantha

than half. For C, 5 out of 18 sophomores preferred salmon, which is a bit less than 30%. For D, juniors made up 30% of those who chose souvlaki, while sophomores made up 20%. D is our correct answer.

4 Mary's average annual salary for her first 6 years of work was $15,000. What raise should Mary request to bring her average up to $15,250 over a total of 8 years?

Notice that n for this problem is 8; the average is

$$15,250 = \frac{(6 \times 15,000 + 2 \times (15,000 + x))}{8}$$

$$15,250 = \frac{120,000 + 2x}{8}$$

$$1,000 = x$$

5 If Paul ate 300% more pizza than Manek ate, and Manek ate an entire pizza, then how many pizzas did Paul eat?

Paul ate *as many* pizzas as Manek *plus* 300%.

So Paul ate ONE pizza PLUS 300% of one.

So Paul ate FOUR PIZZAS! (Paul, you glutton.)

6 Suppose Samantha took the SAT 8 times and her combined scores each time were 1430, 1430, 1480, 1500, 1540, 1600, 1600, x. For which of the following values of x would the median be 1520?
A) 1510
B) 1520
C) 1530
D) 1550

We know that our list includes 8 values, so our median would be the average of the fourth and fifth values. Choices A, B, and C would all become the fifth value in the list and none will yield a median of 1520. Only choice D will become the sixth value, so that 1500 and 1540 will yield our desired median, 1520.

The SAT requires fast thinking in difficult situations. So here's a scenario—you have approximately three seconds to come up with the appropriate response:

A psychotic iguana with a bottle of dishwashing detergent is chasing you and gaining every second. The soft grass you're running on barefoot suddenly ends and you're faced with the option of treading on a minefield strewn with broken glass or walking across a river of flowing lava. Which do you choose?

Answer: Neither, of course! I'd much rather face an iguana (even a psychotic one with detergent) than deal with a minefield or hot lava. So remember, if you really don't like *any* of your choices, then "it cannot be determined from the information given" may be an option.

HEART OF ALGEBRA

WARNING: Serious spoilers ahead. **Do not read** if you want to be surprised by the problems in the Heart of Algebra section.

Okay, you've been warned. Here goes: Heart of Algebra problems are all about algebra. That's the surprise twist. Sorry for ruining it.

Algebra is all about equations, and the fundamental rule for equations is *do the same thing to both sides*. We don't care what *it* is, but do it to both sides. That keeps everything nice and equal. So if your friend is your enemy (friend = enemy), and you want to kill your enemy, you must kill your friend, too (kill your friend = kill your enemy). There. Nice and equal. Well, equal, anyway.

$$x + 36 = 40$$

If you want to solve for x, then do it like this. Subtract 36 from the left *and* subtract 36 from the right:

$$x + 36 - 36 = 40 - 36, \text{ which means that } x = 4$$

Now check it by substituting 4 for x in the original expression:

$$4 + 36 = 40$$
$$40 = 40 \quad \text{Bingo!}$$

Examples:

1. $12x = 24$

    Divide both sides by 12 to get $x = 2$.

2. $3x + 4 = 28$

    Subtract 4 from both sides to get $3x = 24$.
    Divide both sides by 3 to get $x = 8$.

3. Solve for fish:

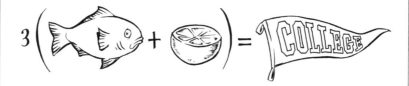

$$3 \text{ (fish + grapefruit) = college}$$

Divide both sides by 3:

$$\text{fish + grapefruit} = \frac{\text{college}}{3}$$

Subtract grapefruit from both sides:

$$\text{fish} = \frac{\text{college}}{3} - \text{grapefruit}$$

Number 3 was a moronic question, you might say to yourself. Yes. It was. But they ask similar questions on the SAT just to see if you know these rules. They might use x, y, and z more than they use fish and grapefruit, but it's the same basic idea.

4. $x - y = 17$

What is $y + 12$?

A) x

B) $x + 5$

C) $x - 5$

D) It cannot be determined from the information given.

Answer:

$$x - y = 17$$
$$x - y + y = 17 + y$$
$$x = y + 17$$
$$x - 5 = y + 17 - 5$$
$$x - 5 = y + 12$$

C is correct.

5. $x + 3 - y = 10$

Solve for x in terms of y.

A) $y + 7$

B) $y + 3$

C) $y - 7$

D) $13 - y$

Answer:

$$x + 3 - y = 10$$
$$x + 3 - y + y = 10 + y$$
$$x + 3 = 10 + y$$
$$x + 3 - 3 = 10 + y - 3$$
$$x = 7 + y$$

A is correct.

Inequalities

Inequalities work the same way as normal equations. Check it out:

$$5x > 40$$

$$\frac{5x}{5} > \frac{40}{5}$$

$$x > 8$$

But there is one crucial difference: When you multiply or divide by a negative, you must *flip the inequality sign.*

$$5 - 6x < 41$$

$$5 - 6x - 5 < 41 - 5$$

$$-6x < 36$$

$$\frac{-6x}{-6} < \frac{36}{-6}$$

$$x > -6$$

In that last step, we flipped the sign because we divided by a negative. There is also a chance that an SAT problem might ask you to chart an inequality on a number line. This is easier if you say the inequality out loud. For example, in the above problem, our answer was "x is greater than -6." So the number line would look like this:

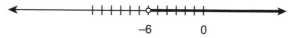

Why did we leave the circle open? Because x cannot *equal* -6. Let's try a tougher one. How about this:

$$x^2 \geq 16$$

Here, there are two possibilities:

$$x \geq 4 \text{ and } x \leq -4$$

Why are there two possibilities? Because $4^2 = 16$ and $(-4)^2 = 16$. Let's try graphing both on the number line.

This time, the circles are filled in because x can be greater than *or equal to* 4 and less than *or equal to* -4.

Systems of Equations

Sometimes the SAT will throw not one, but *two* equations at you. Most of the time, each equation will have *two* variables. We call this a **system of equations**, and this might seem, at first glance, like double the work. But the fact that there are two equations actually makes solving for one or both of the variables *easier*.

There are two methods for tackling this kind of problem. Sometimes the first method is easier, sometimes the second. You should know how to use both of them.

Say you're supposed to solve for x in this system:

$$2x + 3y = 6$$
$$5x + 8y = 11$$

FIRST METHOD: ELIMINATION

Keep them stacked up, then multiply or divide the equations to make the coefficients of either the x's or the y's equal. Sometimes they're equal when you start out. But this time we're not so lucky. Let's say we go with the x's. In order to make the coefficients equal, multiply the top equation by 5 and the bottom equation by 2.

$$5 \, (2x + 3y) = (6) \, 5$$
$$2 \, (5x + 8y) = (11) \, 2$$

You end up with:

$$10x + 15y = 30$$
$$10x + 16y = 22$$

Subtract the bottom equation from the top one:

$$10x + 15y = 30$$
$$- \, (10x + 16y = 22)$$
$$-y = 8$$
$$y = -8$$

Then take either equation and plug in –8 for y and solve for x:

$$2x + 3y = 6$$
$$2x + 3 \, (-8) = 6$$
$$x = 15$$

Pro Tip: If you are graphing these equations on a graphing calculator, their solution is the same as the point of intersection.

SECOND METHOD: SUBSTITUTION

Substitution is an easier method for solving a system of equations in cases when one of the variables isn't multiplied by a number. For example:

$$3x + 2y = 6$$
$$-2x + y = 10$$

Notice that the y in the second equation is all by itself. This is a big fat clue that substitution is the way to go. Start by focusing on that second equation. Isolate y in terms of x by adding $2x$ to both sides, giving you:

$$y = 2x + 10$$

Next, you want to *substitute* that expression for y into the first equation of the system. Then solve for x:

$$3x + 2(2x + 10) = 6$$
$$3x + 4x + 20 = 6$$
$$7x + 20 = 6$$
$$7x = -14$$
$$x = -2$$

Now that you know x, finding y is a breeze. Just plug your x back into the second equation. Then solve for y.

$$3(-2) + 2y = 6$$
$$-6 + 2y = 6$$
$$2y = 12$$
$$y = 6$$

The trick to which method to use depends on what kind of system you're dealing with. If each x and y in the system has a **coefficient** (that's the fancy name for a number that's multiplying a variable), you'll want to stick with elimination. If one of the variables is all alone, go with substitution.

Whether you use elimination or substitution, you still might not be able to solve x and y for both equations. For example, in the equations:

$$4y - 28 = 3x$$

$$y - \left(\frac{3}{4}\right)x = 6$$

No matter how you manipulate those equations, you will never find an x and y that satisfy both of them. What's going on here? Well, the answer might be clear if we convert both to slope-intercept form:

The first equation: $4y = 3x + 28$

$$y = \frac{3}{4}x + 7$$

The second equation: $y = \frac{3}{4}x + 6$

As you can see, those two equations form parallel lines with different y intercepts. Because they never intersect, there is no coordinate pair (x,y) that will satisfy both equations.

Similarly, you might get two equations in which the solution is *all* real numbers. Like so:

$$2y + 13x = 12$$
$$36 - 39x = 6y$$

Any pair of x,y coordinates that works for the first equation will work for the second. This is because the second equation is exactly the same as the first, just multiplied by 3 and with its terms shifted around to different sides of the equals sign. The SAT likes to play games like this, so be on the lookout.

Absolute Value

Absolute value problems also work very similarly to standard algebraic equations, with one key difference: They break into two equations. Here's what we mean.

Samantha's
Theorem*:
$$|-x| = |x| = x$$

*(Okay, this isn't really a theorem. But it is my proprietary Math Fact, and I will sue if you copy it.)

$$|5x + 6| = 66$$

$$5x + 6 = 66 \qquad 5x + 6 = -66$$

Why do we do this? Because whether the expression "$5x + 6$" comes out to 66 or –66, the absolute value sign is going to make it positive 66, so both would work. Now, we just solve both equations in the regular way.

$$5x + 6 = 66 \qquad\qquad 5x + 6 = -66$$
$$5x + 6 - 6 = 66 - 6 \qquad 5x + 6 - 6 = -66 - 6$$
$$5x = 60 \qquad\qquad 5x = -72$$
$$x = 12 \qquad\qquad x = \frac{-72}{5}$$

So the two possible values for x are 12 and –72 / 5.

Plugging In

When faced with complicated algebraic expressions, test takers can get confused or flustered. Although simple problems should be solved algebraically, more complicated problems can be solved in another way. Instead of working through the problem algebraically, consider **substituting numbers for variables**. Choose numbers that are easy to work with, such as 1, 2, or 10. Also try a negative number such as –1 or –2. Zero is useful, too.

Example:
Last year, a town had a population of 2,000 + x. If the population increased by 25 people this year, which of the following expressions represents this year's population?
A) 2,000 + 25x
B) 2,025 + x
C) 5,000 + 25x
D) 5,250 + x

While this can be solved using pure algebra, substituting the number 1 for x is an easy alternative. By doing this, the population was 2001 and then increased by 25, becoming 2,026. By substituting 1 for x in the answer choices, you find that B is correct.

More complicated example:

$$4^x + 4^x + 4^x + 4^x =$$

A) $4^{(x + 1)}$

B) $4^{(x + 2)}$

C) $4^{(x + 4)}$

D) $4^{(x^4)}$

This problem can be solved algebraically, by saying that $4^x + 4^x + 4^x + 4^x = 4 \times 4^x = 4^{(x + 1)}$. If, however, you get stuck or have a difficult time following this method, you can plug in a number for x instead. By saying that $x = 2$, $4^2 + 4^2 + 4^2 + 4^2 = 64 = 4^3$. Therefore, the answer is $4^{(x + 1)}$ or choice A.

Word Problems

One of the Evil Testing Serpent's favorite activities is to disguise algebra problems within word problems.

A phone company charges $4 for the first 3 minutes of an international call, then $.50 per minute thereafter. Which of the following represents the total charge, in dollars, for an international call lasting x minutes?

A) $x(4 + .5)$

B) $.5x + 4$

C) $4(x + 3) + .5$

D) $.5(x - 3) + 4$

There are two ways to do this problem, **translating** and **plugging in**. To translate, we try to convert the language of the problem into an equation. Here, we see that *after* the first three minutes, we start to multiply each minute by $.50. So $(x - 3) \times .50$ will find us the amount we are charged *after* those three minutes. To account for those first three minutes, we just add the four dollars ($+4$). So our final equation is $.5(x - 3) + 4$, or D.

For some people, this is a fine way to solve the problem.

Channel your inner seventh grader. Give in to the urge to plug-and-chug.
—Samantha

If you are one of those people, more power to you. But here at *Up Your Score*, we find it much easier (and less open to stupid errors) to plug in. * Let's say, for example, that our call is seven minutes. The first three minutes cost us $4, then there are four minutes left. If each costs $.50, then altogether that costs $2 more, for a total of $6. Which answer choice yields $6? Answer choice D!

Plugging in is an essential tool for algebraic word problems. Here's the rule of thumb: If you see variables in the answer choice, you should plug in. It will always work.

System of Equation Word Problems

Recently, the SAT has been unleashing word problems that translate into multiple equation problems. You are likely to see two or even three of these in the Math section. And while you totally *can* plug in, we find translating to be the easier strategy. Take a look:

> CanineCorp manufactures at least 75 RoboDogs per month. iLabs cost $350 to manufacture, while E-huahuas cost $200. In the current market, CanineCorp cannot afford to spend more than $25,000 in manufacturing in a single month. If CanineCorp must make at least 15 iLabs and at least 20 E-huahuas per month, which of the following systems of inequalities represents the conditions described, if x is the number of iLabs and y is the number of E-huahuas?
>
> A) $350y + 200x \geq 25{,}000$
> $x + y \leq 75$
> $x \geq 15$
> $y \geq 20$
>
> B) $350y + 200x \leq 25{,}000$
> $x + y \geq 75$
> $x \leq 15$
> $y \leq 20$

C) $350x + 200y \leq 25,000$

$x + y \geq 75$

$x \geq 15$

$y \geq 20$

D) $350x + 200y \geq 25,000$

$x + y \leq 75$

$x \leq 15$

$y \leq 20$

Sure, you can pick a number for x and a number for y, plugging-in style. But then you have to make sure that your x and y follow all those rules laid out in the problem. And that's a lot of rules! We find it much easier to take it rule by rule. Let's start with that first sentence: CanineCorp makes at least 75 RoboDogs. Look for the line of each answer choice that involves 75. We can see they all include "$x + y$," which means the total number of iLabs and E-huahuas. So if the rule says "at least," this means the sum of the iLabs and E-huahuas must be *greater than or equal to* 75. That means we can eliminate answers A and D.

Next, let's look at our remaining answers, B and C. They look very similar, except that answer choice B says that x is *less* than or equal to 15, and y is *less* than or equal to 20, while C says the opposite. Which is correct? Head back to the rules. Where do we see the numbers 15 and 20? "CanineCorp must make at least 15 iLabs and at least 20 E-huahuas." So if x is our number of iLabs, it must be *greater* than or equal to 15, and same goes for the E-huahuas. Our answer is C.

Bonus Algebra: Direct and Inverse Variation

You've done such a good job getting through this algebra section, we've decided to reward you with a smidge more algebra. The very last algebraic concepts are direct and inverse variation. Although you will see only one or possibly two problems involving these concepts, they are pretty simple once you see how they work.

When y is **directly proportional** to x, that means that an equation $y = kx$ can be written (where k is any constant number). For example, $y = 5x$ is a directly proportional equation. On the other hand, when y is **inversely proportional** to x, then the equation is $y = k/x$. The equation $y = 5/x$ is an inverse proportion.

x is inversely proportional to $\sqrt{y}$, and x is 12 when y is 25. What is y when x is 24?

$$\text{If } 12 = \frac{k}{\sqrt{25}} \text{, then } k = 60.$$

So when $x = 24$, our equation becomes $24 = \dfrac{60}{\sqrt{y}}$

$$\sqrt{y} = 2.5$$

y is approximately 6.25

PASSPORT TO ADVANCED MATH

"**A**ttention, ladies and gentlemen, your attention, please. Flight 204 to Advanced Math is now boarding. Please have your passports out and your bags open for inspection."

Okay, so where exactly is Advanced Math, and why do we need passports? Don't worry, Advanced Math just means more algebra. In this section, we will cover exponents, quadratic equations, and functions. If you were comfortable with the previous section, then you will be A-OK with this material as well.

Exponents

The rules for exponents are pretty simple. Know them like the back of your hand.

$$c^a \times c^b = c^{(a + b)}$$
$$c^a / c^b = c^{(a - b)}$$
$$(c^a)^b = c^{(a \times b)}$$
$$c^a \times d^a = (cd)^a$$

1 If the cube root of the square root of x is 3, what is x?

A) 27
B) 54
C) 243
D) 729

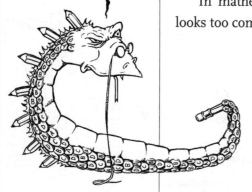

First of all, figure out what they're really asking you. If x is square-rooted and *then* cube-rooted, the answer is 3. What is x?

In mathematical terms, then, it's $3 = \sqrt[3]{\sqrt{x}}$. Because that looks too complicated, try to make it simpler:

$$3 = \sqrt[3]{\sqrt{x}}$$

$$3^3 = \left(\sqrt[3]{\sqrt{x}}\right)^3$$

$$27 = \sqrt{x}$$

$$27^2 = \left(\sqrt{x}\right)^2$$

$$729 = x$$

And D is the right answer.

2 If $3^{(x+1)} = 27^4$, what is x?

A) 9

B) 10

C) 11

D) 12

This question looks impossible because the bases (3 and 27) are different, so we can't apply our exponent rules. What we need to realize is that 27 can be rewritten as 3^3.

$$3^{x+1} = \left(3^3\right)^4$$

$$3^{x+1} = 3^{12}$$

$$x + 1 = 12$$

$$x = 11$$

So our answer is C.

NEGATIVE AND FRACTIONAL EXPONENTS

$x^{-1}, y^{1/2}, z^{-2/3}$

Are you trembling in mortal terror? Don't. Negative and fractional exponents look annoyingly complicated, but they're not. *

To make sense of a negative exponent, simply rewrite the

Annoying? Maybe. Complicated? No way.
—Samantha

number as a fraction with 1 on top, and flip the sign of the exponent. Like so:

$$3^{-2} = \frac{1}{(3^2)}$$

Example: $2x^{-2} = ?$

You should immediately flip it upside down:

$$2x^{-2} = 2 \times \left(\frac{1}{(x^2)}\right) = \frac{2}{(x^2)}$$

Fractional exponents are even easier. Just remember this:

$$x^{p/q} = \sqrt[q]{x^p}$$

AN ENLIGHTENING CARROT DIAGRAM

you need

Power (to pull)

Root (the carrot)   ground = fraction line

So remember, a fractional exponent is just $\dfrac{\text{Power}}{\text{Root}}$.

Example 2: $4^{2/3} = ?$

First, you should raise x to the p power, and then take the q root:

$$4^{2/3} = \sqrt[3]{4^2} = \sqrt[3]{16} = 2.520$$

Also, if you ever see a question that asks you what 1,293,254 to the 0th power is, you can punch it into your calculator, or you can just remember that *anything (that's not zero) to the 0th power is equal to 1*. Even if it's $1,293,254^0$. It's just 1.

RADICAL EQUATIONS

Radical equations are not, unfortunately, equations with extreme political views; they are just equations that use the root sign. When you see something like $\sqrt{x}$, all you have to remember is one thing: Isolate the enemy. Get the radical by itself. The rest is a piece of cake.

Push radicals to the margins to make things easier. That's what the U.S. government attempted to do in the 1960s.

—Samantha

Example: If $\frac{1}{2}\sqrt{x} - 4 = 2$, then what is x?

The first thing you do in a problem like this is to get all the constants on one side. So let's add 4 to both sides:

$$\frac{1}{2}\sqrt{x} - 4 + 4 = 2 + 4$$

$$\frac{1}{2}\sqrt{x} = 6$$

Then, in order to get the radical by itself, you have to divide both sides by (½) or multiply both sides by 2.

$$2\left(\frac{1}{2}\sqrt{x}\right) = (6)\,2$$

$$\sqrt{x} = 12$$

In this case, since x is square-rooted, all we have to do is square both sides to see that x is 144.

Quadratic Equations

Now that we know how exponents work, we can talk about quadratic expressions, which are just algebraic expressions where some component is squared. The big celebrity quadratic equation is $ax^2 + bx + c = 0$. Recognize it from math class? If not, no worries, we will explain it after this important message about factoring.

FACTORING

When you see a quadratic expression in a problem, it's quite likely that in order to find the solution, you will need to *factor*, or break down, the quadratic before you can solve it. Factoring can be an intimidating process. But by asking these five questions, you can make your life much easier.

1. Is there anything in common?

Example: In $3x^2 + 6x$, there's a $3x$ that both terms have in common.

$$3x^2 + 6x = 3x\,(x + 2)$$

2. Is there a difference of two squares?

If both terms are perfect squares, the expression is factorable. Example:

$$x^2 - 36 = x^2 - 6^2 = (x - 6)\,(x + 6)$$

In other words, you can factor 3x out of both terms.
—Samantha

3. Is this a trinomial?

Sometimes, an expression with three terms can be factored into two expressions with two terms each. (We will explain this further below.)

Example:

$$x^2 - x - 12 = (x + 3)(x - 4)$$

4. Is the expression a sum or difference of two cubes?

If both terms are cubes, you can factor them based on these formulas:

$$x^3 + y^3 = (x + y)(x^2 - xy + y^2)$$
$$x^3 - y^3 = (x - y)(x^2 + xy + y^2)$$

Example:

$$8 - y^3 = 2^3 - y^3 = (2 - y)(4 + 2y + y^2)$$

5. Can I group this?

Grouping means to rearrange the terms so that a common factor can be pulled out.

Example:

$$3x^2 + 6x + 5xy + 10y = 3x(x + 2) + 5y(x + 2) = (3x + 5y)(x + 2)$$

SOLVING A QUADRATIC EQUATION

With the power of factoring, you can solve *most* quadratic equations you will encounter. Factoring involves breaking up the quadratic expression (usually the left side of the equation) down from a trinomial—which has the form $ax^2 + bx + c$—into a product of two binomials—which has the form $(dx + f)(gx + h)$. To do this, we're going to use the coefficients of the trinomial (the a, b, and c numbers), as well as the grouping method we covered in the previous section. We're also going to employ the wise, age-old, foolproof system of . . . trial and error.

Here's a sample quadratic equation: $2x^2 - x - 6 = 0$. To the left of the equals sign, we have our happy little trinomial expression (the "$2x^2 - x - 6$" part), and we can recognize that it has the form $ax^2 + bx + c$. First, we are going to need to extract the three coefficients a, b, and c. In this case, $a = 2$, $b = -1$, and $c = -6$.

The game we have to play now is to find two numbers that *multiply* up to the quantity $a \times c$, but also *add* up to the b in the trinomial. So in this case because $a \times c = -12$, we need two numbers that multiply to -12, but also add to -1. Let's try making a list of all the factor pairs of -12 and checking their sums.

-1×12	$-1 + 12 = 11$	(no good)
-2×6	$-2 + 6 = 4$	(no good)
-3×4	$-3 + 4 = 1$	(no good)
-4×3	$-4 + 3 = -1$	(success!)
-6×2	$-6 + 2 = -4$	(no good)
-12×1	$-12 + 1 = -11$	(no good)

So the important numbers we want to save from this whole experience are: -4 and 3. Here's how we'll use those numbers to factor. Let's go back to our trinomial:

$$2x^2 - x - 6$$

We're going to take the middle term (the $-x$) and rewrite it as the sum of two like terms, using the two numbers we just found (-4 and 3). Since that $-x$ can be represented by $-4x + 3x$, we can rewrite the original trinomial as a *four* term expression:

$$2x^2 - 4x + 3x - 6$$

Now we're going to group it by factoring out the greatest common factor of the first two terms and the greatest common factor of the last two terms:

$$2x(x - 2) + 3(x - 2)$$

For the pièce de résistance (pee-ess-duh-ray-zis-tonse) we're going to factor out the common factor in both of these new terms, the $(x - 2)$, giving us:

$$(2x + 3)(x - 2)$$

Voilà, our factored form! To check our work, we can FOIL these two binomials. You multiply the **F**irst terms of each

Factoring is best mastered by practice. Go ask your old algebra teacher for some practice worksheets— you'll gain insane math skills AND crazy admiration from your prof.
—Samantha

binomial together, then multiply the **Outside** terms, then the **Inside** terms, and finally the **Last** terms.

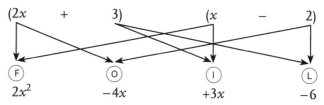

You can see for yourself that when we combine the like terms $-4x$ and $3x$, we get $2x^2 - x - 6$, which is, miracle of miracles, our original trinomial. So we did indeed find the right binomials.

$$(2x + 3)\ (x - 2)$$

Now to solve the whole equation, set each of these two binomial factors equal to zero. Why? Because if the product of two factors is zero, then one of those factors *has* to be zero. Don't believe us? Go ahead, think of two non-zero numbers that multiply to zero. It ain't happening!

So we have:

$$(2x + 3) = 0 \text{ and } (x - 2) = 0$$

Now solve each equation for x. You should come up with two solutions: x can be either $-3/2$ or 2.

Pro Tip: A particularly difficult math problem might ask for *zeroes* of a polynomial. This just means that you need to set the expression equal to zero, then solve for x. For the expression on the previous page ($2x^2 - x - 6$), the question might be "What are the zeroes of the equation $2x^2 - x - 6 = 0$?" To solve it, just set the expression equal to zero ($2x^2 - x - 6 = 0$) and factor it (using the method above) to find that $x = -3/2$ or 2. So our *zeroes* are $-3/2$ and 2. (It's just a mathier way of saying "solve for x.")

All this might have taken you a minute. It might have taken you 20. But don't worry about it—the more problems you do, the better you get at seeing the answer without having to do many calculations.

Not all trinomials can be factored like this, but more on that coming up.

Sorry if this diagram hurts your brain.
Just track the arrows as they go through the letters FOIL and it should make more sense.
—Samantha

Let's try a problem:

> The sum of the two roots of a quadratic equation is 5 and their product is –6. Which of the following could be the equation?
> A) $x^2 - 6x + 5 = 0$
> B) $x^2 - 5x - 6 = 0$
> C) $x^2 - 5x + 6 = 0$
> D) $x^2 + 5x - 6 = 0$

First of all, since the product is negative and the sum is positive, you know that one of the numbers is negative and the other is positive. Start with the product (there are fewer possibilities)—how many pairs of numbers would have a product of –6? The answer: –1 and 6, –6 and 1, –3 and 2, –2 and 3. Then look at the sum. Out of all these pairs, which one has a sum of 5? The pair –1 and 6 satisfies both conditions, so –1 and 6 are the roots.

Next, put those roots down as the answers to a quadratic equation—$(x + 1)(x - 6) = 0$. Then FOIL this out, and you'll get the answer: B.

Pro Tip: In any quadratic equation $ax^2 + bx + c = 0$, the sum of the two roots is equal to $-(b/a)$ and the product of the two roots is equal to (c/a). Try it, it works!

QUADRATIC FORMULA

Sooner or later, you'll try to solve a quadratic equation that looks something like this: $5x^2 - 3x - 4 = 0$. Sometime after the thirtieth try, you'll realize that it doesn't factor nicely. That's where the quadratic formula comes in.

With a trinomial in the form $ax^2 + bx + c = 0$, the two roots are:

$$x = \frac{-b \pm \sqrt{b^2 - 4ac}}{2a}$$

(If you need to convince yourself, try this using a trinomial that you know factors nicely.)

Now back to the more difficult equation:

Solve for x if $5x^2 - 3x - 4 = 0$

Remember: Zero times anything equals zero. Therefore, if either factor equals zero, the whole expression must also be equal to zero.

—Samantha

In this trinomial, $a = 5$, $b = -3$, and $c = -4$.

Plug these into the formula.

$$x = \frac{3 \pm \sqrt{9 - 4(5)(-4)}}{2(5)} = \frac{3 \pm \sqrt{89}}{10}$$

So the two factors are

$$\frac{3 - \sqrt{89}}{10} \text{ and } \frac{3 + \sqrt{89}}{10}$$

The great thing about the quadratic formula is that it will always give you some kind of solution for x, whereas the binomial factoring method doesn't always work out (sometimes the product of $a \times c$ doesn't factor into two numbers that add up to b). Although the quadratic formula is harder to remember, if you practice it enough times, it's the safer choice. Just be extra careful with your signs when evaluating the $b^2 - 4ac$ part (the part under the square root). Our private research indicates that this is the source of 87.42% of all quadratic formula fails.

Functions

A function is just like any other algebraic expression, except we record the input and the output, so that we can *graph* it on a coordinate plane.

$$f(x) = x + 7$$

All this means is that whatever number (x) we input, we add 7 to find our output. It's helpful to make a chart, using x as our input and y as our output, like this:

x	y
-2	5
-1	6
0	7
1	8
2	9
3	10

As you can see, any number (x) that goes in comes out with 7 added onto it. We call all the numbers that can be entered into the function the **domain**, and all the outputs are called the **range**. Annoyingly, mathematicians can also write the same table, substituting "$f(x)$" for "y." The SAT might express it either way.

x	$f(x)$
-2	5
-1	6
0	7
1	8
2	9
3	10

We're going to talk about more ways to use those charts in a bit, but for now, let's create a more complex function.

$$f(x) = 3x - 5$$

Pick a random number—let's say 3. So what is $f(3)$? Simple, replace the x with a 3, and we get $3(3) - 5$, or 4. So far, so good. But a trickier SAT question might ask for $f(4c + 2)$. In this case, we have to replace x not with a number, but with an algebraic expression, like this:

$$3(4c + 2) - 5$$
$$12c + 6 - 5$$
$$12c + 1$$

As if that wasn't fun enough, we can also **combine functions**.

$$g(x) = \left(\frac{x}{2}\right)^2$$

$$f(x) = 3x - 4$$

What is $f(g(6))$?

The trick is to first run 6 through the inside function g, then run *that answer* through the outside function f.

$$g(6) = \left(\frac{6}{2}\right)^2 = 9$$

$$f(9) = 3(9) - 4 = 23$$

Surely that's all the frim-frammery that the SAT can pull with functions, right? Oh no, my friend, there is one last bit of frim-fram. We can also put a *function within an expression*.

$f(x)=y$.
If you don't remember this, then you will be immediately disowned by your family, friends, and society.
—Samantha

Remember:
$f(x)=y$. y is a variable. Use substitution.
—Samantha

If $f(x) = \left(\dfrac{x}{4}\right) + 7$, what is $2f(x) + 9$?

For these problems, we need to replace the "$f(x)$" symbol with its equation. It should now read $2\left(\left(\dfrac{x}{4}\right) + 7\right) + 9$.

$$\left(\frac{x}{2}\right) + 14 + 9 = \left(\frac{x}{2}\right) + 23$$

Sorry! We forgot one last type of function question.

Example 2: The function f, where $f(x) = (1 + x)^2$, is defined for $-2 \leq x \leq 2$. What is the range of f?

A) $0 \leq f(x) \leq 4$
B) $0 \leq f(x) \leq 9$
C) $1 \leq f(x) \leq 4$
D) $1 \leq f(x) \leq 9$

Since f is defined only for $-2 \leq x \leq 2$, that is the domain of the function. To get the range, the best bet is to plug in all the integers between -2 and 2. You won't always have to plug in *all* the numbers, but if it's a small set (and it probably will be) it will be worth your time. No matter what the size of the set, it's usually a good idea to check the end points and the values of x that yield a zero.

x	$f(x)$
-2	1
-1	0
0	1
1	4
2	9

Clearly, the lowest number is 0, and the highest is 9. So B is the right answer. Notice that if you had plugged in only -2 and 2, you would have incorrectly gotten D as the answer instead.

GRAPHING FUNCTIONS

Still with us? Good, because now we get to use those charts. The best thing about functions is that we can graph them and *see* them on the page.

Let's make a table for a new function:

$f(x) = 2x + 5$

x	y
−3	−1
−2	1
−1	3
0	5
1	7
2	9
3	11

A collection of (x,y) coordinate pairs is called a **relation**, and if we plot each pair on the standard xy-plane, and draw a line to connect the dots, then we'll get something like this:

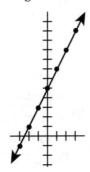

The Evil Testing Serpent likes to test your ability to move back and forth between a function and its graph. Like so:

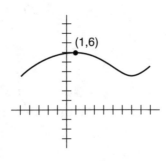

(1,6)

The graph of $f(x)$ is shown above. If $f(z) = 6$, what is $\frac{2z}{3}$?

What we need to understand, looking at the graph, is that if $f(z) = 6$, that means that our *output*, or y, is equal to 6. Can

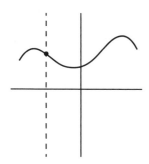

Passes the vertical line test! It's a function!

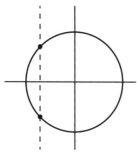

Fails the vertical line test! Not a function!

we tell which input (x) corresponds to the output (y) of 6? Sure, it's the only x point we're told: 1. So $\frac{2(1)}{3} = 2/3$.

Notice how each x-coordinate has only one corresponding y-coordinate. This fact makes our relation a function. A relation is only properly called a function if each x has *only one y* value. On the other hand, when a y value corresponds to more than one x value (such as a horizontal line), the relation is still a function. Confused? Think of it this way: In math class, each student (x) has only one score (y), but the same score (y) can be achieved by many different students (x). It is far easier to tell if a relation is also a function by looking at its graph. If you can draw a vertical line through any part of the graph, and it only touches one point, then it is a function. If your vertical line touches at more than one point (think of a circle) then it is not a function.

SPECIAL FUNCTIONS

We are going to talk about the graphs of particular equations in the Coordinate Geometry section in a few pages, but you should be able to recognize a few special functions.

FUNCTION	LOOKS LIKE	NOTATION	EXPLANATION
Linear	Line	$f(x) = mx + b$	m is the slope, b is the y-intercept.
Constant	Horizontal line	$f(x) = k$	The y value is always equal to k.
Absolute value	V shape with point at (0,0)	$f(x) = |x|$	Makes all negative values of x positive, but positive values stay positive.
Quadratic	Parabola	$f(x) = ax^2 + bx + c$	
Polynomial	Could be lots of things	$f(x) = ax^n + bx^{n-1} + \ldots z$	

POLYNOMIAL DIVISION

Another type of problem you might run into involves "dividing polynomials." If you consult the table above, you can see that a polynomial is any expression made up of unlike terms of variable factors (terms are products that are separated by a + or −). For example, here's a polynomial: $2x^2 - 5x - 1$. Three unlike terms, separated by addition or subtraction. The SAT might ask you what would result if you divided that $2x^2 - 5x - 1$ by a simpler polynomial, something like $x - 3$. They'll write it like this:

$$\frac{2x^2 - 5x - 1}{x - 3}$$

The Serpent expects you to know how to simplify this ratio using something called "polynomial long division." Polynomial long division is a lot like regular long division with numbers, but instead of dividing the digits into each other, you divide the terms into each other. First write it out in long division form, like this:

$$x - 3 \overline{)2x^2 - 5x - 1}$$

Now, much like you might do if we were working with the digits of numbers (instead of the terms of polynomials), you're going to divide the first term of the *divisor polynomial* (the $x - 3$) into the first term of the *dividend polynomial* (the $2x^2 - 5x - 1$), and write the result on top. How many times does x go into $2x^2$? If you divide $2x^2/x$ you get $2x$. So write that on top. Then multiply each term of the divisor again by that quotient term, and write the result *below*. Now you should have:

$$\begin{array}{r} 2x \\ x - 3 \overline{)2x^2 - 5x - 1} \\ 2x^2 - 6x \end{array}$$

Next, you're going to *subtract* the $2x^2 - 6x$ part from the polynomial above. Remember that you're subtracting the *whole expression* so you'll have to distribute the negative sign to both terms. $-(2x^2 - 6x) = -2x + 6x$. Then draw another line and

Remember that you're subtracting NEGATIVE 6x from the trinomial, so you are really adding 6x.
—Samantha

combine terms. The $2x^2$ and the $-2x^2$ will cancel, leaving just an x. Bring down the last term of the polynomial, the -1, and put it next to the x. That gives us:

$$\begin{array}{r} 2x \\ x-3\overline{)2x^2-5x-1} \\ \underline{-2x^2-6x} \\ x-1 \end{array}$$

From here, you repeat the whole process, but divide your $x - 3$ into whatever's below the line, instead of the initial dividend. So now you're going to divide $x - 3$ into $x - 1$. $x/x = +1$, so put that up top next to your quotient $2x$, making a quotient of $2x + 1$. Multiply the 1 back into $x - 3$ and subtract, giving you:

$$\begin{array}{r} 2x+1 \\ x-3\overline{)2x^2-5x-1} \\ \underline{-2x^2-6x} \\ x-1 \\ \underline{-x+3} \\ 2 \end{array}$$

Now at this point, all you have left is just a measly little 2. You might think: "How can I divide $x + 3$ into 2? x doesn't go into 2 at all because it's just a constant!" But not to fear—you don't really have to figure out the division. In polynomial division, this is the *remainder*. This is exactly the same situation at the end of long division with numbers—like if you tried to divide the number 5 into 8 and had 3 left over. You can't divide 5 into 3, so you write the quotient as a fraction with the remainder in the numerator and the divisor in the denominator, giving you $1\frac{3}{5}$. You're going to do exactly the same thing with your polynomial! Take the remainder and put it over the divisor, like this: $\frac{2}{x-3}$. This will be the extra little piece you stick at the end of your quotient polynomial to give the full quotient and remainder:

$$\frac{2x^2-5x-1}{x-3} = 2x+1+\frac{2}{x-3}$$

Because there is a remainder, we know that $(x-3)$ is not a factor of $(2x^2-5x-1)$.
—Samantha

That's the process for polynomial long division. This is a tricky topic and will take some practice to master, particularly if you're not already a whiz at long division with numbers. But it's important to learn because it is likely to appear on the test in some form.

TRANSFORMATIONS

Finally, the SAT might ask you questions about how altering a function affects its graph. Here are a few basic transformations that you will want to know:

We'll take as our basic function $y = x^3$.

$y = x^3 + 5$ Graph is shifted *up* five units

$y = x^3 - 5$ Graph is shifted *down* five units

$y = (x + 5)^3$ Graph is shifted *left* five units

$y = (x - 5)^3$ Graph is shifted *right* five units

$y = (2x)^3$ Graph is pinched horizontally

$y = (\frac{1}{2}x)^3$ Graph is stretched horizontally

$y = 2x^3$ Graph is stretched vertically

$y = \frac{1}{2}x^3$ Graph is pinched vertically

$y = (-x)^3$ Graph is reflected over the *y*-axis

$y = -x^3$ Graph is reflected over the *x*-axis

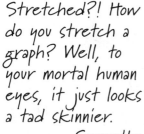

Stretched?! How do you stretch a graph? Well, to your mortal human eyes, it just looks a tad skinnier.
—Samantha

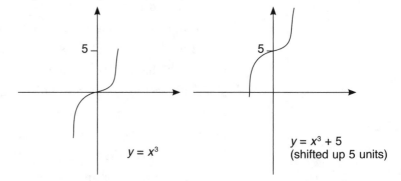

$y = x^3$

$y = x^3 + 5$
(shifted up 5 units)

ADDITIONAL TOPICS

Congratulations! You've reached the last content area for the Math Test. And we've saved the best for last! You've finally reached the (drumrollllllllllll) *Additional Topics*! Did you know that famed physicist Albert Einstein cut his teeth studying *Additional Topics*? Or that the ancient Greek philosopher Anaxagoras was the first to discover *Additional Topics*?

Okay, so maybe this section doesn't have the most exciting name. As you might have guessed, this is a catchall category for "other math stuff the SAT wants to test." Primarily, this means Geometry, and we'll start there. Then we'll talk about Coordinate Geometry, and finally go into the truly random leftovers like complex numbers and trigonometry. Let's dig in!

Geometry Vocabulary

First off, familiarize yourself with the following symbols, definitions, laws, and formulas.

Symbols: ∥ means "is parallel to." $l_1 \parallel l_2$ means line 1 is parallel to line 2.

⊥ means "is perpendicular to." $l_1 \perp l_2$

Congruent angles have equal numbers of degrees. (They fit perfectly over each other.)

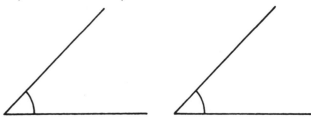

Complementary angles add up to 90 degrees. (If they look complementary, and it doesn't say "not drawn to scale," they probably are complementary. Don't bother proving it to yourself if you're pressed for time.)

Supplementary angles add up to 180 degrees. (Again, if they look supplementary, they probably are.)

Parallel lines cut by another line: These things are full of congruent and supplementary angles. You could try to memorize which pairs of angles are congruent and which pairs are supplementary, but why bother? The ones that look supplementary are supplementary, and the ones that look congruent are

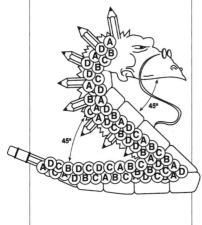

congruent. In some problems, you may need to extend the lines for it to look like this:

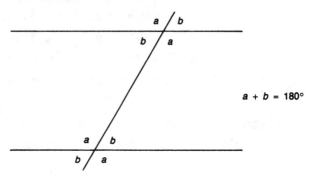

$a + b = 180°$

Parallelogram: Opposite sides are parallel. Parallelograms have two pairs of *equal* (or *congruent*) angles and four pairs of *supplementary* angles. In the diagram, the ones that look equal are equal and the ones that look supplementary are supplementary.

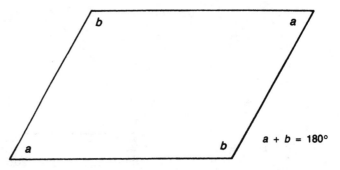

$a + b = 180°$

Triangles: Triangles are three-sided shapes whose interior angles add up to 180 degrees. One very, very heavily tested rule about triangles is the **third side rule**. This states that the length of any side of a triangle has to be less than the sum of the other two side lengths and greater than the difference of the other two sides. Looking at the diagram to the left, which of the following is a possible length of side *x*?

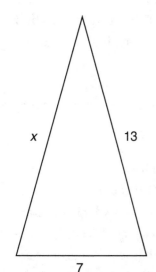

A) 19

B) 20

C) 21

D) 22

The sum of the other two sides is 20, their difference is 6, so $6 < x < 20$. The only answer choice that works, then, is A.

But most triangle questions will deal with one of two concepts: similar triangles and right triangles.

Similar triangles: Though there have been no new developments in similar triangles for more than 2,000 years, they're still in fashion with the SAT. So don your toga and get psyched for the bacchanalian triangle party!

What are similar triangles? Similar triangles are two or more triangles with congruent angles and proportional sides. Here, for example, are two similar triangles:

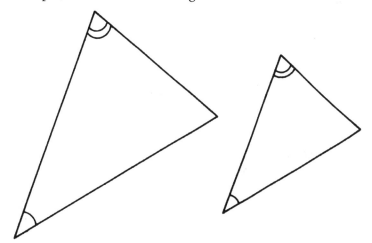

Continuing along this line of thought, here are two similar fish:

Same shape, different sizes.

The technical way to think about similar triangles is that

Don't ever change, similar triangles. We love you just the way you are.
—Samantha

We have different values and our own unique personalities, thank you very much.
—Fish #1

the two triangles have three angles of corresponding measurements. And if you think about it, knowing that *two* of the three angles are the same is enough to ensure that all *three* are the same, since the angles of a triangle always add up to 180 degrees.

So, to jump right in here, what is the measure of angle *x* if A and B are similar triangles?

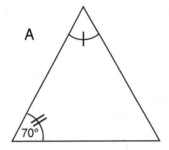
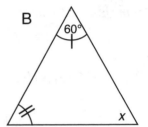

Answer: $x = 50°$. Why? Because both triangles have a 70° angle and a 60° angle. The last angle must be 50° in order to add up to 180°.

*Don't know what those lines over AB and CD are? See page 287.

Here's another one: If $\overline{AB} \parallel \overline{CD}$, then what is θ?*

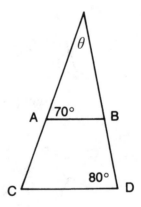

Answer: 30°. The key here is that the triangle includes parallel lines. Remember the congruent angles involved with parallel lines? Sure you do. So think of them when looking at the picture: Angle *B* must be the same as angle *D*, namely 80°. Which brings us to:

Similar Triangle Rule: The top triangle is similar to the big triangle if their bases are parallel.

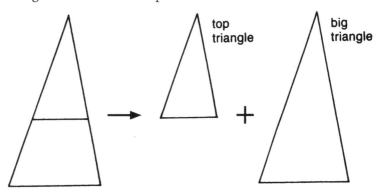

Got it? So if you see a triangle intersected by a line parallel to its base, the new, smaller triangle is similar to the larger.

Side c is the hypotenuse— the longest side and the one not adjacent to the right angle.

—Samantha

Right Triangles: A right triangle is any triangle with one angle that is 90° (indicated by a square in the corner). If you see a right triangle in an SAT problem, there is an 83.72% chance that you will need to use the Pythagorean Theorem to solve that problem. The PT for right triangles is: $a^2 + b^2 = c^2$.

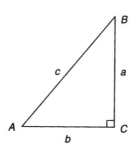

Simple, right? Well, the SAT will often *hide* their right triangles in an innocent-looking word problem.

A window washer leans his ladder against the wall of a building. If the wall is perpendicular to the ground, and the base of the ladder is 5 feet from the wall, and the ladder is 13 feet long, at what height will the top of the ladder touch the wall?

A) 10 feet

B) 11 feet

C) 12 feet

D) 13 feet

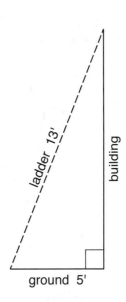

ground 5'

Since the ground and the building must be perpendicular (hopefully), the ladder must be the hypotenuse.
—Samantha

You'll save a lot of effort if you memorize these very common right triangles, also known as Pythagorean triplets:
3, 4, 5
5, 12, 13
8, 15, 17

The first step is to draw a picture.

Now do you see the right triangle? Let's plug in our numbers to the Pythagorean Theorem.

$$5^2 + b^2 = 13^2$$
$$25 + b^2 = 169$$
$$b^2 = 144$$
$$b = 12$$

So C is our answer.

You should also know two special kinds of right triangles. These are given to you in the reference section at the top of the Math section. But it will make your life easier to be able to recognize them. The first is the 30°-60°-90° triangle, whose sides are always in the ratio $1 : \sqrt{3} : 2$.

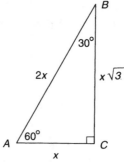

In the 45°-45°-90° triangle, the ratio is $1 : 1 : \sqrt{2}$

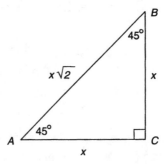

Circles: A circle is a . . . well, you know what a circle is. What you need to remember about the circle for the SAT is that the *radius* is the distance from the center of a circle to any point on its *circumference* (or perimeter of the circle). The *diameter* is twice the radius and connects a point on the edge to its opposite point through the center. This is not to be confused with a *chord*, which just connects any two points on the circumference.

Here are some formulas for the components of a circle:

area = $\pi \times r^2$ (*r* is radius)

circumference = $2 \times \pi \times r$

arc = measure of central angle

arc also = $2 \times$ measure of inscribed angle

Wait, what the hell is all this *arc* stuff? Let us show you:

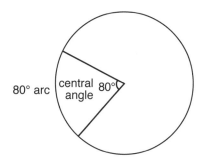

If the central angle = 80°, then the arc would also equal 80°.

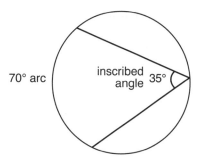

As you can see, the inscribed angle is an angle made by drawing two lines from a point on a circle's circumference. The degree of the arc is always 2 times that of the angle, so if the angle is 35°, the arc is 70°.

Radians: Angles are usually measured in degrees (with 360 degrees in a full circle). However, the SAT will sometimes ask

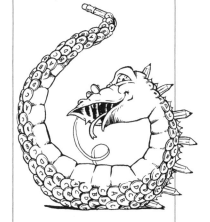

I actually didn't know this. You truly learn something new every day.

—Samantha

you to calculate angles in terms of **radians**. A **radian** is an arc or angle measure equal to one radius length. Because the circumference of a circle is always proportional to its radius, there are always 2π radians in every circle. So 360 degrees = 2π radians. To convert from degrees to radians just multiply by $^\pi/_{180}$. To convert from radians to degrees, just multiply by $^{180}/_\pi$. For example, a 30 degree angle is the same as $(^\pi/_{180}) \times 30 = {^\pi/_6}$ radians.

> **Area:** Area is the region inside a two-dimensional shape.
> *Circle*: area = $\pi \times r^2$
> *Rectangle*: area = length (l) × width (w)
> *Triangle*: area = (½) × base (b) × height (h). The (½) comes in because the triangle is ½ as large as a rectangle with the same base and height.

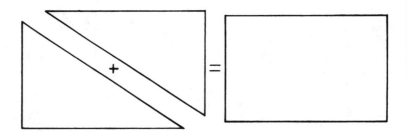

Parallelogram: area = $b \times h$, but the height is *not* one of the sides (unless the parallelogram is also a rectangle).

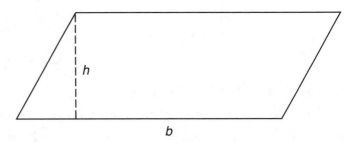

Often, the SAT will require that you find h before you can calculate the area.

Trapezoid: Because a trapezoid has parallel bases of two different sizes, the area is (the average of the two bases) × height.

Imagine chopping the parallelogram along the dotted line and then attaching your newly chopped triangle to the other side. Ta-da, you'd have a rectangle— which is a much easier shape for calculating area.
—Samantha

If you're curious about why these formulas work, ask a math teacher or look up a YouTube video on the subject. But for the SAT, all you have to do is memorize them.

—Samantha

So in this trapezoid:

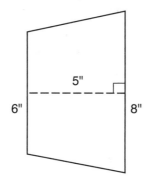

We first take the average of our parallel bases: $\dfrac{(6 + 8)}{2} = 7$, and multiply this by our height, 5, to get our area: 35 in².

Volume: In general, volume is an area times a height.

Rectangular solid: volume = length × width × height

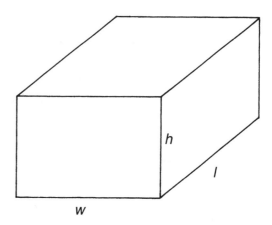

Cylinder: volume = π × r² × height

Sphere: volume = (⁴/₃) × π × r³

Cone: volume = ⅓ × π × r² × height

Pyramid: volume = ⅓ × length × width × height

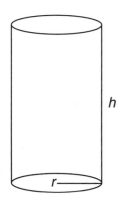

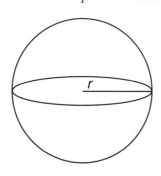

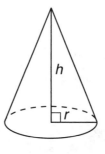

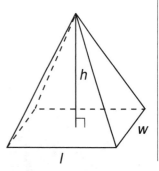

Surface Area, or the amount of area on the surface of a solid, is often seen as lots of little areas added up.

Rectangular solid: surface area = $(2 \times l \times w) + (2 \times h \times w) + (2 \times h \times l)$. Why? Because there are three different pairs of faces.

Cylinder: surface area = $(2 \times \pi \times r^2) + (2 \times \pi \times r \times h)$. The $2 \times \pi \times r^2$ are the two bases (circles), and the $2 \times \pi \times r \times h$ is the rectangle you get if you unroll the side.

Sphere: surface area = $(4 \times \pi \times r^2)$

Important Note: Many of these geometrical formulas are actually printed in the SAT exam instructions. So if you draw a blank, scan the instructions for the formula you need.

We can use these formulas to solve the following questions.

1 Jennifer wants to build a fence (God knows why people are always building fences in questions like these) to enclose a circle with an area of $144 \times \pi$. How much fencing will she need? (Draw a picture. It usually helps.)

Amount of fence = circumference

Circumference = $2 \times \pi \times r$

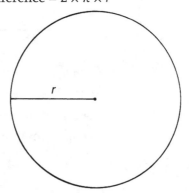

Well, we can't solve it without knowing the radius. So find the radius from the known area ($144 \times \pi$).

$$144 \times \pi = \pi \times r^2$$

$$r^2 = 144$$

$$r = 12$$

Answer: Jennifer needs $2 \times \pi \times r = 2 \times \pi \times 12 = 24\pi = 75.4$ units of fence. She also needs to get a life!

2 What is the measure of angle x if l and m are parallel?

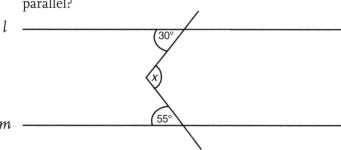

Remember those parallel lines cut by another line? The ones that are full of congruent and supplementary angles? Draw a third parallel line right through the middle of angle x and fill in the angles you know.

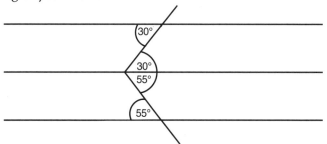

Voilà! The answer: $30° + 55° = 85° = x$.

3 What is the measure of angle x? (A Star Trek cosplayer needs to know.)

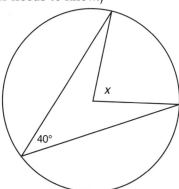

The 40° angle is *inscribed,* so the arc shown is 80°, as is, therefore, central angle *x*.

Answer: 80°

4 Given this parallelgram, what is the measure of angle *x*?

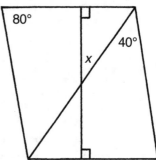

Break down the figure into the following components to find *x*.

First:

The angles in the following figure are supplementary, therefore: $y = 100°$.

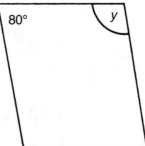

Second:

$z + 40° = y = 100°$

$z = 60°$

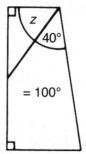

Finally:

$x + 60° + 90° = 180°$

$x = 30°$

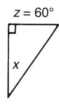

Answer: 30°

5 The Andy Warhol Museum is constructing a giant commemorative soup can with a radius of 5 feet and filling it with Campbell's tomato soup. If the can is filling up at a rate of 50π cubic feet per minute, and it fills in 6 minutes, how tall is it?

5

The first thing to recognize is that if we are talking about *cubic* feet, then we are talking about volume. (*Square* feet are used to talk about area. Plain ol' feet are used to talk about distance in a straight line.) If we already know the volume *per minute* and the radius, what are we missing? The height. Plug our numbers into the volume formula:

$\pi \times 5^2 \times h = 50\pi$

$25 \times \pi \times h = 50\pi$

$h = 2$

On some tests you can change pi to an approximation like 3.14. The SAT is not one of those tests. Leave pi alone!

—Samantha

This tells us that every minute, the can fills up 2 feet in height. If the entire can fills in 6 minutes, then the can is $6 \times 2 = 12$ feet high.

6 The box below is painted so that all of the sides EXCEPT the top, marked with an x, are painted green. The top is painted purple. What percentage of the box's surface is painted green?

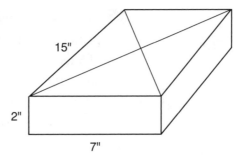

This is a surface area problem. Our length is 15, our width is 7 and our height is 2. So our surface area of the total box is $(2 \times 7 \times 2) + (2 \times 2 \times 15) + (2 \times 7 \times 15) = 298$. We are looking for the percentage of all that surface area except the top, which is $7 \times 15 = 105$. The question, then, is what percentage of 298 is 193 (or $298 - 105$).

$$\frac{193}{298} = \frac{x}{100}$$
$$x = 64.8$$

The answer is 64.8%.

Coordinate Geometry

We already saw a few graphs when we charted our functions. Now, we're going to take a deeper look at how graphs work and how the Serpent likes to test our graph awareness. But first, let's quickly recap some of the basics of coordinate geometry.

While it's usually true that the vertical axis is called the y-axis and the horizontal axis is called the x-axis, the SAT might use other letters instead. This is annoying, but harmless—all the same rules still apply.

This is a basic graph with some points on it.

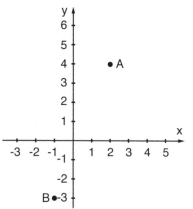

The y-axis is vertical. The x-axis is horizontal. The origin is the point (0,0) where they meet.

Any point on a graph has two coordinates. For example, point A on the graph shown has coordinates (2,4), which means that if you start at the origin and want to get to A, you have to go 2 units to the right and 4 units up. For point A, 2 is called its "x-coordinate" and 4 is called its "y-coordinate." Point B has coordinates (–1,–3).

The next element of coordinate geometry is a line, which connects and extends through two points. Like so:

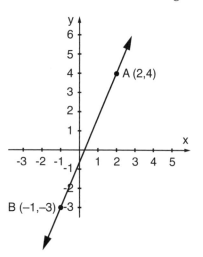

And as soon as we have a line, we also have a *formula* for that line, usually in the form $y = mx + b$. For example, the line to the left has the formula $y = (7/3)x + (–2/3)$. Our m is $(7/3)$ and our b is $(–2/3)$. But what are m and b? The easier one to explain is b, which is our y-intercept, or the y-coordinate of the point where the line hits the y-axis. Just take a look at that line. At which point does it cross the y-axis? At $(–2/3)$. So far, so good.

m stands for slope. * The slope of a line is an indication of how steep it is. To figure out the slope of a line that connects two points (x_1, y_1) and (x_2, y_2), you use the formula:

Why "<u>m</u>"? The world may never know.

—Samantha

$$\text{Slope} = \frac{\text{change in } y}{\text{change in } x} = \frac{(y_1 - y_2)}{(x_1 - x_2)}$$

So, in our line above, $\dfrac{(4) - (-3)}{(2) - (-1)} = \dfrac{7}{3}$.

Another helpful way to think of slope is "rise over run," where rise means *up* or *down* and run means *across*. Going from left to right (or from point B to point A), we went *up* 7 and *across* 3. To continue this line segment, we would go up another 7 and across another 3.

Lines that are **parallel** have the same slope, but different *y*-intercepts. This allows the SAT to write horrifying problems like this:

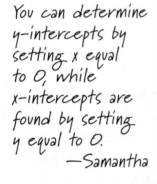

You can determine *y*-intercepts by setting *x* equal to 0, while *x*-intercepts are found by setting *y* equal to 0.
    —Samantha

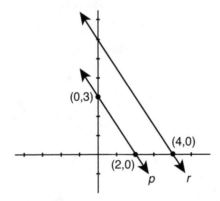

Line *p* and line *r* are parallel. What is the *y*-intercept of line *r*?

With only one coordinate in line *r*, there isn't a lot we can say about it. Luckily, it is parallel to line *p*, which has two coordinates, and can thus be converted to $y = mx + b$ form. *b* is given to us, 3, because it hits the *y*-axis at *y*-coordinate 3.

$$y = mx + 3$$

To find *m*, use the slope formula: $\dfrac{(0 - 3)}{(2 - 0)} = -3/2$

$$y = (-3/2) \, x + 3$$

If line *r* has the same slope, then its formula is:

$$y = (-3/2)\ x + b$$

To find *b*, we can pick our point (4,0), and plug the *x* and *y* coordinates into the formula to solve for *b*:

$$0 = (-3/2) \times (4) + b$$
$$0 = -6 + b$$
$$b = 6$$

To check, let's take a look at our graph. Does it look like line *r* crosses the *y*-axis at 6? It does indeed.

If two lines are **perpendicular**, then their slopes are the negative reciprocals of each other. That mathy term *negative reciprocal* just means "flip the fraction and negativize  it."

What is the slope of a line perpendicular to the line $y = (-4/3)\ x + 4$?

If the slope of the original line is $(-4/3)$, then the slope of the perpendicular line is $(3/4)$.

The SAT can also ask about the **midpoint** and **distance** between two points. There is a formula for distance, and we will tell you that formula, but it is far easier to draw a right triangle. Like in this problem:

What is the distance between points A and B?

*Is this a word? Yes.

—Samantha

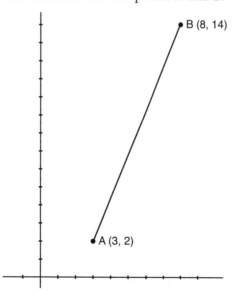

B (8, 14)

A (3, 2)

To find the distance, draw the right triangle for which the line would act as a hypotenuse.

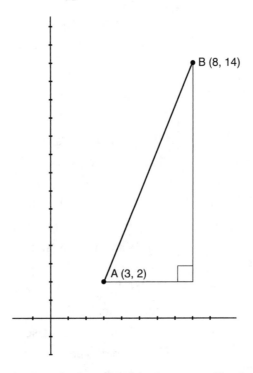

Next, calculate the length of the horizontal leg by finding the difference in the x values: $8 - 3 = 5$. Do the same for the vertical leg using the difference in the y values: $14 - 2 = 12$. Now plug those two lengths into the good ol' Pythagorean Theorem.

$$5^2 + 12^2 = c^2$$
$$25 + 144 = c^2$$
$$169 = c^2$$
$$13 = c$$

The distance is 13.

For those of you who prefer to memorize formulas, here is the monstrous (and easily forgettable) distance formula, from one point (x_1, y_1) to another point (x_2, y_2): *

$$d = \sqrt{(x_1 - x_2)^2 + (y_1 - y_2)^2}$$

*It doesn't matter which point you call "point 1" and which one you call "point 2." You will get the same answer either way.

—Samantha

The midpoint, on the other hand, *is* easier to calculate using a formula, because the formula is much easier to remember. It's just the average of the x values and the average of the y values:

$$\left(\frac{x_1 + x_2}{2}\right), \left(\frac{y_1 + y_2}{2}\right)$$

What is the midpoint between the points (–2,2) and (10,4)?

x-coordinate: $\dfrac{-2 + 10}{2} = 4$

y-coordinate: $\dfrac{2 + 4}{2} = 3$

The midpoint is (4,3).

A FEW MORE SYMBOLS

It's possible you will see these on the SAT, so you should know what they are:

$\overleftrightarrow{AB}$	a line with A and B as points on the line
$\overrightarrow{AB}$	a ray with point A as an endpoint
$\overline{AB}$	a line segment with A and B as endpoints
$\triangle ABC \cong \triangle DEF$	triangle ABC is congruent (equal) to triangle DEF
$\triangle ABC \sim \triangle DEF$	triangle ABC is similar to triangle DEF

CIRCLES

A circle looks pretty familiar, even when plotted on a graph:

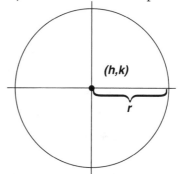

A circle is defined as a series of points that are all equal in distance from its center. Its formula is:

$$(x - h)^2 + (y - k)^2 = r^2$$

Where (h,k) is the center and r is the radius

PARABOLAS: STANDARD FORM, VERTEX FORM, CARTESIAN FORM, OH MY!

A parabola is basically just a bowl shape, and it's what a quadratic equation looks like if you graph it. You'll usually encounter quadratic functions in what's called *standard form*: $f(x) = ax^2 + bx + c$. Standard form is very user-friendly because you can factor it or apply the quadratic formula to find the roots (we covered this on page 256). However, the new SAT will sometimes ask you to recognize a different form, called *vertex form*: $f(x) = a(x - h)^2 + k$. Vertex form is useful for graphing because the numbers h and k in the equation together give you (h,k)—the coordinates of the vertex. The vertex is the minimum or maximum point (the bottom or top of the bowl shape). You can easily tell if the vertex is a maximum or a minimum by looking at the sign of your a value. If a is positive, the parabola opens up, and the vertex is a *minimum*. If a is negative, then the parabola opens down, and the vertex is a *maximum*. So it's helpful to know how to convert standard form into vertex form when you need to find that all-important maximum or minimum point. Converting from standard to vertex form involves a process called *completing the square*. Here's how you do it. Let's start with a sample quadratic function in standard form: $f(x) = x^2 + 4x - 5$. Let's start by rewriting it with some space between the 4 and the –5:

$$f(x) = x^2 + 4x \qquad - 5$$

What we want to do is make that $x^2 + 4x$ part into a perfect square trinomial by adding a number to it. We find that number by dividing the b constant (4 in this case) by 2 and squaring the result. This gives us $2^2 = 4$. We're going to add a 4 and subtract a 4 in that space so that things balance out. (We can't just add something to an expression willy-nilly, since that would cause the algebra gods to smite us. By subtracting the same number we added, we make things balance out and keep the algebra gods happy.)

$$f(x) = x^2 + 4x + 4 - 4 - 5$$

The first three terms form a perfect square trinomial, and it factors into two identical quantities. Factoring just that part, we get $f(x) = (x + 2)(x + 2) - 4 - 5$, which we can rewrite as $f(x) = (x + 2)^2 - 9$. Voilà! We have completed the square and converted from standard to vertex form. Remember that the constants h and k will give us the vertex if we put them together. The 2 is positive, so to fit our original vertex form, we have to switch the sign in order to get $h = -2$. So the x-coordinate of the vertex is -2. The -9 is the k number, or the y-coordinate of the vertex. Since the first term of the polynomial is positive, we know that the parabola opens upward and has a minimum point at $(-2, -9)$.

Beyond standard and vertex form, there's something called *cartesian form*. This form has the benefit of describing horizontal parabolas (which open left or right, and are *not* functions), as well as vertical parabolas (which open up or down, and *are* functions).

The cartesian form for vertical parabolas is $(x - h)^2 = 4c\,(y - k)$

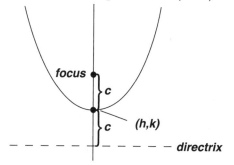

The cartesian form works because a parabola can be defined geometrically as a set of points that all have the same distance from the focus (the top dot) as from the directrix (the dotted line). c is the distance between the vertex (h,k) and the directrix, and is also the distance between the vertex and the focus.

PERPENDICULAR AND TANGENT LINES

When two lines are **perpendicular**, they intersect at right angles. You can immediately tell that two lines are perpendicular if their slopes are opposite reciprocals of each other. For example,

---

"Parabola," by the way, is not pronounced like "pair of bowlers." It's fancier than that, so you have to put the accent on the second "a." Par·á·bo·la.

　　　　—Samantha

$y = -2x + 6$ and $y = \dfrac{x}{2} + 12$ are perpendicular to each other because the slope of the first line is −2 and the slope of the second is ½.

You will usually see tangent lines associated with circles (or any other conic section, for that matter, but the SAT's probably not going to ask about tangents to hyperbolas). Basically, a line is **tangent** to a circle if it makes a right angle with the circle's radius and intersects the circle at one point.

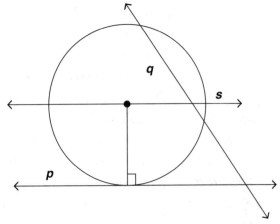

In the circle above, only the line p is a tangent line.

Example 1: A circle of the equation $x^2 + y^2 = 25$ has a tangent line at the point (4,3). What is the equation of the tangent line?

First of all, we have to visualize this circle. Because there's nothing after the x's and the y's, the center of the circle is on the origin (0,0). The radius is the square root of 25, and so it's 5.

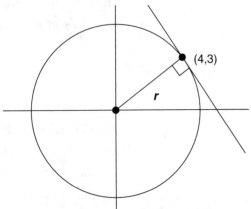

The one advantage of problems that give you less information is that you have fewer elements to consider. The disadvantage is that they're really hard.
        —Samantha

The tangent line is perpendicular to this radius, so we have to figure out what the equation for the radius is at this point. We know the center is (0,0), and the point is (4,3). We can use the **point-slope formula** to derive the slope of the line through those two points. For any two points (x_1, y_1) and (x_2, y_2), we can say $\dfrac{y_2 - y_1}{x_2 - x_1} = \text{slope}$. So:

$$\frac{3-0}{4-0} = \frac{3}{4}$$

So now we know that the slope of this radius is ¾. We're trying to get the equation of the tangent line, so we need the perpendicular slope, which is –⁴/₃.

Now all we have to do is plug everything into an equation:

$$(y - 3) = m\,(x - 4)$$

$$(y - 3) = \frac{-4}{3}(x - 4)$$

And we have our tangent line.

Note that this also could have been written as

$$y = \frac{-4}{3}x + \frac{25}{3}$$

Trigonometry

Trigonometry is an official VSMW, or Very Scary Math Word, and indeed trigonometry *can* get pretty complicated. Luckily, the SAT is going to test you on the basics. The first step is to get comfortable with one very uncomfortable word: **SOHCAHTOA**.

What is that? An ancient Gaelic curse? A new celebrity baby name? Well yes, it is both those things, but it is also an acronym for:

$$\text{Sine} = \frac{\text{Opposite}}{\text{Hypotenuse}}$$

$$\text{Cosine} = \frac{\text{Adjacent}}{\text{Hypotenuse}}$$

$$\text{Tangent} = \frac{\textbf{O}\text{pposite}}{\textbf{A}\text{djacent}}$$

Get it? SOHCAHTOA. (Soh-kah-TOW-ah.) Say it ten times, and you will never forget it.

Here's how it works.

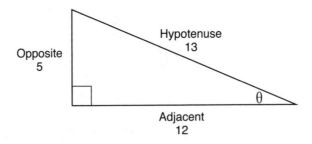

In any right triangle, SOHCAHTOA allows us to say things about the relationships between one of the non–right angles and the sides of that triangle. In the above triangle, $\sin \theta = \dfrac{\text{Opposite side}}{\text{Hypotenuse}}$, or $5/13$. Try this SAT-style problem:

In the triangle below, if $\tan \theta = ¾$, what is $\sin \theta$?

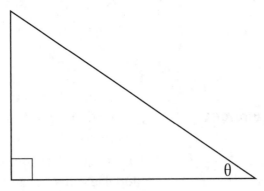

A) ¾

B) ⅘

C) ⅗

D) 5/4

The easiest way to solve this problem is to first draw a right triangle, then fill in the sides.

We know that $\tan \theta = \frac{3}{4} = \frac{\text{Opposite}}{\text{Adjacent}}$, so we know that the opposite side is 3, and the adjacent side is 4. The Pythagorean Theorem tells us that $3^2 + 4^2 = c^2$. $9 + 16 = 25 = c^2$, so our hypotenuse is 5. The problem is asking for $\sin = \frac{\text{opposite}}{\text{hypotenuse}} = \frac{3}{5}$, or C.

Once we are comfortable with SOHCAHTOA, we can start really having fun by pairing it with another sparkly new math toy: the unit circle. Take a look.

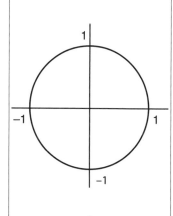

That's a very friendly-looking circle, right? The center is at the origin, and the radius is 1. What could be nicer? So here's the neat trick, and by "neat trick" we mean "terribly intimidating basis for much of trigonometry": Any radius in the unit circle is also the hypotenuse of a right triangle with a horizontal leg of $\cos(\theta)$ and a vertical leg of $\sin(\theta)$. Take a look.

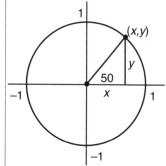

The only information we are given is that our angle (θ) is 50 degrees. But with just that information, we can find the coordinate (x,y) using trig. Here's how.

$$\sin(50) = \frac{y}{1}, \text{ so } y = \frac{\sin(50)}{1}, \text{ or } \sin(50)$$

$$\cos(50) = \frac{x}{1}, \text{ so } x = \frac{\cos(50)}{1}, \text{ or } \cos(50)$$

In other words, with only the angle θ, we can say that the corresponding point on the unit circle is simply $\cos\theta$, $\sin\theta$. This helps us solve difficult-looking problems, like the following.

In the unit circle to the left, which of the following is equal to c?

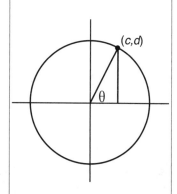

A) $\sin\theta$
B) $\cos\theta$
C) $\tan\theta$
D) $\sec\theta$

Because they are asking about the x-coordinate, we know that we are looking for $\cos(\theta)$, so our answer is B.

Think of it this way: cos represents x, sin represents y, and tan is just sin divided by cos.
    —Samantha

Additionally, the unit circle helps you find the values of trigonometric functions within each quadrant of the graph.

sin: positive cos: negative tan: negative	sin: positive cos: positive tan: positive
II	I
III	IV
sin: negative cos: negative tan: positive	sin: negative cos: positive tan: negative

Imaginary and Complex Numbers

There might be a couple of questions on the Math Test that involve the letter i. If you are not careful, you might assume that this is just another variable, as innocent as x or y. But i is an **imaginary number**, equal to $\sqrt{-1}$. The SAT is not going to get too tricky with i; all you need to know is how i works when it is raised to various powers:

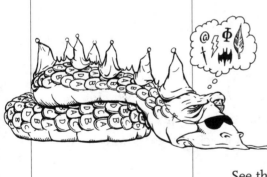
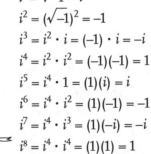

$$i^1 = \sqrt{-1} = i$$
$$i^2 = (\sqrt{-1})^2 = -1$$
$$i^3 = i^2 \cdot i = (-1) \cdot i = -i$$
$$i^4 = i^2 \cdot i^2 = (-1)(-1) = 1$$
$$i^5 = i^4 \cdot 1 = (1)(i) = i$$
$$i^6 = i^4 \cdot i^2 = (1)(-1) = -1$$
$$i^7 = i^4 \cdot i^3 = (1)(-i) = -i$$
$$i^8 = i^4 \cdot i^4 = (1)(1) = 1$$

See the pattern? This repeats ad infinitum, every four integer powers. This comes in handy in problems that involve complex numbers, which combine real and imaginary numbers in single expressions.

What is $(3i + 4)(5 - 6i^3)$?

First, we FOIL this like a standard algebra problem:
$$15i - 18i^4 + 20 - 24i^3$$

Next, we check in on our i values. That regular i stays the same (because $i^1 = i$), the i^4 becomes 1, and the i^3 becomes $-i$. Let's rewrite it:

$15i - 18(1) + 20 - 24(-i)$

$15i - 18 + 20 + 24i$

$2 + 39i$

GRID-IN PROBLEMS

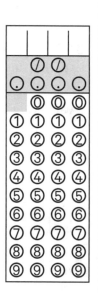

Unlike all other questions on the SAT, grid-in problems allow you to produce your own answer. Finally, a chance to express yourself!

Content-wise, these problems are the same as every other problem on the math test. The downside is that you cannot plug the answers in to back-solve the problem or use the plugging-in strategy. The upside is that you get to have fun bubbling in a slightly different type of bubble-grid.

Take a look at a sample of the grid that will appear on your answer sheet. Notice that at the top is space to write in your answer. However, this is not required—the computer scores only what's in the circles. So don't bother to write in the answer unless you're afraid you'll get confused otherwise.

You can start your answer in any column. Either of these positions is correct:

Both fractions and decimals are accepted. If the answer is ¼, you can use either ¼ or .25. But remember to make decimals as accurate as possible. For instance, ⅔ can be filled in as .666 or .667, but not .66 or .67. Because of this we think it's easier to stick with fractions, when possible.

Important: You can't state your answer in mixed fractions. For instance, 2½ would look like ²¹/₂ (twenty-one halves). So you have to use ⁵/₂ or 2.5.

For some reason, there is a decimal point in the last column: Ignore it. There is no possible answer that will use it.

The largest possible answer on the grid is 9,999 (obviously); the smallest answer is 0. There are no negative answers. If you get a negative number or a five-digit answer, try the problem again.

Here are two real SAT questions to whet your appetite. (Have you ever seen *whet* used in a sentence without *appetite*?)

1 If $(^a/_6)(12b) = 1$, what is the value of *ab*?

Answer:

Remember: You don't have to write in the answer at the top; we did it for clarity.

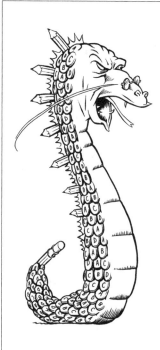

2 The lengths of the sides of a triangle are *a*, 9, and 17, where *a* is the length of the shortest side. If the triangle is not isosceles, what is one possible value of *a*?

Answer:

In this case, you could have written any number greater than 8 and less than 9. If *a* were 9 or greater, it wouldn't be the shortest side anymore. And if it were anything smaller than 8, you couldn't make a triangle out of it (just try drawing it).

A FEW LAST WORDS

Congratulations! You got through the entire math chapter. You are 83.425% more prepared to take the Math Test. To attain that last 16.575% of improvement, keep the following general strategies in mind.

USE YOUR IMAGINATION

As we've said, most of the math problems are word problems. Don't immediately scan your brain for the appropriate formula. Imagine the situation, and walk yourself through it. This will save you time and reduce the likelihood of making a conceptual error.

All math questions are created equally. That's not to say they're equal in difficulty, but they're all worth the same amount of points. So it's a great idea to skip the hardest ones and come back after you've done all the easy ones.
—Samantha

*Fun game: Try to count the number of times we've told you to take practice tests.
—Samantha

GLANCE AT THE ANSWER CHOICES BEFORE SOLVING

Sometimes answer choices aren't simplified. So don't waste time simplifying. Also, you can often work backward from the answer choices by plugging them in and seeing if they work. If you choose this method, start with B or C and determine whether you should try a smaller or larger answer choice. (Answer choices go from least to greatest.)

SKIP AND COME BACK

We explained skipping and coming back on page 33, but this is an exceptionally helpful strategy on the Math Test. Give yourself the chance for second (and third and fourth) reads, and do not allow your frustration with a particular problem to throw you off.

IF YOU HAVE TIME, RE-SOLVE TOUGH QUESTIONS WITH A DIFFERENT METHOD

This is just a great way to ensure you've done it correctly. If you solved it first by constructing an equation, try plugging in and see if you get the same answer.

ON PRACTICE TESTS, PAY ATTENTION TO YOUR ERRORS

When practicing, the *kind* of errors you make matters more than the number of errors. If you got some percentage problems wrong, you know what to study that week!

SPEAKING OF WHICH, TAKE PRACTICE TESTS *

If you haven't already, get ahold of the College Board's *The Official SAT Study Guide* or download the practice tests found at khanacademy.org/sat. Now! Go do it now! Then take a practice Math section. We'll meet you afterward to talk about the not-so-optional optional Essay.

The Not-So-Optional Essay

DOES OPTIONAL REALLY MEAN OPTIONAL?

Here are a couple examples of this sense of the word "optional": "Blinking is optional." "Breathing is optional."

—Samantha

There have been many, many changes made to the SAT Essay in the last year, but the most glaringly obvious change is that the SAT Essay is now described as "optional." That's a pretty strange description for a test section, isn't it? Because if the Essay Test were truly optional, then our answer would be "Thanks, but no thanks."

Unfortunately, describing the Essay as "optional" is exactly the same tactic your mother uses when she wants you to do the dishes. "It is absolutely your choice," she says, "you're nearly an adult, and you are free to make your own decisions about what is fair and what is not. If you think that I have not done my share, what with my birthing you and feeding you and canceling that trip to Sacramento with my great-aunt Claire—who is now dead, by the way—so that I could watch your soccer game, then so be it. I will do the dishes. You go enjoy some television. Be sure to turn up the volume so you're not disturbed by the clattering plates and stifled sobbing."

Doing the dishes isn't really optional, and neither is the Essay. The truth is that the college admissions process is a competition, and choosing *not* to write the Essay puts a big, old LAZY stamp on your application. So, you still need to write it. That's the bad news.

The good news is that the Essay isn't really as tough as it looks. So let's dive in.

NOT *WHAT IS* SAID, BUT *HOW* IT'S SAID

In the Evidenced-Based Reading and Writing Tests, you were asked questions about the meaning of certain passages: What is the point of a certain phrase or sentence? How does it relate to the main idea of the paragraph? Which piece of evidence best supports the author's argument? Are you sure the author said *this*, or did she really say *that*?

On the Essay, you will again be given a passage (and you'll again need to be on the lookout for "evidence"), but the thrust of your job is different. Instead of searching for the meaning, you are searching for the ways in which the author *communicates* the meaning.

The deal here is that the Evil Testing Serpent wants you to

The best part about the new SAT Essay is that you don't have to provide your own ideas; you just analyze the ones in the passage. Well, I guess that could be a bad thing if you're one of those people who likes to talk about themselves nonstop.
—Samantha

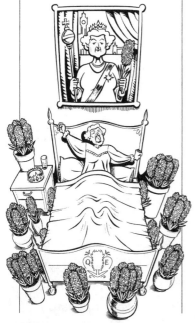

analyze the passage by discussing the evidence, the reasoning, and the rhetorical elements of the writing. Your job is to describe *how* the argument is built, *how* the evidence is used in the service of the argument, and *how* rhetorical devices make the writing more persuasive.

Read the following (made-up) passage by (made-up) author Camilla Fizzlethwaite—it's on a topic that the SAT would probably never cover (hyacinths), but it'll show by example what we mean.

For those who would question the aesthetic supremacy of the stately hyacinth, I have only pity. Are they not aware that Queen Elizabeth, who has made no secret of her disdain for the rose, the chrysanthemum, and the lilac, surrounds her bed with hyacinths so that first thing each morning—before the Royal Bath or any pressing affairs of state— she can gaze upon these unparalleled flowers? Have they not been informed that hyacinths fill the flower shops not only of England, but also those of Spain, and the islands of Trinidad and Tobago, and even the bazaars of remote Afghanistan? At present, the hyacinth can be found on the stamps of thirty-seven nations and in the sketches and watercolors sold along the Seine. For generations, hyacinths have added a much needed touch of class to countless portraits simply by standing in the background. Their popularity speaks more eloquently of their beauty than words could ever hope to do.

What is the meaning of this passage? That's easy: Hyacinths are great. But *how* is this message conveyed? That requires a bit more thinking. There are whole college courses that you can— and should—take on analyzing writing, but the SAT wants you to focus on the big three:

- Reasoning
- Evidence
- Rhetoric

We are going to go into more detail later, but you know what those three things are. Reasoning is the **argument** of the passage. The evidence comprises those **facts, figures, and anecdotes** used to bolster or strengthen the argument. Rhetoric is by far the hardest because it requires that we take a magnifying glass to each sentence. But rhetoric refers to the specific **words and sentences** that help deliver the argument. Let's try a mini-analysis of Ms. Fizzlethwaite's passage to demonstrate how this is done.

> In this paragraph, the author argues that hyacinths are beautiful, primarily by citing their popularity. To make this point, she uses the example of Queen Elizabeth surrounding herself with them, details the variety of widespread locations where the flower is popular, and names a few artistic mediums that include the hyacinth. Her tone is arch and fairly humorous, referring to "the Royal Bath," and personifying flowers by having them "stand in the background" of portraits. She is also authoritative. She does not cite studies to show that hyacinths can be found in Trinidad or Afghanistan. She simply states that they are there, and we are meant to accept it. This authority is also communicated in her precise knowledge of the number of stamps on which hyacinths appear.

See what we did? First, we summarized the argument—that's the easy part—and named the evidence—a bit tougher—then we talked about the rhetoric of the paragraph, including specific words and phrases, to show *how* the argument is stated persuasively. This last bit is the most sophisticated, and we will talk about it in more detail in a moment.

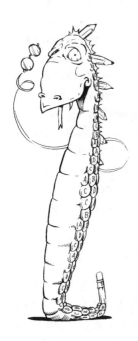

What NOT to Write

Did you notice what we did *not* say in our analysis? We did not simply write about *what* the passage says. This is an easy mistake to make. After all, the Evidence-Based Reading Test is all about *what* the passage says, but for the Essay you need to switch gears to include *how* it says it.

Nor did we agree or disagree with Ms. Fizzlethwaite's point. This is crucial, so we will write it in bold: **The SAT does not care if you agree or disagree.** In assessing your essay, the Evil Testing Serpent cares about your analytic abilities, not your opinion. It wants to know if you can "close read" a text and explain how it works. You could love the text, or you could hate it. The Serpent doesn't give a hoot.

(Also, you might notice that we did not curse. In general, the SAT does not care for cursing, so keep a nearby piece of scrap paper for all of the swear words that will arise during the planning and writing of the essay.)

ONE TEMPLATE TO RULE THEM ALL

There are many ways to plan out an effective analytical essay. One fine strategy is to spend one paragraph talking about the reasoning of the passage, one about the evidence and how it is used, and one about the rhetorical strategies employed throughout. We've also seen successful essays that choose three rhetorical techniques, such as parallel structure, metaphor, and direct address, and dedicate a paragraph to each, showing how each technique augments the argument and evidence of the passage.

But there is a simpler, faster, and more effective essay template than either of these. We call this THE template. Behold:

- Introduction: State your thesis. (2–3 sentences)
- First paragraph: Write about the beginning of the passage (the first couple of paragraphs). Summarize the argument. Point out the evidence and how it is used. Analyze how a few rhetorical choices help deliver the argument. (6 sentences total)
- Second paragraph: Write about the middle paragraphs of the passage. Summarize the argument. Point out the evidence and how it is used. Analyze how a few rhetorical choices help deliver the argument. (6 sentences)
- Third paragraph: Compose a sonnet about thy love's flaxen ringlets, which the sun doth trembleth o'er. Just kidding. Write about the end of the passage. Summarize the argument. Point out the evidence and how it is used. Analyze how a few rhetorical choices help deliver the argument. (6 sentences)
- Conclusion: Restate your thesis. (2–3 sentences)

You might notice that this template is very similar to the way you learned to write an essay in school.
—Samantha

And that's it! Nothing fancy, just a whole bunch of analyzing, then you drop the mic, walk out of the test center, and collapse on the sidewalk in exhaustion.

Let's try this out on a passage we fabricated.

Step 1: Read the Passage (5 minutes)

First things first: The new SAT Essay comes with *a ton* of instructions, like a full page of them. However, the instructions are basically always the same. Read through the standard instructions carefully on a practice test (or two or three), so that you know what they ask and can skip reading them on the actual test. But for now, in a nutshell, the instructions ask you to consider how the author of the passage uses:

• Evidence, such as facts or examples, to support his or her claims.

• Reasoning to develop his or her ideas and to build an argument.

• Stylistic or persuasive elements (word choice, cadence, or appeals to emotion) to add power to the ideas expressed.

Got that? Now, after reading those instructions, we want you to do something a little strange: Forget 'em. Actually, don't totally delete the instructions from your memory banks, but put them aside. We'll come back to them later. For now, you should kick back (not literally, the proctor will yell at you) and read this like you would any newspaper article. Don't go searching for stylistic moves or the underlying argument. Just read to understand the main idea. Give it a go:

Remember— try to convince yourself that you are truly interested in the passage's topic. It will make reading it less of a chore!
—Samantha

ADAPTED FROM BERNIE KRUMPF, "THE REAL DANGER OF VIDEO GAMES"
© 2010 by *The Mississippi Tribune*. Originally published April 10, 2010.

I encountered my first physics problem in the woods of Massachusetts in 1973. I was six years old at the time, and wanted what all young boys want: a stick that would travel downriver faster than my brother's stick. I thought the problem was simple, but soon I was evaluating mass and surface area, buoyancy and wind resistance, ballast, pitch, and yaw. I also received a crash course in the solid American values of perseverance, creativity, and, by the day's end, the acceptance of failure. These days, when I see childen and young adults playing video games, I think back to that Massachusetts summer. Like a game of stick-boat race, video games are undeniably fun. The question is: Do they pay the same dividends?

The issue is more pressing now than ever. The video game industry this year made more than $47 billion, more than half again as much as Hollywood. But that is old news; what's changing is the *amount* of time children and adolescents report playing video games per day. A recent poll published by the U.S. Department of Health stated that the average child plays two hours on weekdays, and four hours per day on weekends. For many, many children—perhaps the majority of children—video games have become the primary mode of having fun.

This is a big deal. Despite its name, goofing around is crucial to a child's development. Dr. Maude Glazier, a neuroscientist at the University of Chicago, in February published a study in *Nature* titled "When Brains Have Fun." Her experiment was elegant in its simplicity. Dr. Glazier took brain scans of children at play and compared these scans to those of children at rest. The images were remarkable: Whole swaths of the brain light up during recreation. "The resulting gains in neuroplasticity, in areas as disparate as the occipital lobe and the corpus callosum," Dr. Glazier writes, "cannot be overstated." The question, then, is whether video games have the same salutary effect as other types of play.

People have long argued that video games are harmful to the developing child. A headline from the *New Orleans Times-Picayune* in 1986 reads, "Video Games Conclusively Linked to Increased Violence in Youngsters." One cover of the *New York Post* in 2007 put it more poetically: "Pixels Poison Prepubescents." This argument, that violent video games produce violent youths, crops up every two or three years, then dies down. It is ridiculous on its face. Ever since the days of painting bulls on cave walls, humans have been able to discern between representation and reality. Just as *Super Mario Bros.* did not cause an uptick in plumbers or jumping on turtles, *Grand Theft Auto* does not inspire teenagers to ride tanks through the streets of our cities.

No, the real problem with video games is that they pose

problems with predetermined solutions. If a door is locked, the gamer needs to find a key. If a kidnapper has taken the president's daughter, the gamer needs to shoot the kidnapper. Even the more sophisticated and difficult video games tend to resemble challenging puzzles. But a puzzle, no matter how complex, is still a puzzle. It has one, or perhaps two, or at best five or six paths toward a solution. But even the simplest real-world activity—be it an organized sport like soccer, or a disorganized sport like a stick-boat race—has infinite possibilities and solutions. Real life games reward creativity, effort, and orthogonal thinking in a way that no video game can. The reason for this is fundamental: Humans, crafty as we are, can never re-create reality's staggering plenitude of opportunity and failure.

After the passage, you will read a prompt like this:

Write an essay in which you explain how Bernie Krumpf builds an argument to persuade his audience that video games have a negative effect on a child's development. In your essay, analyze how Krumpf uses one or more of the features in the directions that precede the passage (or features of your own choice) to strengthen the logic and persuasiveness of his argument. Be sure that your analysis focuses on the most relevant features of the passage.

Your essay should not explain whether you agree with Krumpf's claims, but rather explain how Krumpf builds an argument to persuade his audience.

Step 2: Plan the Essay (20 minutes)

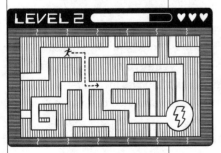

Resist the urge to start writing right away. All around you, you'll hear pencils scratching on paper, and you may think that everyone else is well under way writing perfectly polished prose. But the trick to writing perfectly polished prose is to think before you write.

Start by thinking in general terms, and then get more detailed. First, let's take two minutes to answer the question: What is the argument?

Krumpf is arguing that video games are bad. Why are they bad? Because video games require that players find a predetermined solution, rather than experiment and create their own solutions.

*In SAT world, everything that is presented in the passage is right and just and magnificent. End of story.
—Samantha

(Now, many of you are probably cooking up quite a few arguments of your own. Has Krumpf ever played *Minecraft*? Has he played *any* open-ended, massively multiplayer games? Resist this impulse! Your job is to reveal how the essay persuades—how Krumpf uses evidence to build his argument and how his writing effectively conveys his points. It's not your job to point out the flaws of his argument or to present alternatives.)*

Now that we know the argument, let's take eight minutes to outline the logic, and dig out the evidence he cites for each point. At this point, we want to go *back* to each paragraph, and summarize the argument. Like so:

1. Krumpf evokes a memory of a real-life game that made him think in productive ways and learn some life lessons. His evidence is this recollection. Ends it with a question that he will answer in the rest of the essay.

2. He shows the stakes of the question by demonstrating the popularity of video games. His evidence is a sales figure and a poll from the U.S. Department of Health.

3. He shows that play is important to brain development. His evidence is a scientific study from the journal *Nature*. Ends with another question to move the argument forward.

4. He shows that typical explanations for the destructive nature of video games are silly. As evidence, he provides a ridiculous headline. He argues against this interpretation with comically exaggerated examples.

5. He provides his own explanation for the shortcomings of video games. He appeals to the reader's experience to argue that video games are less beneficial than real-life games.

As we said previously, we're going to write about the beginning, middle, and end of the passage. We now know the argument and pieces of evidence we will discuss. Next, let's delve into the rhetorical choices Krumpf makes throughout his essay.

But First: What Exactly Is Rhetoric?

Rhetoric = the subtleties of the author's language.
—Samantha

Your word balloon is below us.

That's an UNDERSTATEMENT.

When you talk about a writer's rhetoric, you are talking about why a writer writes *this* way as opposed to some other way.

When Fizzlethwaite writes that hyacinths add "a much needed touch of class to countless portraits simply by standing in the background," she is making a choice to express an idea in a particular way. She could have expressed this same idea like so: "Hyacinths are often seen in the backgrounds of portraits, where they have the effect of making the image prettier." Same idea, but said differently. Why is the first one better? Why is the phrase "a touch of class" more fun to read? Why do we enjoy that they are "standing in the background"? When we answer these questions, we are talking about rhetoric. In this example, we might say that "a much needed touch of class" is cheeky, a bit ironic, a little funny. By personifying the hyacinths, we are given the slightly ridiculous image of flowers as low-paid background actors. The addition of that adverb "simply" emphasizes how effortlessly they expend their charm.

This kind of analysis is not easy. Critics make a good living by doing this sort of reading-with-a-magnifying-glass. With a bit of practice, you'll get the hang of it. But because you don't have *that* much time to practice, here's a handy list of rhetorical devices.

Allusion: referring to an outside text (often literary), story, or legend. *Example*: "Like a modern-day Jay Gatsby, my two-year-old seemed discontented at his own party."

Repetition and Amplification: a repeated word or phrase, which is often emphasized through this repetition. *Example*: "Did I flinch? I never flinch. I'm not a flincher."

Parallelism: parallel structure or word choice that often emphasizes a similarity or difference. *Example*: "On Sundays, my habit was to wake up at seven for a morning run. My brother's habit was to wake up at two p.m. for an afternoon snack."

Hyperbole: exaggerated language. *Example*: "When Daria realized the grocery store was sold out of her favorite cereal, her head exploded."

Understatement: the opposite of hyperbole. *Example*: "The baby two rows down cried miserably and loudly throughout the flight from New York to Paris. It was noticeable."

Metaphor: using one thing to describe another. *Example*: "His rage was an avalanche, obliterating everything in its path."

Simile: a metaphor that uses the words *like* or *as*. *Example*: "Your kisses are like the state fair: occasional and underwhelming."

Personification: attributing human characteristics to a non-human. *Example*: "The car had not been used in years, and complained bitterly when Sam tried to start it."

Irony: a very broad term that can be used in many ways. The basic idea is that you express yourself using language that usually connotes the opposite of your true meaning. That might sound overly technical, but you use irony all the time. *Examples*: "I overslept, I broke my heel, I burned my thumb, and then I got dumped. Overall, it was a triumphant day." *Or*: "Mr. Halverson, with his greasy shirt, sauce-stained pants, and mismatched shoes, was the very essence of gentility and dash."

Back to Planning!

So, let's take our paragraphs and spend another eight minutes finding some rhetorical choices and analyzing why the evidence serves the argument. (For clarity's sake we wrote full sentences—your notes will likely be, well, more note-like.)

Beginning: Opens with a joke to engage the reader—setting up ("what all young boys want") with an unexpected punch line ("a stick"). Contrasts the word "simple" with "buoyancy," "wind resistance" and "ballast" to emphasize the complexity of what we would assume to be a very basic activity. He ends the first paragraph with a question. This both engages the reader—who wants to know the answer to this question—and creates a more conversational tone.

Middle: Establishes the importance of the topic by stating the high number of hours kids spend on video games. Goes on to demonstrate the importance of play in general by citing Dr. Glazier and the highly respected journal *Nature* (giving his argument PhD backing). Dr. G's quote includes some ten-dollar words like "neuroplasticity," "occipital lobe," and "corpus calossum." These words further serve to ground his argument in hard science. Krumpf contrasts the simple phrase "goofing around" with a serious one, "a child's development"; the contrast shows that the stakes of his argument are more serious than they might initially appear. He again ends a paragraph with a question, which helps propel the reader from one paragraph to the next, which is an answer to that question.

End: In the fourth paragraph, Krumpf chooses two headlines to establish that condemning video games is not new. The first is a standard newspaper headline, but the second is sillier, which emphasizes his point that the idea that video games cause kids to become violent is itself hysterical and overblown. He uses the words "crops up" to define the discussion, as if it were a weed that sprouted again and again. In the last paragraph, he uses parallel structure when defining video-game challenges in order to emphasize their simplicity. He then opposes this simplicity with the complex requirements of real-world games.

At long last, we are ready to take two minutes formulating our thesis for the introduction and conclusion. "What?!?!" You are perhaps saying, "Write our thesis at the *end* of eighteen minutes of planning? That is crazy." No, it is very sane. In an analytical

The phrases and jargon that the author uses are important because they reveal the <u>tone</u>, which is something you might want to mention in your essay. For more on tone, see page 316.
—Samantha

essay, your thesis is nothing more than a hyper-reduced version of your findings. This hyper-reducing is tough to do, unless of course you have an incredibly helpful formula for thesis statements. Lucky for you, you *do* have an incredibly helpful formula for thesis statements. Here it is:

In (author's name)'s essay, (he/she) argues that (argument). To make (his/her) point, (he/she) cites (describe evidence), (rhetorical choice), and (rhetorical choice).

Here's ours: In Krumpf's essay, he argues that video games do not help children develop as effectively as real-world games do. To make this point, he cites scientific studies and uses humorous contrast, rhetorical questions, and parallel structure.

And that's it! Now, some of you might be objecting that 20 minutes is a *long* time to plan. But here's the deal: The Evil Testing Serpent cares about the *quality* of your thinking and the *organization* of your essay far more than the brilliance of your expression. In other words, you do not need to take the time to sound fancy, brilliant, or even that polished. You need to be clear, and your thoughts need to be developed. That means you should prioritize planning way higher than writing.

You may be tempted to create a fancy-schmancy thesis statement. Don't. There is no wooing the SAT graders.

—Samantha

Step 3: Write the Essay (20 minutes)

You know everything you need to say; you planned it all out. Now all you have to do is write it. And listen up, Oscar Wilde: There are no points for clever turns of phrase. Just be clear. Here's our first draft:

In his essay "The Real Danger of Video Games," Bernie Krumpf argues that video games are less beneficial for a child's development than real-world games. He does not take the common position that video games make kids violent; rather he says that video games are like puzzles that do not allow kids to come up with their own solutions. In making his argument, Krumpf cites scientific studies and makes use of humorous contrast, rhetorical questions, and parallel structure.

Krumpf opens the essay with a story from his childhood, arguing that a youthful game of "stick-boat race" gave him a lesson in physics, as well as training in some virtues that would serve him well. This all sets up his argument, in the last paragraph, that real-life games encourage creative thinking and force you to learn life lessons. He opens the paragraph on a humorous note, stating that "what all young boys want" is nothing more than a "stick that would travel downriver faster than my brother's stick." This reminiscent tone is continued in the next sentence, but then the word "simple" is contrasted with "bouyancy, wind resistance, and ballast" to emphasize how the basic activity involved complicated problem solving. He ends the paragraph with the question, "Do they pay the same dividends?" This rhetorical question does three jobs at once. It lets the reader know that this question will guide the essay, it makes the tone more conversational, and it encourages the reader to keep reading in order to learn the answer.

Before he outlines his argument against them, Krumpf wants the reader to understand that video games are a more serious topic than one might initially expect. He cites a U.S. Department of Health study that reveals the enormous number of hours that kids spend on video games, and establishes the significance of these hours by quoting Dr. Maude Glazier in a study she published in the jornal *Nature*, in which she emphasizes the importance of play for brain development. The use of technical, specialized terms like "neuroplasticity," "occipital lobe," and "corpus callosum" lend weight to her authority. But the author's use of the phrase "goofing around" at the start of the third paragraph lends the essay a certain folksiness and lets the reader know he's not losing sight of the fact that he's talking about the simple act of play.

Krumpf wants to distance his argument against video games from others that decry them on different grounds. He spends a paragraph disputing those who call video games overly violent and manipulative. He chooses two newspaper headlines to serve as examples of this argument. The first is straightforward, but the second, "Pixels Poison Prepubescents," demonstrates how ridiculous these popular arguments can be. He uses the term "crops up" in order to characterize these arguments as invasive pests, rather than serious intellectual positions. In his concluding paragraph, where he states that video games do not encourage creative thinking, he uses parallel structure to emphasize the simplicity of video games. "If a door is locked, the gamer needs to find a key. If a kidnapper has taken the president's daughter, the gamer needs to shoot the kidnapper." This serves his final thesis: The complexity of real-world games is more beneficial.

By the time we get to Krumpf's argument in the last paragraph, the reader is prepared to accept his point as valid, because he has established the seriousness of the issue (by citing the *Nature* article and the U.S. Department of Health study) and because he has distanced himself from sillier arguments (by citing the ridiculus *Post* headline). When we get to his final point, we are in a better position to accept it as a worthwhile and important agument.

Step 4: Smooth, Polish, Edit (5 minutes)

An interesting thing happened during the writing of our first draft. Our conclusion is a bit different, and a bit *smarter*, than our introduction. This happens *all the time* when writing a 50-minute essay. You may not realize it, but you think while you write, so your first draft conclusion is often wiser than your first draft intro. By the end, we realized that we were talking about how Krumpf uses rhetoric and reason to *prepare the reader* for his argument in the final paragraph. In our last few minutes, let's go back and change the introduction to make it look like this was our point all along!

Here's the new intro:

> In his essay "The Real Danger of Video Games," Bernie Krumpf argues that video games are bad for children's development. He does not take the common position that video games make kids violent; rather he says that video games are like puzzles in that they do not allow kids to think creatively or devise their own solutions. In the opening paragraphs of his essay, alongside scientific evidence, Krumpf uses humorous contrast, rhetorical questions, and ridiculous comparisons to prepare the reader to accept his final argument as serious and worthwhile.

Ta-da! Now it looks like we were brilliant from the start! Finally, let's correct any spelling or grammar mistakes. We hid four misspellings in the text. Can you find all of them?

HOW IS THE SAT ESSAY SCORED?

*Bigger is better. This is not golf.
      —Samantha

The SAT Essay will receive three separate scores on a scale of 2–8. You want 8s, not 2s. * The way it works is that you are given a 2–8 score on Reading, a 2–8 on Analysis, and a 2–8 on Writing.

The Reading score grades your understanding of the main idea of the passage. This is the "easiest" score, insofar as you will tank on this only if you majorly misread the passage. The Analysis score is based on your understanding of the argument, the use of evidence to back up the argument, and the stylistic moves used to persuade or guide the reader. Finally, the Writing score is based on your writing ability. They are looking for an orderly progression of ideas throughout the paragraph and the essay, precise word choice, and a variety of sentence structures.

These scores are added up to get your total score, though on the score sheet they will break it down so you can see just where you triumphed, and just where you messed up.

HOW TO WRITE GOOD

That last score, the Writing score, will judge you on how well you've written the essay. So . . . how do you write well? Hopefully, you have been working on this in many classes in high school and, to be honest, we could write a whole separate book on this topic, entitled *Up Your Sentence: The Underground Guide to Writing*. But here we only have the space to give you a few helpful guidelines and tips.

1. BE SPECIFIC.

Bad writing: Krumpf doesn't like video games.

Better writing: Krumpf says that video games offer fewer benefits than real-world games.

Best writing: Krumpf argues that video games provide a lower level of creative and intellectual engagement than even the most basic real-world games.

The more accurately you can restate, describe, and analyze the passage's argument, the wiser you will sound. By the same logic, writing specifically about your own points and arguments will make you sound like the owner of a fine-grained intellect. And who doesn't want a fine-grained intellect?

2. VARY YOUR SENTENCE STRUCTURE.

Bad writing: Krumpf appeals to sentiment in his first paragraph. He appeals to the authority of a respected journal in his third paragraph. He appeals to general experience in his concluding paragraph.

Better writing: Krumpf starts the essay by appealing to senti-ment. He then appeals to the authority of a respected journal in

Be as specific as you can without getting stuck on any one point— time is of the essence.
—Samantha

his third paragraph and to general experience in the conclusion.

Best writing: Krumpf uses a variety of argument types in his passage. He appeals to sentiment in the beginning, to authority in the middle, and to general experience at the end.

Reading the same kind of sentence over and over puts the brain to sleep. Mix it up! If you've just written a longer sentence with lots of clauses, wake up the reader by following it with a short, punchy sentence. *

For a long time, I thought short sentences were bad. Untrue. Monotonous sentences are bad.
—Samantha

3. SPICE UP YOUR LANGUAGE.

When writing about writing, people tend to use the words *writes* and *says* a lot. Try these better, more interesting, more precise verbs:

Argues	Reiterates	Juxtaposes
Asserts	Underlines	Conceives
Posits	Bolsters	Imagines
Insists	Reinforces	Stresses
Implies	Clarifies	Highlights
Infers	Conveys	Disputes
Proposes	Describes	

When describing the tone of the passage, consider using some of these tone words.

Here it is. The all-important tone.
—Samantha

Analytical: picking things apart to find causes and effects; usually not very emotional. *Example*: The actor's melancholy can be partly attributed to his failed audition, but it was the sudden onset of the measles that really brought him down.

Cynical: believing in only the worst of human nature or events. *Example*: The idea that a high schooler's awareness campaign will have an iota of impact on controlling carbon emissions is patently preposterous.

Detached: uninterested or disconnected; having no emotional reaction. *Example*: There's an enormous meteor heading right at us. In other news, I'm thinking about adopting a parakeet.

Equivocal: ambiguous, difficult to interpret; often unnecessarily wordy. *Example*: Upon second thought, I have come to the conclusion that I am ready to confess that I am not yet willing to admit that I won't be confessing to the crimes in question.

Facetious: reacting to a situation with (often inappropriate) humor. *Example*: Remember when that guy fell and broke his arm and shattered three ribs? I caught it on camera—it's *hilarious*.

Incredulous: disbelieving, often in reaction to surprising news. *Example*: You're telling me that the moon really *is* made of cheese? *Ha!* I'll believe it when I see it . . . or taste it.

Jocular: joking, playful, inoffensively humorous. *Example*: If the moon is a ball of cheese, I've eaten four moons already today.

Laudatory: praising someone or something, often to excess. *Example:* Your interpretive dance was delivered with conviction, elegance, and grace; I am convinced you are the single most talented interpretive dancer alive.

Pedantic: intended to instruct or preach, often in an unneeded or annoying way. *Example:* You asked me for a copy of the *magazine* my short story was featured in, but it's actually called a *literary journal*. It's a very important distinction, and I felt it was my duty to enlighten you.

Authoritative: speaking with knowledge or experience; confidence, often earned through specialized knowledge or experience.

Example: In the course of getting my PhD in television, I have watched the entirety of every TV show ever made, scored them against my Super-Advanced TV Quality Criteria, and polled literally every TV viewer in the world. Now, I can firmly say that *Game of Thrones* is the best show ever.

WHY YOU SHOULDN'T HATE THE ESSAY

The new SAT Essay is not easy. It is long, and it comes at the end of a taxing standardized test. It asks you to dig pretty deep into a text. The only way to make this section easier is to practice. Luckily, there are a number of practice essay prompts, as well as sample essays at collegereadiness.college board.org/sat/inside-the-test/essay.

Difficulty aside, we here at *Up Your Score* think the new Essay is pretty excellent. Here's why: It asks you to do precisely the same kind of thinking you will do in a college humanities course. The ability to look closely at a text, take it apart, and discover what makes it tick will give you an enormous leg up in college. Taking the time to work on these skills now, in other words, will pay big dividends in the near future. (Do we sound like your parents talking? Sorry!)

Finally, another big bonus of developing your analytical skills is that it makes reading much more enjoyable. Once you become attuned to the subtle ways that writers do their thing, their writing will open up like a . . . like a . . . like a *flower* or something. Whatever, we're not writers. We're just humble SAT gurus; leave us alone.

Is a *treasure chest* a better metaphor? What else opens? A closet? A clam? Yeah! Let's try that again:

Once you become attuned to the subtle ways that writers do their thing, their writing will open up like a clam.

Nope, that sucks even worse. Yeesh, writing is hard.

If you ask a teacher to take a look at some of your practice essays, they might feel flattered and see you as a go-getter. Ain't nothing wrong with that.

Guessing,

or Defeating
the Impostors
from Hell

IMPOSTORS FROM HELL

One day, soon after its self-inauguration as Supreme Commander of the High School, the Evil Testing Serpent woke up and realized it was dissatisfied with the SAT. Apparently, its torturous questions didn't always fool students. Scores were much higher than it wanted them to be. It felt sad, or the nefarious, serpentine equivalent of sadness. The Serpent saw that students would get math problems wrong and that *their wrong answer* wasn't one of the choices. So they tried the problem again and got it right the second time. Other times, when they couldn't do one of the cruel math or reading questions, they would guess randomly and, out of sheer luck, get it right. This sort of thing just wouldn't do.

The Serpent had two brilliant ideas. One, it decided to include wrong answers that students would most likely come up with if they made an error. * Two, it included answers that would tempt students away from the correct answer. It called these tricky wrong answer choices Impostors. With this concept incorporated throughout the SAT, students would once again live in fear. The Serpent chuckled hideously. It knew that its delicious years of tyranny would continue . . . forever.

*Picking off the weak—just natural selection at work.
    —Samantha

Okay, don't get frightened. We didn't mean to scare you. Actually, the truth is that the Serpent didn't plan on *Up Your Score*. We've gone deep into its system of Impostors and discovered that, if you use them properly, they actually make the SAT easier. In this section, we show you several techniques to recognize Impostors, avoid them, and best the Serpent by using them to help you find the right answer.

Impostors are used in both the Evidenced-Based Reading and Writing Tests and the Math Test. They are the tempting answers that look right but aren't.

For an example of a reading Impostor, look at this question:

Among the answer choices, the Testing Serpent deliberately includes the wrong answers a student would most likely come up with.

"He is often lauded for pursuing a philosophy that is progressive in spirit and yet practical in application."

In line 15 (cited above), the word "spirit" means

A) apparition
B) psyche
C) disposition
D) sentiment

To get this one right, you have to realize that the word *spirit* stands in for something like "in theory" (a big clue is that it is contrasted to "in application"). The answer choice that is closest to "in theory" is C, disposition. But do you see how somebody who wasn't paying close attention could be misled? The Serpent deliberately put two answers in there—choices A and B—that a student would be drawn to if they weren't considering the context for the word. When you see *spirit*, your first thought is probably related to ghosts or your inner being. A and B try to lure people into answer choices that relate to this kind of "spirit."

Answer D, sentiment, is an even more devious Impostor. The word *sentiment* is three inches away from correct. *Character* is a better word to describe the quality of a philosophy or argument —sentiment more often refers to a feeling or opinion. Choosing between these two is tough, but the Impostors make it easy to not even make it to that point.

Here's another example:

"Borrowing from the Roman emperors who placated their subjects with gladiator fights and opulent circuses, the prime minister sealed his victory in the 1998 election by sponsoring a lavish centennial celebration that earned him the admiration of even his fiercest critics."

In line 6 (cited above), the main reason the author compares political practices from two distant eras in history is in order to:

A) condemn the showiness of the prime minister's political style.

B) illustrate the inspiration behind a calculated decision.

C) prove that political behaviors will never change.

D) identify the primary causes of the prime minister's failure.

Keen-eyed readers will recognize quickly that D is wrong because it suggests that the prime minister failed, whereas the passage is talking about his success. But A, B, and C all seem like reasonable possibilities. A is a tempting Impostor, for the PM's style is certainly being described as showy, but is it a condemnation? Not really, because the sentence asserts that his critics came to admire his tactics. C might seem correct because a continuance is being demonstrated. But the language of that answer ("prove" and "never") is way too extreme. This leaves us with B, which is hidden, in the classic SAT style, in the language of abstraction. Again, just approaching questions carefully and thoughtfully can keep you safe from most Impostors.

The Math Test includes Impostors that are the answers students would get if they used the wrong method to solve a problem. The Serpent makes sure that if you screw up in the way it hopes you will, the wrong answer you get is one of the answer choices. For instance, the first question on one SAT Math section reads:

If $x + y = 2$, then $x + y - 4 = $?

A) -2

B) 0

C) 2

D) 6

The correct answer is A, but the Evil Testing Serpent made sure that C was one of the choices in case some frazzled student left the minus sign out of the answer. It also made sure that D was there just in case some confused young scholar added the 4 instead of subtracting it. He also made sure that B was there in case a space case decided that *x* and *y* were each equal to 2. So, in this example, the Impostors are B, C, and D.

GUESSING, THE SAT, AND THE SPECTER OF WORLD DESTRUCTION

A PULITZER PRIZE–WINNING PLAY

Cast

A sagacious guru who has read *Up Your Score*
His naive disciple, who has not

Disciple: To guess or not to guess? That is the question.
Guru: Guess, my child, guess.
Disciple: But why should I guess on a question if I'm most likely to get it wrong?
Guru: Isn't it obvious, my child? There is absolutely no guessing penalty on the SAT. If there is a 20 percent chance of getting it right on the Reading and Writing Test, and a 25 percent chance of getting it right on the Math Test, and a 0 percent chance of losing any points, only a fool would not guess.
Disciple: If it's so obvious, what makes you a guru?
Guru: I'm a graduate of Guru Gary's Online School of Advanced Wisdom.
Disciple: Sounds like a useful degree. Can I ever become a sagacious guesser like you?
Guru: It's a good thing you asked. I can recommend an invaluable book that has an incredible section about guessing. It's called *Up Your Score*. It's a masterpiece, really. Buy some copies for your friends and family.

So just how valuable is this guessing stuff, anyway?

Incredibly valuable. We did two experiments on the old SAT

(which penalized you for wrong answers) to prove that guessing really works. First, we took the test by looking only at the answer choices without reading any of the questions. We got an average combined score of 660. Although that's not going to get anyone into Harvard, it was 260 more points than would be expected from someone with no knowledge of the questions. Our second experiment had two parts. Ten kids took the test and left blank all the questions they couldn't do. Next, we had them read this chapter and then guess on all the ones they had left blank. Their scores increased by an average of 35 points, and they guessed correctly on 40 percent of the questions that they had left blank. *¡Ay caramba!* Pretty good improvement for a simple application of the five basic guessing rules, which we'll now discuss.

THE FIVE RULES OF GUESSING

RULE 1: **ONE OF THESE THINGS IS MOST LIKE THE OTHERS.**

If you have no idea what the correct answer is, choose the one that looks the most like all the other answers. This works because the Testing Serpent is going to make his Impostors look as much as possible like the correct answer. Use the Impostors to show you the path to the correct answer.

For example, if the answer choices are:

$$\text{(A)} \quad \frac{\sqrt{3}}{7} \quad \text{(B)} \quad \frac{\sqrt{3}}{2} \quad \text{(C)} \quad \frac{-\sqrt{3}}{2} \quad \text{(D)} \quad \frac{3}{2}$$

you should choose B. Why? Because three out of four choices have $\sqrt{3}$ in them, the correct answer probably has a $\sqrt{3}$ as well, so you can eliminate choice D. Since three out of four choices have a 2 in the denominator, the correct answer probably does, too; so eliminate A. Since three out of four answers are positive, the answer probably is, too; eliminate C. This leaves B as the best guess.

RULE 2: ON THE MATH TEST, THE PROBLEMS INCREASE IN DIFFICULTY AS YOU GO ALONG.

The first problem in a Math section should be easy; the last problem should be hard. This should be taken into account when you guess. If, on one of the questions near the end of a subsection, the Serpent puts in an answer choice that can be arrived at through a simple calculation, it is probably an Impostor. Look at the following problem, which was the last in the section:

> What is the ratio of the area of a rectangle with width w and length $2w$ to the area of an isosceles right triangle with a hypotenuse of length w?
>
> A) 8 / 1
> B) 4 / 1
> C) 2 / 1
> D) 1 / 4

If you do not know how to do this problem, or if you don't have time to do it, or if you have a personal grudge against the word *hypotenuse*, you should keep in mind that this question is likely the hardest in the section, so you should eliminate answer C because it is a simple ratio of the two numbers that are in the problem (i.e., $2w/w$, or $w/2w$). If that was all you had to do to solve this problem, it would have been easy and therefore it wouldn't have been the last question in the section.

You could actually solve this problem by drawing the following sketch:

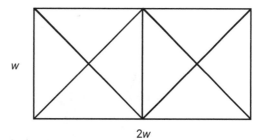

The sketch immediately shows you that 8 isosceles right triangles with hypotenuse w fit in 1 rectangle with width w and length $2w$. In other words, the rectangle is 8 times as large as 1 triangle. So the answer is A.

RULE 3: CHOOSE AN ANSWER THAT CONTAINS THE NUMBER REPRESENTED IN THE MOST ANSWER CHOICES.

This rule pertains to a type of question that comes up occasionally in math questions in the following nasty format:

> Let x and y be numbers such that $-x<y<x$.
> Which of the following is true?
> I. $|y|<x$
> II. $y>0$
> III. $x>0$
>
> A) I only
> B) II only
> C) I and III only
> D) I, II, III

Following Rule 3, in this example you should pick an answer that has a I in it because I shows up three times in the answer choices, whereas II and III show up only two times each. This works because, if indeed I is true, the Evil Testing Serpent considers any wrong answer with a I in it to be an Impostor. If you have no idea at all about whether the other statements are true, select I only. However, if you have a hunch that statement III is correct as well, then you would go with C because that contains both I (which shows up the most) and III, which you think might be correct.

Sometimes there is a tie between two numbers. Say I and II showed up three times each. In this case, choose an answer that has both I and II in it.

Of course, if you think the best answer is one that I doesn't appear in, go with that. **Don't use any of these rules against your better judgment.**

Be wary of "never" and "always" in answer choices. They tend to imply absolute statements.

—Samantha

RULE 4: IN READING PASSAGES, BEWARE OF ANSWER CHOICES THAT EXPRESS AN OPINION TOO STRONGLY OR THAT MAKE AN ABSOLUTE STATEMENT.

For example, without even reading the passage, we can make a good guess on this SAT question:

> The author's attitude toward Aristotle's writings is best described as one of
> A) unqualified endorsement.
> B) apologetic approval.
> C) analytical objectivity.
> D) scholarly dissatisfaction.

Choice A is making too absolute a statement. While the authors of SAT reading passages are likely to take a positive stance toward their subject, they almost never make an "unqualified endorsement." You might also eliminate choice C because it is redundant. To be "analytical" is pretty much the same thing as to be "objective." You can tell that the Serpent had to find two-word Impostors that would match the real answer, so it used redundant words in choice C. So that leaves B and D, but you can eliminate D because it is saying something negative about Aristotle, so the correct answer is B.

As a general rule, avoid answers that take an overtly negative view of the passage's subject matter. The College Board rarely criticizes people (especially über-important historical figures like, say, Aristotle), so choose an answer that is friendlier to the subject without being an absolute statement.

RULE 5: IN THE WRITING SECTION, LOOK FOR THE ANSWER THAT IS *UNLIKE* THE OTHERS.

You will often want to flip Rule 1 in the writing section. Take a look at this question (it's the kind where you are presented with alternative phrasing and asked to choose among the choices).

For years, Drake struggled as an artist, trying to break into the death metal scene. When he started rapping, <u>furthermore</u>, he found success.

A) no change

B) moreover

C) however

D) additionally

Notice something familiar about A, B, and D? The words *furthermore, moreover,* and *additionally* all mean basically the same thing! In what situation would *furthermore* work, but *additionally* would not? We can't think of one. Answer choice C, *however,* is the only outlier. So that must be our answer.

SOME MORE GOOD ADVICE

If you are stuck on a problem and need to guess, you should also try skipping and coming back. It is very, very, very common to *mis*read a problem. If you move on, take a crack at a couple of other problems, and then come back, you greatly increase your chances of reading it correctly. Unbeknownst to you, while you're answering the next questions, your brain is still processing information from the one you skipped. When you come back to the problem, you will be able to start fresh *and* you will still remember the question. This will help you either find the answer or make a more educated guess.

Finally, you should know that guessing on a question is no substitute for knowing the answer. If you know the right answer, don't guess a different answer. When you're taking the SAT, second-guessing yourself is almost always a bad idea. You know a lot of things. Be confident!

CHAPTER 8

But Wait! You Also Get . . .

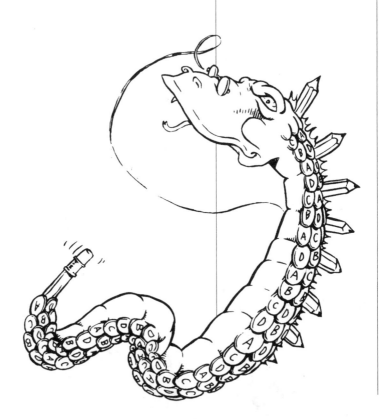

Other test prep guides offer info only on the SAT itself — Evidence-Based Reading and Writing Test, Math Test, and Optional Essay, and then it's over and out. But we here at *Up Your Score* know there's more to SAT success than just choosing the correct answers. For crucial stuff like insights on how to best fill in the little answer bubbles, how to deal with a nasty proctor, what to wear on test day, and much more, read on!

LITTLE CIRCLES

Robert Southey, the author of "The Three Bears" and arguably the worst poet ever, once said, "The desert circle spreads like the round ocean." He was referring, of course, to the metaphorical relationship between circles and the SAT.

Circles are quite significant in that there are many of them that you will have to fill in during the course of the test. This is about how to fill in those little circles.

Undoubtedly, you've had to fill in lots of little circles in your life. You probably never gave much thought to technique or speed. In fact, until the publication of *Up Your Score*, no one had ever researched the science of filling in circles. We were the first.

Our original groundbreaking study showed that some students spend an unimaginably wasteful 2.3 seconds per circle. At that rate, they will spend 7 minutes and 4 seconds of their total testing time filling in circles. For "O-lympic" competitors, we developed the In-to-Out Circle Method, which enabled students to reduce their time to an unprecedented 0.4 seconds per circle, saving almost 6 minutes of time to spend working on the test.

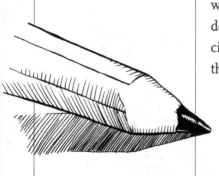

In-to-Out Circle Method

So how obsessive do you have to be about filling in the circles? As it turns out, optical scanning machines are far more advanced than anyone could have possibly imagined. Advances mandated by Congress after the 2000 Florida election fiasco have created machines capable of reading people's minds before they even select an answer. One such machine narrowly missed being elected president of Bolivia. The machines used to grade SATs employ a similar technology. They scan through your answers and search for a pattern—for instance, if you decide to fill in only the left half of every circle, the machine will recognize this pattern and realize that it is your way of marking an answer. As long as you are consistent, you could draw a phallic picture in every little circle and the machine would not give it a second thought. Still, doing so probably isn't time efficient, so we wouldn't recommend it.

Whatever you do, **avoid** the following time-wasting methods of high school students who are not familiar with our groundbreaking research:

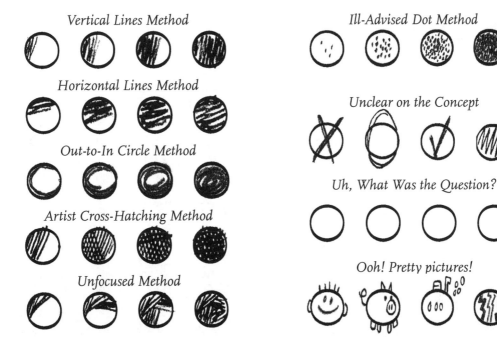

Vertical Lines Method

Horizontal Lines Method

Out-to-In Circle Method

Artist Cross-Hatching Method

Unfocused Method

Ill-Advised Dot Method

Unclear on the Concept

Uh, What Was the Question?

Ooh! Pretty pictures!

To perfect your technique, follow these rules:

1. Leave the point of one of your pencils dull. Although you don't want to use a dull pencil on the Math section (you want a good pencil for scratch work), it will save you time filling in the circles on the verbal section because the more surface area the point of your pencil has, the better coverage a single line will provide.

2. Although you don't want your arm to be too stiff, you should press hard on the answer sheet. The darker the mark, the more likely the scanner is to see it. This is an important factor since you won't necessarily be filling in your circles all the way.

3. On the math grid-in questions, there is space above the grid to write in the answer. But the computer registers only the circles, so you don't have to waste time writing in the answer.

4. Practice, practice, practice. Try to get your time below 0.3 second per circle. Following are a bunch of circles for you to practice on. If you get your time below 0.1 second, you may be able to qualify for the O-lympics.

	A	B	C	D			A	B	C	D			A	B	C	D
1	○	○	○	○		9	○	○	○	○		17	○	○	○	○
2	○	○	○	○		10	○	○	○	○		18	○	○	○	○
3	○	○	○	○		11	○	○	○	○		19	○	○	○	○
4	○	○	○	○		12	○	○	○	○		20	○	○	○	○
5	○	○	○	○		13	○	○	○	○		21	○	○	○	○
6	○	○	○	○		14	○	○	○	○		22	○	○	○	○
7	○	○	○	○		15	○	○	○	○		23	○	○	○	○
8	○	○	○	○		16	○	○	○	○		24	○	○	○	○

CURSING CURSIVE

*I feel old.
—Samantha

In recent years, the SAT has started asking students to certify that they aren't cheating by copying down a statement in cursive. Since many kids barely ever use script these days * (or never learned it in the first place), here's some space to practice.

I hereby agree to the conditions set forth in the test regulations and certify that I am the person whose name, address, and signature appear on this answer sheet.

YOGA AND THE SAT

In order to succeed on the SAT, it is most important to use your mind. If you arrive at the testing area without your mind, you are sure to do poorly on the test. (There have been reports of test takers in California who scored above 800 without their minds; these rumors have been investigated and have been found to be vicious hoaxes.) Most of this book is devoted to training the mind to meet the intellectual challenge that the SAT presents. However, a certain amount of physical conditioning is necessary as well. Each year, thousands of students all across the nation suffer from muscle fatigue, leg cramps, and spinal curvature as a direct result of the SAT. Yes, the SAT can be a grueling, bone-breaking, lung-collapsing experience for the ill-prepared. How can this be? How can taking a test be so physically draining? Simply stated, all the misery is caused by the beastly little desk pictured on the next page.

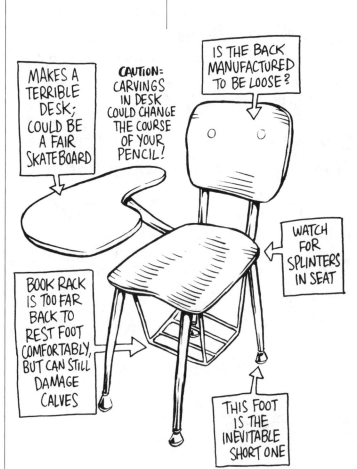

MAKES A TERRIBLE DESK; COULD BE A FAIR SKATEBOARD

CAUTION: CARVINGS IN DESK COULD CHANGE THE COURSE OF YOUR PENCIL!

IS THE BACK MANUFACTURED TO BE LOOSE?

WATCH FOR SPLINTERS IN SEAT

BOOK RACK IS TOO FAR BACK TO REST FOOT COMFORTABLY, BUT CAN STILL DAMAGE CALVES

THIS FOOT IS THE INEVITABLE SHORT ONE

And well you should gasp! This demented version of a chair, or something much like it, will be your home during the three or four of the most important hours of your high school career. Equipped with hardly ample desk space of about one square foot, this chair undoubtedly will have you making a fool of yourself as you attempt to keep your test booklet and answer sheet together on the desk and not let them fall all over the floor. They will fall on the floor anyway, making a rustling sound, and you will wind up annoying everyone in the testing hall.

If you are left-handed, the situation will be even worse. You will wind up with the book on your lap and the answer sheet on the desk—leaving your left arm wrapped across your body to mark the circles. This is misery. Demand from the proctor a more appropriate place to take the test. But he will probably just laugh wickedly and enjoy watching you suffer.

To make matters worse, the legs of the chair are usually too short and the edges too sharp. If you're not careful, you'll cut yourself and there'll be blood everywhere. And if you don't maintain good posture (practically impossible), you'll wind up in traction with a slipped disc. Only the strong survive.

But there is hope. For help, we suggest you turn to knowledge that has existed for centuries in the Eastern regions of the world. The ancient art of yoga, we have found, offers the most relevant conditioning for the serious-minded. If you practice the

above Sun Salutation sequence, starting at least a month before the test, you will suffer minimal discomfort from your immediate surroundings during the test.

THE SAT AND THE INTERNET

Most of you already know all the fun stuff you can do on the Internet. You can download any Adele or Ed Sheeran song you want, you can play Grand Theft Auto with someone in New Zealand, you can even make a website for your cat. And, for your extreme convenience and pleasure, you can also prepare for the SAT on the Internet. We've spent countless hours checking what's out there. Here's what we've found.

As we've mentioned one million times already, the College Board's website (collegeboard.org) is surprisingly peppy for such a stuffy organization. You can register for most of the SAT services we've described, and it offers advice not only on test taking, but choosing a college and getting financial aid. There's even a "store" where you can buy books and software and a "library" where you can review documents. They also have a "Question of the Day," which is a good place to see SAT practice questions. *
You can view the daily question online, or you can sign up to get one emailed to you each day—which is an easy way to integrate SAT prep into your routine. We recommend that you save this for a Friday or Saturday night when you're looking for a good time.

*You can also download this as an app. I'm a fan of apps.
—Samantha

As we mentioned in Chapter 2, the College Board has teamed up with the website Khan Academy to create exercises and videos that are geared specifically to the new SAT. Check this out at khanacademy.org/sat. Khan offers full-length SAT practice tests, which you can take timed or untimed, that come with explanations of every problem. It is basically mandatory that you look at these tests. Khan even provides an analysis of your strengths and weaknesses and suggests areas where you need work.

What's more, the non-SAT instructional math videos on Khan's site are particularly strong. The explanations can be helpful, quick refreshers on long-forgotten concepts. You can rewind and replay Sal Khan's videos as often as you want and, unlike a live tutor, he will keep explaining the concepts with the same dorky enthusiasm and humor. Definitely give the website a try.

Several SAT schools now have online versions of their courses that are less expensive than their classroom offerings and have the excellent advantage that when these courses start to bore you (and you will get bored if you expect the other guys to be as witty and charming as we are), you can always log off.

The Princeton Review's site (princetonreview.com) is pretty good. You can take a practice test, sign up for a local "Strategy Session," and get lots of college advice. Kaplan's website (kaptest.com) covers territory similar to The Princeton Review's, and their SAT course itself seems solid enough.

CHEATING

Cheating is rampant at many test centers. Among the cheating methods we have encountered are sharing answers during the breaks between sections, peeking at other people's answer sheets, communicating answers through sophisticated body language codes, leaving a dictionary in the restroom and looking up words during the breaks, and even having one student take the test for another student.

Two kids at Larry, Manek, and Paul's high school cheated by using the following method. Since their last names were Basset

and Bates (the names have been changed to protect the guilty), they knew that they would be sitting near each other during the test. Basset was a math whiz and Bates was a vocabulary guru. So when the proctor turned around, they traded tests. Basset did Bates's math sections and Bates did Basset's verbal sections. They both did very well and—what a surprise—they both got exactly the same score.

Another way of cheating that we heard of involved using M&M's. Throughout the test, one kid would eat different-colored M&M's, each one standing for a letter—yellow for A, green for B, etc. The other kid would watch her and know what the right answer was. The problem with this method is that the College Board creates several tests for every date that the SAT is offered, and proctors distribute them randomly throughout your testing center. So the person sitting next to you is not necessarily taking the same test as you.

Should you cheat? No. You should not cheat. You see, there's nothing wrong with beating the system by learning what you've learned in this book because, although we do teach you a lot of tricks, we don't break any rules. But if you beat the system by breaking the rules, you are doing something that's wrong. You will feel guilty and wish you hadn't done it. When your friends who didn't cheat don't get into their first-choice colleges and you do, you will feel awful. Just ask Basset and Bates.

A Gray Area

Cheating by getting answers from other people is clearly wrong. The most common form of cheating, however, does not involve getting answers from others. The most common method of cheating is working on a section of the test after the time allotted for that section is over. At the bottom of every section, the SAT warns you in big, bold letters:

STOP

IF YOU FINISH BEFORE TIME IS CALLED, YOU MAY

CHECK YOUR WORK TO THIS SECTION ONLY.

DO NOT TURN TO ANY OTHER SECTION IN THE TEST.

Cheating by glancing at a neighbor's answer sheet is likely to be a losing proposition; not all tests have the sections in the same order.

At many test centers, no one checks what section you are on. We would estimate that about half the kids at our test centers cheated by using this method. The five of us were good kids and didn't. But after the test, when we realized how many of our friends had done this, we felt we were at an unfair disadvantage for not having done it.

Clearly, this kind of cheating is not as bad as getting answers from other people. You could argue that when your future is in the balance, why not borrow a minute from the Math Test to work on a reading passage that you didn't quite finish, especially if half your classmates are doing it?

On the other hand, it's still cheating.

Note: The parents of one of our past guest editors dabbled in the dark art of proctoring and would like to point out that the Evil Testing Serpent instructs all proctors to expel from the testing center anyone who cheats using this method. Also, doing so is immoral and will invite bad karma.

IS THE SAT BIASED?

In past years, the SAT has been called unfair. Why? Because of its alleged bias against women, minorities, and the poor, who as a group consistently do worse on the tests than rich white males.

Basically, the test is a fast-paced game that stresses speed and strategic guessing. (Unfortunately, it's used to predict success in college, which does not necessarily depend on speed or strategic guessing.) This type of test favors the way archetypal American boys behave.

Gender Bias

On average, girls scored about 30 points lower on the old SAT than boys did, with most of the points lost on the Math Test. Although many people argued that boys are better math students or girls' grades are inflated, research has shown that in high school and college, girls get better grades and are more likely to graduate. The SAT, therefore, has consistently underpredicted the performance of female students in college. (The main thing the SAT claims to do is predict college performance.) Partly in response to objections to a perceived gender bias, in 2005 the College Board added the Writing Test (on which girls tend to score slightly higher) to the SAT in order to balance out the gender gap on the Math Test. In the years since, we have seen arguments and counterarguments about whether the SAT is biased, and it will probably be a long time before we reach a firm consensus. Unfortunately, you do not have a long time to wait. Luckily, by reading this book and learning how to take the test, girls can score higher than boys.

Racial Bias

The following were the average scores (out of a possible 2400) for various racial and ethnic groups in 2015:

Asian American	1654 (or about 1100 on the new scale)
White	1576 (or about 1050)
Native American	1423 (or about 950)
Mexican American	1343 (or about 900)
Puerto Rican	1347 (or about 900)
Other Hispanic	1345 (or about 900)
African American	1277 (or about 850)

Some minorities may do worse on the SAT because of income bias (see below); in general, minorities have lower incomes than whites do.

The SAT tried to bridge the racial gap in 1970 by the lame gesture of adding one reading passage per test concerning minorities. The new test tends to include a passage by or that references a minority. (How that's more than a Band-Aid solution is beyond us.)

Income Bias

Richer kids tend to do better on the SAT than poorer kids. This may be the most difficult bias to overcome; it is certainly the most blatant. First, low-income students frequently do not have the educational opportunities that more privileged students have. Another very widespread problem is SAT coaching. Many people who can afford it shell out about $900 to take an SAT prep course. This gives those students an advantage. However, you, the informed consumer, paid only $14.95 for this book and will have your score, and your consciousness, raised immensely.

One of the College Board's main goals in redesigning the SAT for 2016 was to level the playing field by eliminating some of the more esoteric and specialized vocabulary. It has been argued that testing words like *anodyne* and *pusillanimous* serves little function other than to reward those who grew up in households where those words were used. It still remains to be seen whether this change will affect the gap in scores between wealthier and poorer test takers.

A TEST TAKER'S GUIDE TO PROCTORS

SAT proctors tend to be selected haphazardly, and for the most part they do not give a flying poo about your life or your problems. They're paid only a pittance, not enough to make them care.

Sure we're being harsh, but we've interviewed students at many schools, and we have heard some nasty horror stories about incompetent and ignorant proctors. On each test date, students across the nation go in to take the SAT in what they hope will be a fair environment. Instead, some of them must cope with bumbling idiots who forget to read instructions, eliminate break time, talk while you work, or give incorrect responses to student questions (responses like "No, you shouldn't guess"). Many proctors simply haven't learned how to do their job. They are given a proctor's manual with specific instructions on what forms of ID are acceptable, how far apart to seat people, what to do if there's a fire alarm, etc. But because no one ever checks

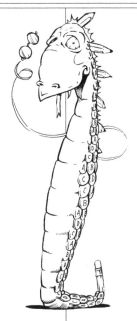

The Greek word proktos *means "anus." So does the English word* proctor.

on them, they usually are left to say and do whatever they want. Here, once again, we discover the Evil Testing Serpent doing its foul work. It insidiously fails to insist on the quality of the proctors it selects.

Proctors come in three varieties. The first and most prestigious model is the Test Center Supervisor (TCS)—a popular item, but available only in limited quantities. The TCS is in charge of the whole test center. She's supposed to hire all of the underling proctors, procure rooms, and maintain contact with the College Board.

Next in the pecking order is the supervisor, the big shot in each room. The supervisor is the dude who reads the directions in a clear and carefully modulated voice. ("Please read the directions as I read them aloud to you. . . .") The supervisor is in charge of all the proctors in his room.

The plain old proctors are the people who hand out the tests and answer sheets and make sure you don't cheat. (Sometimes the proctor is the same as the supervisor.)

Proctors are selected by the test center. Often local teachers are chosen as proctors—people whose faces are familiar to students. Supervisors are paid in proportion to the number of students taking the test, and proctors are paid a flat fee.

Because your proctor may not know all the facts, it is necessary for you to find out everything you need to know about the SAT before the test date. We hope this book has answered all of your questions. If it hasn't, spend some time poking around at collegeboard.org. Your guidance counselor should also have SAT resources available for you. If you still have an unanswered question, get a life.

If you happen to get good proctors, thank them, hug them, and put them in your pocket to keep as a pet. However, you should be prepared for a bad one and know how to cope. This will save you from getting screwed.

So be on guard against a bad proctor. To misquote the

Beastie Boys, "You've Got to Fight for Your Right to SAT."

Your liberties, so generously granted to you by the College Board, include the following:

1. You have the right to 80 (or 65, or 35) silent minutes to work on each section. The minutes begin after the proctor has finished reading all instructions, not before!

2. You have the right to a five-minute break at the end of each hour or so.

3. You have the right to use the test booklet as scrap paper.

4. You have the right to have your seat changed for a legitimate reason. The proctor, of course, decides whether your reason is "legitimate" or not. Being placed at a right-handed desk when you are left-handed, having the sun in your eyes, and sitting with water dripping on your head from a ceiling leak are all examples of legitimate reasons. Wanting to sit next to your girlfriend is not.

5. You have the right to retain what you've stored in the memory on your calculator.

6. You have the right to breathe.

If any of these rights is violated, speak up. If one of the proctors says something you think is questionable or even admits that he doesn't know something, go ask the supervisor, who we can only hope knows what she's doing. Never be afraid of "authorities" who actually know less than you do about their own jobs. Be polite, but insist. Remember, it's your future that hangs in the balance.

WHAT'S THE BEST WAY TO PREPARE THE DAY BEFORE THE SAT?

There is much disagreement about the ideal way to prepare during the 24 hours before the test. Each of the authors of this book has a favorite method. Choose the one that best suits your personality.

1. LARRY'S METHOD: BE PREPARED.

Preparedness is the key. Start your day with a healthy breakfast

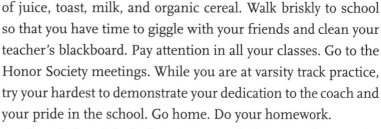

of juice, toast, milk, and organic cereal. Walk briskly to school so that you have time to giggle with your friends and clean your teacher's blackboard. Pay attention in all your classes. Go to the Honor Society meetings. While you are at varsity track practice, try your hardest to demonstrate your dedication to the coach and your pride in the school. Go home. Do your homework.

Spend the night before the test relaxing—watch a movie, practice your clarinet, play Scrabble. Don't bother with last-minute studying except to look at your list of the ten words that have given you the most trouble. Put six number 2 pencils with unblemished erasers, your ID, two calculators, and your admission ticket by the door. Say your prayers, and go to bed early.

2. MANEK'S METHOD: BE MELLOW.

Tranquillity is the key. Skip school the day before and relax—turn off your phone, lock the door, and put a cloth over your goldfish bowl so you won't be distracted. Lie down on the floor with your favorite potato and breathe deeply. Starting with your toes and progressing to your earlobes, calm your entire body; feel yourself losing control of your muscles. When you're marvelously mellow, put your most prized possessions in the microwave and melt them. If you feel alarmed at this stage, then you're not totally tranquil—go back to the beginning and try biofeedback.

When you are entirely free of tension, center your thoughts on how wonderful it will feel to be done with the test, while pronouncing solemn and meditative syllables of wisdom. Close your eyes. Sleep.

3. PAUL'S METHOD: GET PUMPED.

Adrenaline is the key. Do not prepare for the SAT the day before. Instead, try to build up as much anxiety and fury as possible in your tortured, nerve-racked body. Do calisthenics. Mosh to hardcore ska. Invite a few friends over and engage in a primal screaming session. Beat your body repeatedly with knotted cords and whips. Break lots of glass. When morning comes,

make sure that your pulse is above 250 beats per minute, then break open the test center doors and destroy the test with your awesome animal energy.

Organizing materials such as your pencils, ID, and admission ticket the night before does not improve your score or general well-being. Disorganization forces you to think fast and deal rationally with unusual situations and problems such as those tricky questions that will undoubtedly appear on the SAT. Finally, don't go to bed the night before the test. You can catch up on your sleep the first year that you're dead.

4. MICHAEL'S METHOD: BE SUPERSTITIOUS.

Superstition is the key. Find three live rhubarb plants, a number 2 pencil, a proctor, and a college brochure. On the last full moon before the test, boil all of these together in a Teflon cauldron; simmer until golden brown. Chant the following:

"O great *Up Your Score* lords, give me the strength to defeat the College Board! I am the Gatekeeper, and I will do as you command!"

If a black cat crosses your path, stab a mirror with a silver dagger.

The clothes you wear on the test day are very important: If the test is on a rainy day, wear a raincoat. However, if the test is on a day when the Red Sox are playing at home, wear two pairs of socks. If there has been an earthquake during the past week anywhere in Canada, make sure you wear a blindfold during the test (you can take it off during the breaks). Follow these rules, and you are destined to score well.

5. SAMANTHA'S METHOD: BE FOCUSED.

Beginning three months prior to the test, limit your diet to only number two pencils and broccolini. Two months before the test, summon all proctors within a ninety-mile radius to your backyard to play Go Fish. A month before the test, lock yourself in the janitorial closet of your testing center. Write your requests

for food and water only in sequences of small, filled-in bubbles. Stare at this book for nineteen hours per day, and spend the other five hours discussing essay topics with the cleaning supplies. A day before the test, begin standing on your head to make all blood flow to your brain and strengthen its logical power. Either your head will explode, or you will ace the SAT. It's a risk worth taking.

6. LARRY, MANEK, PAUL, MICHAEL, AND SAMANTHA'S METHOD: BE TOGETHER.

Togetherness is the key. The SAT is a dismal, lonely ordeal. You are isolated not only during the almost-four pathetic hours of solitude that is the test, but also during long, bleak minutes of studying with nothing but this book to keep you company. We have confirmed that the College Board has offshore investments that profit right around testing time, when millions of students rush out to buy pet rocks.

BUT YOU ARE NOT REALLY ALONE! There are millions just like you who no longer need to suffer in silence! Comrades, on the night before the test, share your feelings about the College Board with your fellow test takers. Vent your thoughts by sending a pointed email message to the College Board via the "Contact Us" page of their website and sharing your frustrations on Facebook.

Together we will be strong! And when the sun rises on Saturday morning—we will prevail!

Each of these methods has its merits. People using the first method tend to get higher scores, people using the second method get spiritually enriched, people using the third method die young, people using the fourth method get locked up, people using the fifth method can join a Zen monastery afterward, and people using the sixth method get a warm fuzzy feeling. No matter which method you use, be sure to read the wisdom on page 355 on the night before the test. Don't peek at it before then.

SNEAKY SNACKING

Ever since the Evil Testing Serpent increased the length of the SAT to practically three days, it very generously allows students to bring in snacks. (We know this is just to keep its victims alive longer in order to continue torturing them.)

You're not allowed to eat food during the test, and in any case, doing so would waste valuable time. Instead, snack during the breaks. Choosing your SAT menu can be lots of fun. Here are a few guidelines and suggestions:

1. Nothing noisy: no potato chips, carrots, or tuna casseroles (at least not the kind with cornflakes on top)
2. Nothing sticky: no cookie batter, maple syrup, toffee, or super glue
3. Nothing big: no turkeys, cotton candy, or melons
4. Nothing smelly: no Limburger cheese, kimchi, or fried fish

No melons. Absolutely no melons. Trust us on this one.
—Samantha

As long as you stay within the guidelines, we leave the specific choices up to you. However, we do recommend the following recipe.

SWEET AND TASTY 800 BARS

½ pound butter (2 sticks)
1 (1-pound) box dark brown sugar
3 cups flour
3 eggs
1 teaspoon vanilla extract
2½ teaspoons baking powder
2 jumbo Hershey bars (the kind with the little squares)

Melt the butter and let it cool until you can put your nose in it for three seconds and feel no pain. Stir in the brown sugar. Then add the flour slowly. Beat the eggs and add them one at a time. Add the vanilla and baking powder. Break the chocolate bars into squares with <u>you're fingers</u> and add them to the batter.

    A) NO CHANGE
    B) your fingers

C) someone else's fingers

D) you are fingers

Answer: B

Take a glob of the batter and eat it. (Don't you wish all recipes said that?) Pour the batter into a buttered baking dish with a volume of 216 cubic inches. If the pan is 2 inches deep and 12 inches long, how many inches wide is it?

A) 8

B) 9

C) 10

D) $8x - 5$

Answer: B

Preheat the oven to the average of 100°F and 600°F. Place the pan in the oven until the bars turn golden brown on top—35 minutes in a standard oven, 40 minutes in a slow oven.

When the bars are golden brown, remove the pan from the oven. Now you can cut them into whatever shape you choose—we'd enjoy biting the heads off of little Evil Testing Serpent–shaped bars, but that's just us.

In terms of getting your food into the test center, we recommend one of those hooded sweatshirts with the pockets in the front. These can hold a lot of food, and the food is easily accessible. It also keeps the food hidden from all the other starving test takers around you. It's a jungle in the test center. Purses or backpacks are also useful. Just don't do what Larry did. He cleverly stashed a chocolate bar in his back pocket. Before he had a chance to eat it, two of the Musketeers had melted, leaving an embarrassing brown stain.

FASHION AND BEAUTY TIPS

Just as it's important not to be hungry during the SAT, it's also important to be comfortable. You don't want to waste time wishing you'd worn looser jeans or that your shirt wasn't

KEEPING TRACK OF TIME

scratchy. Make sure you dress in layers no matter when your test date is. The test room could be heated, air-conditioned, both, or neither. Be prepared for any climate. Bear in mind that cardigans and sweatshirts that zip up the front are easier to wriggle out of quickly than garments you have to pull over your head. Avoid loose, floppy sleeves; as fashionable as they may be, you don't want to have to keep swishing them out of the way to fill in your answer sheet. The same goes for bangle bracelets (which also have a tendency to jangle annoyingly). Finally, a lucky pair of socks or the underwear you wore when you won the basketball tournament couldn't hurt.

Cut your fingernails so you don't waste time biting them; the same goes for your cuticles. If you like, paint your nails a soothing color like a pastel green or a blue that reminds you of the ocean.

Hair care is also very important. Even if you're otherwise attired in your oldest, floppiest sweats, go to the test with squeaky clean hair—it'll make you feel pulled together and competent. Plus, its brilliant shine might distract other students and therefore increase your percentile score. Also bear in mind that the month before the SAT is no time to start growing your hair out. The last thing you want is to be constantly pushing your hair out of your eyes and cursing yourself for ever aspiring to have Fabio locks.

Wear a good watch. A darn good watch. (But not a smart watch.) In unfavorable circumstances, there might not be a clock in the testing area. Even if there is, you don't want to keep looking up nervously at the clock and risk spraining your neck.

Choose your watch carefully. Digital ones are preferable because in the heat of the moment you might forget how to read an analog watch. * If you never wear a watch, bring one to put on your desk. A small travel clock will do the trick as well. Whatever kind you choose, make sure your timepiece doesn't beep, or if it does, that you know how to turn off the sound. Otherwise, you risk being the object of intense hatred by the other test takers.

If you're not a morning person, try to trick your body on testing day. Go to sleep early on Friday and wake up a few hours before you take the SAT. Your body will think that it is two or three hours later than it really is. You'll feel like you are taking the SAT at 11:00 instead of at 8:30.

It's important to remember the start time! A nice proctor (isn't that an oxymoron?) who knows what she's doing will write the start time on the blackboard, but because you'll mostly be staring at the test booklet, write the start and end times there at the top for easier reference. Or on your hand. But don't smudge it on your sweaty forehead. Check the time on your trusty watch occasionally, with increasing frequency near the end of a section. But don't freak out—it's only to help you pace yourself better.

Done early? Go back and check your answers, duh. Still have time left? (Wow!) Check them again. Sometimes neuroticism works to your advantage . . . and you're stuck in that chair with nothing else to do anyway.

STICK IT IN YOUR EAR

At this point in the book, we would like to recommend that you find two cylindrical objects, rub them back and forth between your fingers, and then insert them into two of your body's orifices simultaneously.

The orifices are your ears and the cylindrical objects are foam earplugs. These little squishy thingies are great. They cost about a dollar a pair at your local pharmacy—a small price to pay for cutting out most of the distracting noises in the testing hall. They are comfortable once you get used to them. In fact, some people we know at college have become addicted to them and can't study without them.

When you put in the earplugs, you suddenly hear your own breathing more intensely and sometimes even your own heartbeat. These are precisely the things that you are supposed to listen for when trying to meditate. So once you get used to it, you'll find yourself concentrating and relaxing with a meditative intensity.

SATITIS

What should you do if you wake up on test day and don't feel well? Panic, beat your fists against the wall, and curse the fates.

Then sit back and assess how you feel. If you really feel vile, consider postponing the test and asking the College Board for a refund. If, however, you just have a cold, slight nausea, and a mild headache, you should still take the SAT. First of all, your "illness" could just be nerves, in which case it might go away after you take a shower. Even if it doesn't, adrenaline might well carry you through the test (you can go home and allow yourself to wallow in your symptoms afterward), and you won't have the SAT looming in front of you for another few months. Take some cold or headache or tummy medicine as long as you're certain it won't make you drowsy. (It's very difficult to succeed on the SAT if you take the test while you are sleeping.) Try to relax and breathe deeply and focus on the test, not on your scratchy throat, runny nose, watery eyes, throbbing head, clogged sinuses, or aching stomach. And remember, the SAT nauseates everyone. Finally, if you know you didn't do well, just cancel your scores.

Bring tissues— even if you're feeling completely fine. A runny nose is the worst thing that could ever happen to you, ever.
—Samantha

CANCELING COUNSELING

If, after the test, you think you might have screwed up, that's only natural, and you shouldn't worry about it. However, if you *know* you screwed up—for example, you made some grievous error like choosing D for all the writing questions or falling asleep during a section—then it is probably wise to cancel (see below). But don't cancel just because you made a few stupid mistakes. It's normal to feel uncertain and nervous about how you did right after the test. Manek was troubled by a couple of dumb errors he'd made, but after some stressing and sulking, he remembered that a couple of mistakes aren't a huge deal. Give it a few days and you will probably feel better about your performance.

The simplest way to cancel is to fill out a Test Cancellation Form before you leave the test center. However, if you decide to cancel after you've left the center, you must notify the College Board by the Wednesday after the Saturday or Sunday you took the test. (For details, go to collegeboard.org.)

If you cancel, your score report will read "Absent or Scores Delayed." **Important Note:** If you took multiple SAT Subject Tests on one test date and you cancel one score, you're really canceling them all. So think twice!

THE SSS

In its spare time, the Evil Testing Serpent likes to play match-maker. This is why it invented the Student Search Service (SSS). The SSS (sounds like something the Serpent would say) is like a computer dating service, except that instead of matching sexually frustrated singles, it matches colleges with potential students. It's free, and it's a good way to get lots of mail, so you might as well do it. However, if you're eco-conscious, you may not want to waste all that paper. One way to save trees is to share college brochures with your friends.

To enroll in the SSS, you opt in when you register for the PSAT/NMSQT, SAT, or an Advanced Placement test. It involves filling out a questionnaire. Unless you're a compulsively ethical person, there is no reason why you have to tell the truth when answering the questionnaire. If you have no artistic ability, but you still want to see the pretty pictures in the brochures that the art schools send out, then select the option that says you got an "A or Excellent in Art and Music." Also, do not be modest when answering the questionnaire. If you're good at something, say that you're great at it. That way you'll be sure to get mail from the colleges that are interested in that skill. The way it works is, colleges will search a database of SSS participants based on certain criteria like gender, ethnicity, expected graduation date, GPA, and intended major. If you turn up in the college's search results, you're deemed a prospective fit for that institution and they will send you information and brochures, either by email or good old-fashioned snail mail.

Another similarity between the SSS and a dating service is that they both make mistakes, matching you up with some real losers. The "Registration Bulletin" claims that you will get mail only from schools with "the academic programs and other features you find important." This is false. If you put on the questionnaire that you are an Alaskan native who wants to study philosophy and has no mechanical ability, you may still get mail from the Crump School of Interplanetary Auto Mechanics.

SATING FOR DOLLARS

I would not be at Vanderbilt without my SAT score. It didn't just get me in— it scored me a sweet scholarship, too.

—Samantha

After you ace the SAT, you will decide that, because you are such a good, involved student with a kick-butt SAT score, you could get into a prestigious college. You will develop a passion for this particular college, but your dreams of attending will be crushed when you learn that it costs about three times as much as you can possibly afford. *

At this point, you have several options. You could turn your back on the material world and join a socialist commune where money is not an issue. You could create a Kickstarter charity campaign called "Educating Our Future Leaders" and solicit everyone in your address book. You could sell your little brother, but you probably wouldn't make enough money.

Or you could try to win some scholarship money. Ask your guidance counselor about scholarship opportunities and research them online (try fastweb.com, cappex.com, or college scholarships.com) or in the library in the most recent scholarship books you can find. Many of these books are huge and daunting, but you will soon realize that you don't qualify for many of the scholarships in them unless you live in Santa Fe, your birthday is February 29, and you're a direct descendant of an original signer of the Declaration of Independence. Although scholarship applications are less fun to fill out than tax forms, they can be much more rewarding. Please note that the cost of a college can be a misleading indicator of whether you can afford it. Some of the most expensive colleges have the best financial aid options.

SOME OTHER THOUGHTS ON GETTING INTO COLLEGE

Remember, the SAT is only one aspect of your college application. If your score isn't that strong, make sure the rest of your application is.

GRADES AND COURSES

These should always be your first priority. Colleges usually insist on a minimum standard of grades and courses before they even look at the rest of an application.

And, drumroll please for the most cliché advice of all time: Be yourself. If you're funny, be funny. If you're inspirational, be inspirational. If you're a compulsive liar, well then, maybe you shouldn't be yourself.
—Samantha

ESSAYS

College admissions officers read hundreds of essays—your goal is to write one that will stick in their minds. You might want to reveal something about yourself in your essay that didn't come out in the rest of your application. Sure, you can write about your summer job, but realize that many others will probably write similar essays about their summer experiences. Make yours stand out. Humor can be effective, but if the admissions committee doesn't find your witticisms funny, it's worse than not using any humor at all. So make sure you get feedback on your essays before you send them in. (This goes for all essays, not just humorous ones.) Show them to your family, your friends, your teachers, your plumber. However, don't let any of your readers write the essay for you—it should always reflect you.

EXTRACURRICULARS

These are secondary to grades, but they are becoming more important. No one wants a school full of do-nothing dweebs. (If you are a do-nothing dweeb, change your ways now. There is still hope!) One extracurricular that is irresistible to colleges is organizing and leading something socially responsible. Ask yourself what your school or community needs, and then get your friends to work with you on a project, such as a recycling program, a canned food drive, or a community rhubarb garden. Being a leader (editor of the school paper, captain of the basketball team) is more impressive than just being a member of a club that meets once a week. And one last bonus tip: One activity that you've taken seriously is a lot more memorable than seven or eight activities. So if you are currently racing from the chess club to the glee club to the French culture appreciation society, you might be wasting a lot of energy. Pick the one or two extracurriculars you like best, and excel in them.

RECOMMENDATIONS

A great recommendation can make a big difference. Ask teachers who know you well and who you think have good things to say about you. Try to choose someone with whom you have a real connection—the teachers you actually think you'll want to see at your high school reunion in ten years. If you are reading this book in early junior year, you still have time to cultivate a relationship with a teacher. And if it's later than that, well, it's never too late to start.

SPECIAL TALENTS

Colleges need running backs for their football teams and violins in their orchestra. Even if you haven't been recruited by the Bears and aren't the next Itzhak Perlman, make sure your colleges know about any special talents that you have. One of our past guest editors, who originally was deferred Early Action at MIT and Cal Tech, got into both Regular Action after sending an application update that included info about the guest authorship and a percussion audition tape for the band and orchestra conductors at each school. Of course, we at *Up Your Score* believe that we were the deciding factor, but the tapes couldn't have hurt.

PARTING WORDS OF ADVICE

(To Be Read the Night Before the Test)

I'm not telling you how many times I took the SAT. Let's just say it became a hobby.

—Samantha

Dear Reader,

Congratulations! You've made it through (or else you're peeking at the end of the book). You have your ID, your admission ticket, three sharp number 2 pencils and one dull pencil, a calculator or two with charged batteries, and some good food to bring into the test all waiting by the door. Maybe you've studied everything in a day; maybe you started with verbal flashcards four and a half years ago. Who cares? It's over now; no amount of studying the night before the test is going to help you significantly.

If you need a boost of confidence, just remember that there are people out there who will be taking the test tomorrow without having read this book first. (Unthinkable, isn't it?) If you botch the test, you'll just take it again on the next test date. ✱ If you don't get into the college of your choice, you can choose another one that probably doesn't cost as much and has a better football team.

We hope you enjoyed our book and learned a lot. Our objective was to teach you how to take the SAT, but we hope that along the way you learned some stuff that will help you for the rest of your life. At the very least, you're now an expert on grammar rules, but if we did our job right you are a cleverer test taker and a better thinker than you used to be.

All of us authors went through the same thing you're going through right now. We know how you feel. There is a lot of pressure. It feels as if someone is scratching fingernails on your mental chalkboard.

So go outside and look at the stars. There are lots of them and they're trillions of miles away. In the Grand Scheme of the Universe, how big a deal can the SAT be? Chill. You're going to cruise tomorrow. Sit back. You only live once . . . and then they send you your score report.

Good luck,

Larry, Manek, Paul, Michael, Samantha

WHO ARE THESE PEOPLE, ANYWAY?

LARRY BERGER

Larry Berger is the CEO of Amplify, a digital education company. He cofounded Wireless Generation, an educational software company, in 2000. He has written two other books: *I Will Sing Life*, a book about children and poetry, and *Tray Gourmet: Be Your Own Chef in the College Cafeteria*. He graduated summa cum laude from Yale and went on to be a Rhodes Scholar at Oxford. At Yale, he codirected the Children in Crisis Big Sibling Program and the Booksgiving Book Drive. He expands to three times his normal size when placed in water.

MICHAEL COLTON

Michael Colton is a screenwriter in Los Angeles who has written for film (*Penguins of Madagascar*) and television (Adult Swim's *Childrens Hospital*). He also appeared regularly as a panelist on *I Love the '80s*, *Best Week Ever*, and other shows on VH1. Before moving to L.A., he cofounded the web magazine *Modern Humorist*; before that he was a staff writer for *The Washington Post*. He graduated from Harvard University, where he wrote for the *Lampoon* and *The Crimson*. Check out michaelcolton.com for more info and a pretty picture of doves.

MANEK MISTRY

Manek Mistry grew up in Ithaca, New York, and received his undergraduate and law degrees from Cornell University. He lives and works in the Pacific Northwest, where he is heckled by his employees. A special talent is that he can eat his own weight in bacon. Each time he does, he gains a few pounds, which means he has to eat even more bacon the next time, which causes him to gain even more weight, which . . . Hey, wait a minute!

PAUL ROSSI

Paul Rossi graduated from Cornell University and earned a master's degree in educational psychology from Hunter College. He currently teaches high school math and philosophy in New York City. He enjoys playing ultimate frisbee and delta blues guitar, and he appears occasionally in contemporary dance performances. One day, he will learn how to surf.

SAMANTHA BINDNER

Samantha grew up in a small beach town in South Carolina called Pawleys Island, which is kind of an island but not really. However, she *is* a professional mermaid (that and *Up Your Score* guest editor are the best jobs for bragging rights, she's learned). When she became sick of life underwater (well, below sea level, at least), she grew some legs and packed her bags for Vanderbilt University. Like a select few other college freshmen, she does not have a meticulous life plan laid out just yet. But pay her a visit at Vandy and she might just be your tour guide.

WHIZ KIDS WANTED

Attention, readers: The search is on for guest editors of *Up Your Score*! Are you a culturally savvy and articulate student who used *Up Your Score* to achieve a perfect (or near-perfect) SAT (or ACT) score? Are you interested in fame, fortune, and the rest of the prodigious perks that go along with revising and promoting upcoming editions of the series? Then we want to hear from you! For more information, visit upyourscore.com or write to info@workman.com.

Join the
Up Your Score
team!